Conciliatory Democracy

This publication is part of the DFG-funded Cluster of Excellence "The Formation of Normative Orders" at Goethe University Frankfurt am Main.

Martin Ebeling

Conciliatory Democracy

From Deliberation Toward a New Politics of Disagreement

Martin Ebeling
Berlin, Germany

ISBN 978-1-137-57742-9   ISBN 978-1-137-57743-6 (eBook)
DOI 10.1057/978-1-137-57743-6

Library of Congress Control Number: 2016948717

© The Editor(s) (if applicable) and The Author(s) 2017
The author(s) has/have asserted their right(s) to be identified as the author(s) of this work in accordance with the Copyright, Designs and Patents Act 1988.
This work is subject to copyright. All rights are solely and exclusively licensed by the Publisher, whether the whole or part of the material is concerned, specifically the rights of translation, reprinting, reuse of illustrations, recitation, broadcasting, reproduction on microfilms or in any other physical way, and transmission or information storage and retrieval, electronic adaptation, computer software, or by similar or dissimilar methodology now known or hereafter developed.
The use of general descriptive names, registered names, trademarks, service marks, etc. in this publication does not imply, even in the absence of a specific statement, that such names are exempt from the relevant protective laws and regulations and therefore free for general use.
The publisher, the authors and the editors are safe to assume that the advice and information in this book are believed to be true and accurate at the date of publication. Neither the publisher nor the authors or the editors give a warranty, express or implied, with respect to the material contained herein or for any errors or omissions that may have been made. The publisher remains neutral with regard to jurisdictional claims in published maps and institutional affiliations.

Cover image © Patrick Batchelder / Alamy Stock Photo

Printed on acid-free paper

This Palgrave Macmillan imprint is published by Springer Nature
The registered company is Macmillan Publishers Ltd.
The registered company address is: The Campus, 4 Crinan Street, London, N1 9XW, United Kingdom

Editorial Note

In an effort to write in a gender-neutral fashion, I have made occasional use of the pronoun "they" as a singular pronoun.

The Chicago Manual of Style states the following with regard to this issue:

> On the one hand, it is unacceptable to a great many reasonable readers to use the generic masculine pronoun (he) in reference to no one in particular. On the other hand, it is unacceptable to a great many readers either to resort to nontraditional gimmicks to avoid the generic masculine (by using he/she or s/he, for example) or to use they as a kind of singular pronoun. Either way, credibility is lost with some readers.[1]

The Cambridge Guide to English Usage, however, conveys a more permissive attitude. It states,

> Those who find it uncomfortable can take advantage of the various avoidance strategies mentioned under he and/or she, to be used when grammatical liberties with they/them/there are unthinkable. Yet that kind of response to singular they/them/their is no longer shared by the English-speaking

---

[1] *Chicago Manual of Style* (2010): sect. 5.46.

population at large. Writers who use singular they/them/their are not at fault.[2]

Furthermore, it notes,

> The appearance of singular they/them/their in many kinds of prose shows its acceptance by English writers generally. It recommends itself as a gender-free solution to the problem of agreement with indefinite pronouns and noun phrases.

I thus hope that my credibility does not suffer from taking this grammatical liberty.

---

[2] *The Cambridge Guide to English Usage* (2004): p. 538.

Introduction

How ought we to react to our persistent political disagreement with other citizens? In response to this question, I introduce a new conception of democracy which I call *conciliatory democracy*. Its key innovation is to bring the ongoing debate in contemporary epistemology about the significance of so-called *peer disagreement*, disagreement between equally competent judges of an issue, to bear on political disagreement and decision-making. After providing arguments for such epistemic equality in politics, I contend that citizens ought to pursue the *epistemic conciliation* of their conflicting judgments. The ideal of epistemic conciliation, finding a middle ground *between judgments*, thus replaces the ideals of consensus and of a compromise of interests at the center of much of democratic theory today. Drawing on insight from public choice theory and the social sciences all too often neglected in contemporary political philosophy, I furthermore show that, and why, multi-party electoral competition tends to produce conciliatory outcomes, i.e. political outcomes which correspond to the epistemic conciliation of the divergent positions constituting the input to democratic decision-procedures. This argument brings to the fore another important innovation of my proposal, namely an elucidation of the epistemic role of political parties in modern democracy.

In sum, this book delivers an altogether novel response to a question at the heart of democratic theory. It is innovative in its epistemic approach, in its elucidation of the vital role of political parties, and in reconciling various strands of democratic theory. Additionally, it solves what we can call *the meta-problem of democratic theory*: to develop a theory that produces an overlap of the normative with the epistemic dimension of democracy.

The fundamental question that plagued me when I started thinking about the issues at the heart of this book was the question of how to deal with the problem of political disagreement in politics. For a long time, I had thought about this question exclusively from a normative vantage point, and consequently treated political disagreement primarily as a moral problem. However, it increasingly struck me that we underestimate its epistemic dimension. Often, disagreement confronts us as an intellectually unsettling experience because we do not regard those we disagree with as moral analphabets. Often we disagree with friends (and foes) to whom we ascribe roughly equal moral competence about intricate matters of justice and politics. This phenomenon points to the epistemic significance of political disagreement, which has not received much uptake in democratic theory. Once we view disagreement as a moral and an epistemic problem, we face the question of how political philosophy ought to address each dimension and how it ought to bring the answers it gives along each dimension into harmony.

I developed the ideas presented in this book at a time when two seemingly unrelated events occurred. One of them was the 2012 US presidential election; the other was the 300th birthday of the cultural critic, writer, and political philosopher Jean-Jacques Rousseau. While it is difficult to perceive at first sight, I believe that a closer look reveals a theme bridging the time and distance between Rousseau's thought and contemporary events. What I have in mind is his distinct vision of politics and democracy, which contrasts sharply with the dire state of politics we sometimes observe in contemporary societies. It is this contrast which can enlighten our understanding and enable a critique of our political practices. US-American society today is deeply divided on issues ranging from economic policies to the permissibility of abortion, same-sex marriage, minority rights, attitudes to climate change, and approaches to foreign policy. What is more, the different sides seem united only in their mutual distrust and their belief that they are the true guardians of the common good, while all others hide their ulterior motives under a fake display of common good orientation. Furthermore, many people judge the intellectual level of political discourse in US-American politics as regrettably low and attribute it to an ill-informed public. The 2016 presidential election was a prime example of what has become known as post-factual politics and included racist and misogynist attacks desguised as challenges to the seemingly oppressive dictates of political correctness.[1]

Admittedly, we do not have to read Rousseau to find this state of affairs deplorable. However, reading Rousseau brings to light an alternative which is, in many respects, very attractive. It is the ideal of a society in which independent and adequately informed citizens cast their vote according to their sincere judgment about what lies in the interests of all. Furthermore, these citizens possess the virtue of intellectual humility. They do not simply discard the judgments of their fellow citizens, but accord them a weight equal to that of their own. This, again, contrasts with the intellectual high-handedness with which actors on both sides of the aisle often dismiss those with whom they disagree. A telling example is a joke which spread after the re-election of George W. Bush in 2004. Reportedly, young Democrats designed a map displaying both coasts in blue and labeled the remaining regions of the country, all in red of course, "the crazy bits in between."[2] We can easily imagine the joke going the other way. Contrast this with Rousseau's teachings, who advocated the virtue of intellectual humility in politics and even thought that in some circumstances citizens could readily admit that it was their own judgment that might have been mistaken.

Surprisingly to our eyes and ears, he also thought that near unanimity is the outcome we should expect of a vote and that more widespread disagreement is a sign of a state in decline. This is, we readily agree, for various reasons an unacceptable position for any conception of democracy fit for complex and pluralistic societies. However, it should not distract us from Rousseau's insight that the political judgments of reasonable citizens carry epistemic significance and do so because independent,

---

[1] Unfortunately, the level of discourse has hit a new low in the 2016 presidential primaries. The general critique applies to other democratic societies just as well, of course.
[2] This anecdote is reported in a news article available at http://www.dailymail.co.uk/news/article-2223828/The-huge-divide-Obama-Romneys-ideology-makes-election-campaign-divisive-recent-memory.html#ixzz2Y5NPoPAp; accessed on July 4, 2013.

adequately informed, and sincere citizens ought to assign equal weight to the judgment of each citizen, including their own. It is this insight which motivates an ideal of democracy as the practice of epistemic conciliation of the conflicting judgments of citizens who regard each other as, what I shall call, *equal epistemic authorities*, i.e. as prima facie equally reliable judges of the rightness of political decisions according to a procedure-independent criterion of rightness. If citizens and their representatives leave behind a manipulative rhetoric designed to divide rather than to convince and engage in sincere public deliberation about the issues at stake in decision-making, there comes a point when they ought to regard others as equally informed and their disagreement as rational and reasonable. In these circumstances, their best bet at getting it right is to seek a middle ground between their judgments. This is one central conclusion of this book. The other central conclusion is that this epistemic conciliation of conflicting judgments is the work of a complex array of democratic institutions, as we find them in different forms in modern democracies. This is why I call the conception of democracy I advance on these pages *conciliatory democracy*.

In what follows I provide an overview of the chapters in order. Apart from the first, which explores the roots of the conciliatory conception of democracy in Rousseau's political philosophy, each chapter provides a building block of a complex argument. This comprehensive argument for conciliatory democracy ties together the normative and epistemic dimensions of the conception. The reader interested in the internal complexities of the ideal along both normative and epistemic dimensions, and how they interact, will find it rewarding to digest the book in its entirety. However, I tried to construct each chapter in such a way that it advances an argument which can stand the test of public scrutiny without relying on the other chapters.

There are thus many ways in which one can approach this book. The first chapter presents an interpretation of Rousseau's philosophy with a focus on his analysis of the epistemic significance of political disagreement. The normative dimension of democracy and the normative significance of political disagreement are the focus of Chap. 2. The epistemic significance of disagreement constitutes the subject matter of Chaps. 3 and 4. Chap. 5 brings the previous arguments together and introduces the idea of epistemic conciliation as a political ideal. It also argues that democracy can have a dynamic toward conciliatory outcomes. Chap. 6 substantiates this claim with a detailed discussion of the vital role of political parties in modern democracies and the centripetal dynamics of multi-party electoral competition. Chap. 7 picks up the various threads running through the book and explains how the epistemic and the normative dimensions of democracy relate to each other in the conciliatory conception of democracy. To arrive at a fair evaluation of the conciliatory conception laid out in this final chapter, however, requires a careful weighing of the arguments I develop throughout the book.

Chapter 1—Rousseau's Insight
In the opening chapter I offer a distinct interpretation of Rousseau with an emphasis on the epistemic significance he attributed to political disagreement. More than anything else, it is this insight, which connects his conception of democracy with the conciliatory conception of democracy, that I advance in the remaining chapters. However, the connections are manifold and the shared outlook comprises many more themes. The first is the idea that the exercise of political power should aim at justice and that this aiming-at-justice is what conveys legitimacy on political institutions and the wielding of political power. A political order does not count as legitimate, in Rousseau's eyes, just because it secures peace and solves basic cooperation problems. It has to recognizably advance, to an equal extent, the fundamental, shared interests of citizens, the most important among them being the preservation of their freedom. This already points to the second point of convergence between Rousseau and my proposal. It is the claim that the idea of reciprocity is at the heart of a publicly defensible conception of justice. Rousseau rejects theological justifications for the exercise of political power and limits permissible justifications to those which are accessible from a shared standpoint of citizens, i.e. their common reason, and can hence count as *public* justifications. This demand of public justifiability of the political order and the exercise of political power is the normative bedrock implicit in Rousseau's political philosophy and the ground on which stands much of what comes

later.[3] Importantly, Rousseau subjects to it not only the institution of a political regime but also the ongoing exercise of political power. He then builds his own conception of legitimacy around the idea of the general will. The general will is an intriguing and somewhat mysterious concept, and Rousseau's attribution of the general will to a moral and collective being with a self, a life, and a will of its own (SC, I, 6,10) can mislead us into interpreting him as postulating a supra-individual subject as its carrier. However, it is evident from his writings that the general will is general because it has its foundation in the fundamental, shared interests of citizens. Hence, each citizen shares this general will, and it is thus the will of *each* citizen *as an individual*. I interpret this idea of a general will of each and every citizen as an idea of public reason and a forerunner of contemporary conceptions thereof.[4] The justification of the exercise of political power is reasonably acceptable to all reasonable citizens because it draws on a shared foundation. This accessibility from a shared perspective of all citizens makes it a *public* justification.

After laying bare the structure of the general will, I then explain the normative and epistemic role Rousseau attributed to democratic procedures. While doing so, I discuss a part of Rousseau's political philosophy that has received little attention thus far and which I nevertheless take to be fundamental to his project. It is Rousseau's insight that political judgments are of epistemic significance as equally reliable indicators of the general will. I show that, according to him, we ought to regard our own judgments about the common good with suspicion because our selfish biases are bound to distort them, even when we do our level best to be objective judges. Rousseau goes on to claim that we ought to uphold this suspicion until we have received confirming evidence in the form of a nearly unanimous judgment of all citizens. Only then are we justified in exercising political power. The reason for this requirement of near certainty is the overriding interest in freedom, which citizens can only preserve when their exercise of political power corresponds to the requirements

---

[3] It was Kant who first made this demand explicit.
[4] Cohen mentions that Rawls viewed his two principles of justice as an attempt to spell out the content of the general will; cf. Cohen (2010): p. 2. Rawls later argued that these principles figure as "political values" in the content of the public reason of a well-ordered society; cf. Rawls (1996): p. 223ff.

of their general will. Hence, the avoidance of false positives, i.e. laws which are *not* expressions of the general will, is of prime importance. And, as a matter of institutional design, we should consequently endorse decision rules with a high supermajoritarian threshold.

But how come agreement with others can have this effect on the confidence we place in our judgment? This part of Rousseau's political philosophy turns on his analysis of the epistemic significance of political disagreement. Rousseau thought that the citizens' judgments about the content of the general will, i.e. the common good, are equally reliable because, if certain conditions hold, the legal regulation of society is simple and the common good fully evident to all citizens. If they regard themselves as equally reliable, it is only rational for them to react as he recommends they do. They ought to increase confidence in their judgments when a majority of citizens agrees with them, and decrease confidence in their judgments when a majority of citizens disagrees with them. If the latter is the case, this can lead to a demand of moral deference. If citizens disagree with a vast majority of citizens, they ought to regard the judgment of the majority as correct and their own as mistaken. This position raises some intriguing questions about the role of procedure-independent and procedure-dependent evidence in the general will and how the two relate to each other. I will show that, according to Rousseau, procedure-dependent evidence, i.e. the extent of dis-/agreement revealed through a decision procedure, constitutes higher-order evidence which undermines the evidential role of the procedure-independent, first-order evidence in the independent judgments of citizens. I then turn to the normative dimension of democratic procedures and propose a reading of Rousseau's conception of sovereignty as the epistemic and normative authority of the people. I close the chapter with a few brief remarks on how Rousseau conceived the role of the lawgiver in his conception of democracy and sovereignty. Rousseau answers the question of the extent to which the institution of a well-ordered society depends on the acts of an external force, a wise politician who legislates the fundamental laws of society. The answer, however, brings with it a second question; that of the authority of the lawgiver to legislate, given that it is *the people* who are sovereign. At the same time, it is also a question about the authority and the task of political philosophy. To what extent can the *philosopher* "legislate" the criteria of legitimacy, given that it is the people who are sovereign? This question stays with us well into the next chapter.

Chapter 2—The Ideal of Deliberative Democracy

After thus sinking my anchor in the depths of the history of philosophy, I shift my attention to contemporary debates and to the ideal of deliberative democracy in particular. This ideal shares many aspects with Rousseau's democratic theory. First and foremost, it shares the conviction that citizens ought to exercise political power according to their sincere judgments about the common good. Furthermore, those advocating the ideal usually share the basic normative assumption that political legitimacy is tied to the public justifiability of the political order from a standpoint shared by all reasonable citizens. However, they add a crucial thought to this normative framework. It is the idea that legitimacy, and hence public justifiability, in one way or another presupposes ongoing practices of public deliberation. Citizens have to engage in public debate, justify their positions vis-à-vis others, and try to understand the position of those who do not share their social background, or who make their judgments based on information not available to them. The backdrop for this insertion of actual deliberation into a conception of legitimacy is a twofold complication of thinking about these matters. Stating the issue in simple terms we can say, first, that the world has become more complicated, and second, that political philosophy has become more complicated. The first point is straightforward. Modern societies are far from the ideal of simplicity Rousseau championed. Instead, their regulation requires tremendously complex legal frameworks. Another aspect of their complexity is that citizens face very different circumstances in their lives, be it because of their economic position, their cultural or religious affiliations, their gender, their race, or other attributes and identities. In short, modern societies are pluralistic, and in such pluralistic societies, laws and public policy are bound to affect citizens in different ways, making it more difficult to judge the effects of a proposed law or policy without actively seeking to take the perspective of the other. Hence, one reason why legitimacy presupposes actual deliberation is that the claim that a law aims at the common good or justice is not credible when no such attempt has been made. Another consequence of this social complexity is that what the common good, or an equal treatment of the interests of all, demands in these circumstances remains opaque. In other words, the common good is not, *pace* Rousseau, fully evident to all reasonable citizens. However, if legitimacy demands that the aiming-at-justice of the exercise of political power is intelligible to citizens, deliberation is necessary to justify its exercise in light of a reasonable conception of justice.

This leads to the second complication. At least in the eyes of some philosophers, the enterprise of political philosophy has become more complicated. They believe that it no longer suffices to postulate the existence of fundamental, shared interests to justify political institutions or the exercise of political power. What might have been regarded as a rock-solid foundation of philosophical systems in the age of Enlightenment no longer serve this role. Political philosophers, they argue, have to accommodate the fact that reasonable people disagree about these assertions and about what might give value to life. Accommodating this reasonable disagreement requires that we leave (most) questions of the substantive legitimacy of specific laws and regulations to the deliberating public. In this view, when it comes to political legitimacy, the philosopher's task is a limited one. What we can do from "outside" the deliberative process is to specify certain formal criteria that justifications have to meet in order to be reasonably acceptable to all. Hence, according to the ideal of deliberative democracy, a publicly justifiable political order is one in which citizens debate the pros and cons of legislative proposals, including the justice of political decisions, and in which citizens justify how they intend to exercise political power over others.

I take this ideal as a starting point and investigate how precisely we ought to conceive the connection between political legitimacy and actual deliberation. My investigation into this question leads me to distinguish two versions of this deliberative standard of legitimacy. One version ties legitimacy to the ideal of consensus, the other is more respecting of reasonable disagreement between sincerely deliberating citizens and settles for public justifiability in terms of reasonably acceptable justifications. The latter version thus presumes that there is more than one conception of justice which can be reasonably claimed to be a reasonable interpretation of the criterion of reciprocity. After tentatively adopting this more plausible latter version, I focus on how deliberative democrats conceive the legitimacy of decision procedures. I argue that it is at this point where actual deliberation and legitimacy come apart. Modest as its claims might be, political philosophy has to step up to the challenge and develop criteria of procedural legitimacy whose validity is not a function of deliberation among citizens. The philosopher, in other words, has to adopt the role of the Rousseauian lawgiver.

If we then extricate what the deliberative standard of legitimacy implies for the procedural legitimacy of political decision-making, we find that its normative content does not carry us very far. Prima facie, it seems that it justifies nothing more than a presumption in favor of equal influence of all citizens over political outcomes. This idea is so weak, though, that it is even compatible with equality of negative influence, i.e. no influence for anyone. However, when recalling that the role of deliberation is to produce reasonably acceptable judgments regarding the merits of the proposals at stake, we can understand that the decision procedure has to be one which selects among "post-deliberative" judgments. Hence, a decision procedure not only needs to be fair, in the sense of providing equal influence over outcomes; it also needs to be judgment sensitive. This consideration thus gets us a significant step closer to what deliberative democrats want, namely a theory of democracy which incorporates the ideal of deliberation with democratic methods of decision-making. Yet there is more than one decision procedure which fits the bill, and with the resources of a deliberative conception of democracy exhausted at this point, we can only note that our hopes of deriving from it a more specific vision of democracy have been disappointed.

At this point, it is tempting to invoke epistemic merits of democratic procedures. We could claim, for instance, that certain democratic procedures not only have a tendency to select reasonably acceptable options, but that they have a tendency to select *the best* among a set of reasonably acceptable options. This bestness-tracking claim, however, is itself subject to the normative criterion of reasonable acceptability. In other words, all reasonable citizens, even those on the losing side of democratic decision-making, would have to have reason to accept the claim that the procedures have a tendency to select the best option. To devise such an argument is a very difficult task, which I take up in the final chapter. The solution comes in the form of a re-injection into democratic theory of Rousseau's insight that political disagreement between equal epistemic authorities carries epistemic significance. Eventually, this observation leads me to propose the conciliatory conception of democracy.

Chapter 3—The Epistemic Authority of Citizens

Before advancing to this argument, however, I first explore the epistemic circumstances of political disagreement. I then defend the claim that, given certain background conditions, reasonable citizens ought to regard each other as *equal epistemic authorities*, i.e. as prima facie equally reliable judges of the rightness of political decisions according to a procedure-independent criterion of rightness. A defense of the claim that reasonable citizens ought to regard each other as equal epistemic authorities is paramount to a rejection of moral elitism. The latter is the thesis that political expertise is unevenly distributed across the population. I offer four interlocking arguments to show why the commitment to equal epistemic authority is justified in the context of ongoing decentered deliberation about sufficiently complex issues and multi-party electoral competition. Building on three of these arguments, I offer a fifth. It shows why persistent political disagreement need not be irrational, i.e. due to cognitive error on the part of some participants, or unreasonable, i.e. the product of insincere reasoning.

The first four arguments come in two sets. The first set comprises *the argument from multidimensional complexity* and *the local knowledge argument*. Both of these suggest that citizens should have only relatively low confidence in their judgments about whether or not a political decision would advance the justice of their society. The first argument makes, and subsequently unpacks, the claim that the question of whether a decision would advance the justice of their society is tremendously complex and thus very difficult to answer with any degree of confidence. I argue that, in part, this is simply due to the fact that our understanding of what considerations bear on it has grown dramatically, and the task of integrating expertise along various dimensions of complexity into political expertise overextends our individual cognitive resources. In light of this, Rousseau's idea of a fully evident common good appears almost naïve. The local knowledge argument draws on the observation that in a decentered deliberative process, no participant can gain knowledge of, what I call, the global validity status of their arguments. Participants inhabit only one of many deliberative spheres and do not know how the arguments they regard as valid in their sphere would fare in others. The ongoing deliberation in other spheres might have produced arguments that defeat or undermine the justifications offered in one's own. Hence, knowledge of the validity status of arguments is always restricted to a local context and those engaged in this context remain ignorant of the reasons others have for their disagreement. Given the fact that the assumption is justified that those who disagree with us do so for reasons which might potentially defeat our own, our own reasoning ought to be suspect to us. Hence, the conclusion is the same as above: the credence citizens have in their judgments about the common good, or whether or not a political decision would advance the justice of their society, should be relatively low.

The second set of arguments aims to close the remaining gap in reliability between citizens. The first in the set is *the practice-based argument*. The point is a simple one. The more we deliberate, the more level we should expect the reliability of our judgments to be. Ongoing practices of deliberation disperse information widely and give citizens opportunities to exercise such crucial moral competencies as mutual perspective-taking. In the context of this argument, I offer an interlude on J.S. Mill's epistemic political elitism and show how this tendency of ongoing deliberation to level the reliability of judgments has the potential to undermine his moral-elitist political philosophy. Even if we start with the assumption that moral elitism is correct, the claim becomes less plausible, the more citizens engage in deliberation with other citizens. I also show how intra-level disagreement can undermine relations of epistemic trust between representatives and the electorate. The second argument in the set, *the argument from institutional expertise*, draws on the epistemic benefits of core institutions in modern representative democracies. The most important among them are political parties. Civic conceptions of democracy, such as deliberative democracy and the conciliatory conception, ought to conceive political parties as translating the abstract value judgments of citizens into specific proposals for public policy and institutional reform spanning a whole range of policy sectors, and ideally not interfering with the intended effects of other public policies or institutions. As collective epistemic agents they thus translate abstract value judgments into sufficiently coherent and sufficiently complex conceptions of justice (see also Chap. 6; Representative Democracy and the Role of Political Parties). A vital aspect of the role of political parties, and representative institutions more generally, is that they infuse, so to speak, the judgments of ordinary citizens with expert knowledge not available to them, and which citizens possess to an unequal degree. The institutions of modern representative democracies thus help to level the reliability of the judgments of citizens as they enter into political decision-making through their vote.

Fusing three of these arguments—the argument from multidimensional complexity, the local knowledge argument, and the practice-based argument—I develop a fifth argument, *the debate room argument*. This argument shows that political disagreement between reasonable citizens engaged in ongoing deliberation about sufficiently complex issues need not be unreasonable, i.e. the outcome of insincere reasoning, or irrational, i.e. based on erroneous reasoning. This leads us back to the question of how citizens who regard each other as equal epistemic authorities and as equal normative authorities ought to react to political disagreement.

Chapter 4—The Epistemology of Political Disagreement
In this chapter, I focus on one part of this question. More specifically, I answer the question of how citizens ought to react *rationally* to disagreements with others whom they regard as equal epistemic authorities. The answer I develop in this chapter is another crucial building block in the overall argument for the conciliatory conception of democracy. It establishes the claim that the rational reaction to certain types of disagreement is to be *conciliatory*, i.e. to seek to conciliate one's judgments with the conflicting judgments of those whom one regards as equally reliable judges of the matter at stake.

I first elucidate the notion of *epistemic peerhood*, around which a lively debate has developed in recent years among philosophers with an interest in the epistemology of disagreement. In short, an *epistemic peer* is someone you regard as equally reliable in answering a given question. The term is thus an obvious analogue to the term *Equal Epistemic Authority*. At the center of my discussion is the *Equal Weight View* and an epistemological principle named *Independence*, which those accepting the Equal Weight View ordinarily endorse. According to the Equal Weight View, it is rational to alter the credence in one's belief in cases of peer disagreement when there is no independent reason not to do so. Roughly, an independent reason is a reason that is independent of the reasoning either one of you offers in support of your views. In some cases, the Equal Weight View recommends an increase in credence. In others, it prescribes *epistemic conciliation* of the credence levels of epistemic peers.

While I argue that the Equal Weight View cum Independence cannot be the final answer to the question under discussion, the fundamental aim of this chapter is to defend the claim that disagreeing epistemic peers ought to seek to conciliate their judgments in certain paradigmatic cases. I do so by showing that other views on the subject of peer disagreement are either implausible or inconsistent. Furthermore, I defend Independence against a number of challenges and, in doing so, I show that it proves to be a more resilient principle than often supposed. However, its resilience comes at too high a price. The problem is its implausible consequence that the (global) downgrading of the epistemic status of one's opponent in a disagreement is *never* permissible if there is no independent reason to do so. Once an epistemic status is assigned to another person it becomes insensitive, even to a long and evolving history of agreement and disagreement. Based on this insight, I present an objection to the Equal Weight View that is itself based on a strong reading of Independence. To salvage the conclusion of the Equal Weight View that disagreeing peers ought to conciliate their judgments, I offer a weaker reading of Independence that limits its significance to the permissibility of the local downgrading of the epistemic status of one's peers. This presupposes a distinction between two types of downgrading, *local* and *global*, which I introduce and then explain. I supplement the Equal Weight View—now equipped with a weak reading of Independence—with a dynamic model of epistemic peerhood, which bases the permissibility of global downgrading on an evolving history of high-confidence dis/agreements. I argue that even when there is no independent reason to alter the epistemic status of others, it can be permissible to do so. The drivers behind an up- and down-grading dynamic are high-confidence dis/agreements. I then return to the question of how the reasonable citizens of a well-ordered society ought to react rationally to political disagreement. Based on the dynamic model of epistemic peerhood just canvassed, I develop a conception of public reason as the shared reason of all reasonable citizens, which I call *Democratic Public Reason*. I identify some high-confidence agreements among reasonable citizens about matters of morality, including their commitments in the area of political morality, and argue that these agreements constitute the epistemic frame of their low-confidence disagreements about other matters of justice. On the level of these low-confidence judgments, reasonable citizens ought to seek to conciliate their judgments with those of their fellow citizens.

Chapter 5—Conciliatory Democracy

This is where the conciliatory conception of democracy finally enters the picture in full. Everything I have said so far leads up to the claim that the conciliatory conception of democracy is the right answer to the question, "how ought the reasonable citizens of a well-ordered society who regard each other as equal normative authorities and as equal epistemic authorities to react to their rational and reasonable political disagreements?" However, some vital steps in the argument for conciliatory conception are still missing, and this chapter starts to address them.

Before explaining in this and the following chapter why the complex set of decision procedures in modern democracies is unique in its tendency to produce outcomes which correspond to conciliatory judgments, I show how an epistemic conciliation of judgments about justice is possible and what it consists of. I use two examples to achieve this: the first is disagreements about distributive justice; the second is disagreements about the permissibility of abortion. As we shall see, the conciliatory conception of democracy can easily accommodate disagreements about distributive justice. Later on, we will also see that conciliation of judgments about distributive justice need not mean that citizens simply reach a middle ground about just levels of inequality. Epistemic conciliation can work along an ideological dimension encompassing various conceptions of justice along with their ingredients, for instance, institutions that structure the distribution of resources and institutions that compensate for some of the effects of inequality. Disagreements about the permissibility of abortion, on the other hand, are trickier. There are various ways to analyze this latter case and, depending on the analysis, we can draw different conclusions. Next, I show in a general discussion of conciliatory democracy and the politics of compromise that the idea of epistemic conciliation can gain traction on a great variety of issues which also lend themselves to political compromise in the traditional sense. The commonality of the ideas of conciliation and compromise is that, in many cases, the possibility of compromise also depends on the existence of a scalar dimension to the issue at stake. Conciliation equally presupposes such a scalar dimension. Hence, it seems that many ordinary issues of politics are potentially subject to the demand to seek epistemic conciliation. It further suggests that the morally adequate reaction to some political disagreements, namely to seek a fair compromise, leads to similar outcomes as the rationally adequate reaction, which is to conciliate the conflicting judgments of reasonable citizens.

In a subsequent step I spell out the idea of epistemic conciliation and its practical implications more fully. If the issue at stake has a scalar dimension, epistemic conciliation engenders moving along that scale and results in a uniquely rational reaction to the disagreement in question. Prima facie, there are many issues which do not seem to have this required scalar dimension, a problem I explore using the example of the abortion controversy. At first sight, we seem to be confronted with a binary choice, i.e. a simple yes or no type of question. If this holds true, then the conciliatory conception of democracy runs aground in these tricky waters. I do suppose that this happens with some political issues. However, this admission only shows that democratic theory and democratic choices are multifaceted and more difficult to come to grips with than some philosophers suppose. Yet I also believe that many contested issues which do not strike us as suitable candidates for epistemic conciliation (or compromise) can be re-described as issues with a scalar dimension. The abortion controversy is a point in question. If we explore the debate in more detail, we quickly come to understand that there are indeed many scalar dimensions to it. If we analyze the issue thus, we become aware that, in spite of appearances, there is ample room for epistemic conciliation. I believe that this point extends to many other political conflicts and hence, that they, too, fall into the scope of the conciliatory conception of democracy.

The primary example I usie in this chapter is disagreements about distributive justice. Clearly, such disagreements remain important in contemporary politics. Furthermore, conflicts about the just distribution of resources are often part and parcel of conflicts about other issues. I first use the example of disagreements about just tax rates to illustrate the idea of epistemic conciliation in this field. Then I discuss more comprehensive disagreements about distributive justice involving broader institutional questions and moral principles. I argue that epistemic conciliation can be issue specific and comprehensive, and that conciliatory democracy can achieve both.

This claim leads to the next vital step in the argument. I show that a complex array of democratic institutions taken together has a robust tendency to produce conciliatory outcomes, i.e. outcomes which correspond to a conciliatory position in political disagreements. The institutions in question are those we find in most modern democracies: representative institutions; and multi-party electoral competition. The inclusion of these institutions in a theory of democracy is an important aspect in which the conciliatory conception of democracy broadens the scope of deliberative conceptions of democracy. Swimming against the stream of contemporary political philosophy, I employ rational choice and game theoretical approaches to political analysis to support my claim. Before moving on to an in-depth discussion of Anthony Downs's spatial model of party competition in the following chapter, I dedicate the second part of Chap. 5 to a discussion of Duncan Black's Median Voter Theorem, which demonstrates the in-built tendency of majoritarian decision-making to conciliatory outcomes.

Chapter 6—Representative Democracy and the Role of Political Parties

Downs's theory is particularly helpful in the context of my argument because it describes the effects of multi-party competition on policy outcomes, and the role of political parties in modern democracies. It shows how political parties position themselves along an ideological dimension which structures the policy space of a polity. It also describes how *party ideologies* serve as information shortcuts for citizens. Apart from providing such information shortcuts, political parties perform an additional crucial epistemic function in modern democracies. They provide the infrastructure to collectively develop a sufficiently consistent and sufficiently specific set of public policies that integrate expert knowledge with its members' more abstract preferences. They thus unburden citizens of a task which they could not perform if left to their own devices (see also in Chap. 3 the section on The Argument from Institutional Expertise).

However, the model as developed by Downs and like approaches are ill-suited for those conceptions of democracy which reject their "realistic" assumptions of narrowly self-interested agents and politics as an arena of elite competition for power and privilege. It thus comes as no surprise that deliberative democrats, to the extent that they engage with them at all, do so in order to reject Downs's model, rational choice, and game theoretical approaches in general. This adversity, however, does not allow them to draw on their many insights when reflecting on democratic decision procedures and democracy in general. I show how the insights of Black, Downs, and others can be put to use for a civic conception of democracy by replacing its motivational premises with the idea of reasonable citizens who seek to promote the justice of their societies. As I show, this move does not affect the core predictions of the approaches under discussion. Multi-party electoral competition in representative democracies and processes of coalition formation maintain their tendency to converge on the median voter position. Furthermore, we can now conceive *party ideologies* as *conceptions of justice* which structure the policy space. Thus, we can describe the tendency to converge on the position of the median voter as a tendency to produce conciliatory outcomes, i.e. outcomes which correspond to the conciliatory position in comprehensive disagreements about justice. This result completes my argument for the conciliatory conception of democracy.

Chapter 7—Connecting the Dots

In this final chapter, I clarify certain aspects of the conciliatory conception of democracy, such as the epistemic authority of democratic decision-making over citizens, the general ambitiousness of its epistemic claims, and I recapitulate how the argument for the conciliatory conception embeds an epistemic claim in the normative framework of deliberative democracy. Furthermore, I discuss how the ideal of conciliatory democracy can bear on non-ideal circumstances. In a concluding remark, I then show how the conciliatory conception produces a congruence between the normative and epistemic dimensions of democracy and thus constitutes an answer to both the normative and the epistemic significance of political disagreement and a solution to the meta-problem of democratic theory.

Contents

1 Rousseau's Insight   1

2 Deliberative Democracy and the Normative
   Authority of Citizens   37

3 The Epistemic Authority of Citizens   87

4 The Epistemology of Political Disagreement   123

5 Conciliatory Democracy   169

6 Representative Democracy and the Role
   of Political Parties   203

7 Connecting the Dots   249

Bibliography   263

Index   265

List of Figures

Fig. 5.1	Unrelated dimensions at right angles to each other	197
Fig. 5.2	Correlated dimensions, showing party positions projected on the principle left–right dimension	198
Fig. 6.1	Two-party competition with centrist majority	217
Fig. 6.2	Party competition with multimodel voter distribution	218
Fig. 6.3	American party movements on a left–right scale, 1952–1992	220
Fig. 6.4	German party movements on a left–right scale, 1953–1994	221
Fig. 6.5	Dutch party movements on a left–right scale, 1952–1994	222
Fig. 6.6	Hypothetical conditions at four stages on the representational process used to illustrate how distortions and biases are evaluated. Conditions: (1) the median voter, MV, is located at +3; (2) Party C is located at +5 and is the party closest to the median voter; (3) Party D, at +10, becomes the parliamentary median through mistranslation from the electoral system; (4) Party C and Party D form the government, and their weighted mean position is +8	241

List of Table

Table 6.1 Policy-, vote-, and office-seeking parties   235

List of Abbreviations

DI *Discourse on the Origin and Foundations of Inequality among Men OR Second Discourse*, in: Rousseau (1997a). References to part and paragraph (DI I.2 = part 1, paragraph 2)
E *Emile or On Education*, in: Rousseau (1979)
GM *Geneva Manuscript*, in: Rousseau (1997b)
LM *Letters Written from the Mountain*, in: Rousseau (2001)
LtoM *Letter to Mirabeau*, in: Rousseau (1997b)
PE *Discourse on Political Economy*, in: Rousseau (1997b), References to paragraph (PE, 1 = paragraph 1)
SC *Of the Social Contract*, in: Rousseau (1997b). References to book, chapter, and paragraph (SC I.2.3 = book 1, chapter 2, paragraph 3)

1

Rousseau's Insight

Up until this day, Jean-Jacques Rousseau remains one of the most enigmatic thinkers of the social contract tradition. He was a brilliant rhetorician whose rhetoric at times obfuscated what he intended to say. Because of this, the interpretation of his philosophical oeuvre presents a challenge to any modern reader and even to his contemporaries.[1] Moreover, as much as I would want to, to explicate all considerations that would have to go into an adequate portrayal of Rousseau's "system" within the confines of this chapter is an impossible undertaking.[2] With this precautionary remark in place, I will lay out a reading of his political theory that could be called retrospective, not in the obvious sense that I am looking at Rousseau through the many layers of ideas and experiences that sedimented into a modern

---

[1] During the French Revolution, the Jacobin leaders Marat, Saint-Just, and Robespierre publicly extolled Rousseau's teachings or, more to the point, a radically distorted version of them.

[2] Fortunately, a number of excellent books discussing these issues in more detail and broader scope have been published recently. In particular, I refer the reader to Cohen (2010) and Neuhouser (2008). These authors have rehabilitated and explored Rousseau at unprecedented depth for the English-speaking world. For the German-speaking context, see the equally excellent Fetscher (1975) and Herb (1989).

© The Author(s) 2017
M. Ebeling, *Conciliatory Democracy*,
DOI 10.1057/978-1-137-57743-6_1

perspective, but through the prism of the conciliatory conception of democracy I defend in this book.

In a very broad sense, then, this conception of democracy is an heir to Rousseau's democratic theory as I construe it in this chapter. Because this conception is informed by my reading of Rawls and Habermas, among others, the reader will detect the undertones of contemporary political philosophy of a broadly Kantian variant.[3] However, we should note that what one of the two, John Rawls, "regarded as important in Kant's political philosophy he attributed to Locke and Rousseau."[4] As for Jürgen Habermas, I believe that his refusal to engage at a deeper level with Rousseau is due to him misreading Rousseau's theory.[5] It is *also* for these reasons, then, that I believe it will ultimately prove its worth to go back in time before Rawlsian and Habermasian Kantianism, before Kant himself even, to the philosophy of Jean-Jacques Rousseau.

The connections between Rousseau's thought and my own ideas presented in this book are manifold. They will to some extent become apparent in the reconstruction I offer in this chapter and more so when I lay out the conciliatory conception of democracy in subsequent chapters. The three most important points I shall make about Rousseau are the following: (1) a reading of Rousseau's doctrine of the general will as a conception of public reason; (2) the epistemic and normative dimensions of democratic decision procedures; and (3) Rousseau's insight that the judgments of citizens can have epistemic significance as equally reliable indicators of the content of the general will. As the title of the chapter suggests, this last point is the most important one.

---

[3] The objective to tease out what connects rather than what disconnects Rousseau from contemporary political thought might serve as a justification for not engaging with the indeed radical criticisms, misunderstandings, and misappropriations to which Rousseau's oeuvre has so often been subjected. See Cassirer (1963), Durkheim (1960), and Bloom (1997) and the critique of their views in Cohen (2010): pp. 34ff.

[4] Freeman (2007): p. 22.

[5] Contrary to Habermas's understanding of Rousseau, I will expound a reading that does not portray him as advocating "an ethical reading of popular sovereignty"; cf. Habermas (1996): p. 101f. See also Maus (1996).

The General Will as a Conception of Public Reason

Rousseau's most distinctive and opaque contribution to social contract theory is the idea of the general will (*la volonté générale*). Its role in his conception of legitimacy is crucial, yet it is difficult to extricate the exact content of the idea from the layers of rhetoric we find in Rousseau's writings. Beneath the at times obfuscating rhetoric, however, there emerges a clear conception, or so I will try to demonstrate, of the general will. In the interpretation I offer in this chapter, the general will is not the will of a supra-individual being; and neither is it the emergent property of a procedure. Instead, I interpret it as a conception of public reason that stems from and applies to each citizen because it derives from their fundamental, shared interests. The general will is not necessarily connected to actual acts of willing of citizens, though it has to be willed in actuality in order for it to manifest itself in and shape their society. However, it is the *constant* will of all citizens, even when it exists only in potentiality, because it supervenes on their fundamental interests; and it is the *dominant* will of all citizens because the supreme importance of these interests trumps whatever importance citizens give to other, non-fundamental interests. This is the gist of Rousseau's answer to the question of why obedience to laws expressing the general will is not contradictory to the freedom of citizens. They remain free because the general will is an expression of what they would have wanted, had they had a proper understanding of their enlightened self-interest. This direct appeal to *the reason of each citizen* in justifying the exercise of political power makes the general will a conception of *public reason*. If the political life of a community is regulated by this public reason of all citizens, all remain as free as before they entered the political state because they can gain a proper understanding of the rationality and the justice of the exercise of political power over them. In this sense, the justification for the exercise of political power is *accessible* to them in a way that it is not when political power is wielded by, for example, a Hobbesian monarch who is at liberty to regulate his realm according to his private reason, that is, as he sees fit. Citizens can be given a justification that they could accept from their own point of view and in light of their shared reason. In this sense, Rousseau's doctrine of the general will is a response to a demand of the *public* justifiability of the exercise of political power.[6]

Thus, we can conceive the role of the general will in Rousseau's thinking as engendering a conception of legitimacy which ties legitimacy to public justifiability. This commitment to the normative criterion of public justifiability is one aspect of Rousseau's political teachings which makes him a relevant reference for the purposes of this book. It reappears at various instances in Chap. 2 where I discuss the normative significance that political disagreement in conciliatory democracy bears on the formal features of the epistemic argument for democracy I offer in Chaps. 5 and 6.

This leads us to the most obscure but also the most distinctive part of Rousseau's political philosophy, the general will (*la volonté générale*). In spite of its obscurity, or maybe because of it, the idea of a general will that guides the collective actions of a polity still resonates in contemporary theories of democracy and is worth exploring in more detail. As I interpret it, it emerges as a forerunner in the history of ideas to a genuinely *public reason*. It is not the reason of a private individual, such as the Hobbesian monarch, which *replaces* the reasons of their subjects and thus overcomes their plurality only by suppressing it.[7] Instead, it is the idea of a reason in which all citizens participate because it is rooted in their fundamental and *shared* interests. Hence, it is a reason that is accessible from the perspective of all citizens. Rousseau believed that it is only under this condition, when social and political institutions and the exercise of political power correspond to a reason that is public in the sense of being accessible, and accessible because it is grounded in certain commonalities, that their legitimacy can be guaranteed. Legitimacy thus presupposes public justifiability. In this reading, Rousseau's political philosophy is the first example of a conception of legitimacy which deeply influenced Kant and other important contemporary Kantian streams in political philosophy. The idea of shared interests of citizens undergoes a non-metaphysical interpretation and

---

[6] Cf. Waldron (1987).
[7] Cf. Gauthier (1995); also Gaus (2003): Chap. 3.

reappears in Rawls's political conception of free and equal persons.[8] The formal and substantive constraints conceptions of deliberative democracy place Rousseau places on the legitimizing general will, on the other hand, return in the shape of formal and substantive constraints on the reasons citizens invoke in public deliberation, as discussed in Chap. 2. What is distinctive about Rousseau's approach, however, is his focus on decision procedures. One question that keeps him occupied is which decision procedures allow the general will to express itself in the form of law. Importantly, the answer to this question has a crucial epistemic dimension and will form the subject of the following section. I begin, then, by laying out Rousseau's idea of a general will as a conception of public reason.

Rousseau claims that through the social contract there comes into being an entity that is a moral and collective being with a self, a life, and a will of its own (SC, I.6.10). This "public person" is called "republic", "body politic" (ibid.), or sometimes "sovereign" (OC, III, 55), though the use of the latter term is usually reserved to denote its members in their capacity as citizens. It "*can be looked upon* as an organized body, alive, and similar to a man's" (PE, 10; my emphasis). The metaphor only goes so far, however. He makes clear that the republic is "*only* a moral person" (OC, III, 57; my emphasis) and "only *a being of reason*" (ibid.; my emphasis) that owes its life to the deliberate act that gave it its unity and existence. The will of this being of reason is the general will.

The Form of the General Will This will is general in its form and its content. It is general in form because it is the will that applies to the citizenry as a whole. Hence, one dimension of its generality is *the generality of application*. Furthermore, it does not attend to any individual or determinate affairs and lose its rectitude when it does (SC, II. 4.5+7). In other words, it considers its objects in the abstract. This dimension of generality is *the generality of the object*. Hence, the formal structure of the general will has an inbuilt momentum of formal equality in that it cannot apply to any particular person or group but only to all equally; and it cannot single out any one person or group and endow them with privileges,

---

[8] Cf. Rawls (1996): pp. 29ff.

or interfere with particular actions.[9] Rousseau explains: "Thus by the very nature of the pact every act of sovereignty, that is to say every genuine act of the general will, either obligates or favors all Citizens equally" (SC, II.4.8). Furthermore, the form of the general will imposes substantive limits (or an expectation thereof) on its content. These derive from the fact that "since the condition [that parties to the social contract agree to a total alienation of their rights] is equal for all, no one has any interest in making it burdensome to the rest" (SC, I.6.6). This is because when reasoning about what each ought to sacrifice for the good of the state and the community, "there is no one who does not appropriate the word *each* to himself" (SC, II.4.5). Thus the formal structure of the general will together with the self-interested reasoning of citizens produces "an admirable agreement between interest and justice which confers on common deliberations a character of equity" (SC, II.4.7), "and justice is nothing but this equality" (LM, 301).[10]

The Content of the General Will This formal structure of the general will is closely tied to *the generality of its content*. Rousseau tells us that "to be truly such [a will that is general], [it] must be so in its object as well as in its essence, [...] it must issue from all in order to apply to all" (SC, II.4.5). This last remark suggests that the formal feature of the general will, its application to all, can be explained in terms of *the generality of its source*. This way of putting it is ambiguousand can easily be misunderstood as meaning that all citizens must actively authorize a will of "the public person'" or "the body politic" (or, which is the same, author a law), or in any other way actively signal their consent, in order for it to be general. Rousseau anticipates this misunderstanding and points out that

---

[9] This does not preclude any public acknowledgment of differences. The state can very well reward citizens for their merit. However, the attainment of these public honors must be possible for all. Furthermore, the relevant type of merit must be such that it strengthens the state and hence promotes the shared interests of all citizens. Rousseau is adamant, though, that a certain type of privileges cannot be awarded to anyone, namely those which place a person or group above the law (PE, 20).

[10] Quoted after Cohen (2010): p. 42.

"what generalizes the will is not so much the number of voices, as it is the common interest which unites them" (SC, II, 4, 7).[11]

More specifically, the end of the institution of the state and the content of the common good is the shared interest in "securing the goods, the life, and the freedom of each member through the protection of all" (PE, 19). Importantly, then, the common good is not to be understood in aggregative terms. For instance, Rousseau did not want to say that the state ought to maximize aggregated pleasure or individual satisfactions of its members. Instead, it ought to be understood in distributive terms as the fundamental interest of *each* member in their life, goods, and freedom. Hence, Rousseau also states that "to sacrifice one innocent person for the safety of the many, I hold this to be one of the most execrable maxims that tyranny ever invented, the most false that might be advanced, the most dangerous that might be accepted, and the most directly contrary to the fundamental laws of society" (PE, 32). Satisfying this interest in one's life, goods, and freedom is no simple matter, of course. Especially the last bit, the interest in securing the freedom of all, involves all the intricacies of Rousseau's political philosophy.

The Scope of the General Will The form and the content of the general will impose limits on its scope. Most significantly, the content of the general will limits its scope (1) to *fundamental, objective* interests *shared* by all citizens (2) to the means necessary to advance them. Citizens certainly have subjective preferences not shared by all. To impose these on others through the use of political power, however, would make the will governing the affairs of a society a particular will. This, of course, violates the requirement that citizens are bound only by their own will and would result in the dependence of the will of some citizens on that of others. Another way of expressing this thought is that the private reason of some citizens would replace and trump the public reason of all citizens in the exercise of political power. Such a relation of dependence would not preserve the freedom of all. Hence, it would violate the

---

[11] However, Rousseau states elsewhere that "[f]or a will to be general, it is not always necessary that it be unanimous, but it is necessary that all votes be counted; any formal exclusion destroys generality" (SC, II.2.1, fn). We shall later see, however, that his reasons for believing thus are different from the ones presently under discussion.

social contract. In other words, it would make the use of political power *illegitimate* and *oppressive*.

This is why Rousseau says that "it is solely in terms of this common interest that society ought to be governed" (SC, II.1.1), and that "the Sovereign [...] cannot burden the subjects with any shackles that are useless to the community" (SC, II.4.4). The bounds of their right over their subjects are the bounds of public utility (SC, IV.8.31), and "[s]ubjects therefore only owe the Sovereign an account of their opinions insofar as those opinions matter to the community" (ibid.). What part of "his power, his goods, his [civil] freedom" (SC, II.4.3) a member of society has to sacrifice is determined by the Sovereign, "who is alone judge" (ibid.) on these matters. This right of the sovereign, that is, *of the citizens taken collectively*, should not put their well-being at risk, however, "since the condition [the total alienation of one's rights to the sovereign] is equal for all, no one has any interest in making it burdensome to the rest" (SC, I.6.6).

Law as the Expression of the General Will While the body politic as a whole and each citizen respectively has a general will—or, maybe more accurately, a will that is generalizable—it finds its expression in laws. Laws are the acts through which the general will manifests itself in society (SC, II.6.7). This alone imposes strict conditions on what can count as law, and not just any act of legislation qualifies. In order to be law, that is, an expression of the general will, it has to share the threefold generality of the general will: (1) the generality of its application; (2) the generality of its object; and (3) the generality of its source (in the fundamental interests of all citizens) (SC, II.6.5–6). Because these conditions are rarely met in the societies of his time (and neither in contemporary ones), he states that "upon closer examination, very few Nations would be found to have laws" (SC, III.15.8).

Rousseau says: "It is to law alone that men owe justice and freedom" (PE, 19). The reasoning behind this claim should by now be obvious. Law secures civil freedom, that is, a sphere of freedom of action that is protected from state interference, because its scope is limited to the common good (SC, I, 8, 2); and it ensures political freedom because it is the expression of the will of self-legislating citizens. Laws are merely "[r] ecords of our will" (SC, II.6.7), which is why the people can be both subject to it and remain free. In other words, law "is this celestial voice that dictates the precepts of *public reason* to every citizen, and teaches him to act in conformity with the maxims of his own judgment, and not to be in contradiction with himself" (ibid.; my emphasis).[12]

Justice as Reciprocity Furthermore, according to Rousseau, members of a society governed by the general will do not only owe justice to the law; he makes the even stronger claim that the law cannot be *un*just! However, this is not because "it has justice as its basis" (GM, II.15), but because "it is against nature to want to injure oneself" (ibid.). In the Rousseauian framework, which ties the idea of justice to the idea of reciprocity, law secures justice because it is not possible to further one's interests without through the same act furthering the interests of all.[13] We can call this conception of reciprocity "reciprocity of advantage."[14] According to Rousseau, the idea of justice as reciprocity is the only idea of justice that is reasonable for human beings. While we might conceive a divine justice, it is beyond the reach of our understanding and of reason. He thus states:

> All justice comes from God, he alone is its source; and if we knew how to attain it at so great a height, we should need neither government nor laws.

---

[12] In addition, Rousseau argues that the existence of enforceable rules is a necessary precondition for any rule, including the law of nature, to become morally binding. His reasoning is that the demand to comply with rules is justified if and only if the expectation is justified that compliance does not bring about disadvantages that are owed to the non-compliance of others. The public proclamation of rules by the state and a state capable of enforcing them are thus preconditions for citizens to justifiably be subject to any such demand. In this sense, the existence of laws and the state is prior to morality.

[13] This is owed to the fact that law applies to all and does not attend to particulars. These formal characteristics of law can only secure justice, however, when there is *a sufficient degree of equality of circumstances* so that law, in spite of its generality, cannot serve the interests of a class of privileged citizens who tailor the laws to their particular interests. If the condition of sufficient equality of circumstances is not met, legal equality "is only apparent and illusory; it serves only to maintain the poor in his misery and the rich in his usurpation" (SC, I.9.8 fn.; see also PE, 34–35). This demand of a more substantive equality among citizens is based on their interest to preserve their freedom defined as independence from the will of others. Hence, freedom is the basic value and a sufficient degree of equality of circumstances a means to secure it.

[14] In more abstract terms, reciprocity of advantage denotes the idea that social institutions advance the interests of citizens according to an appropriate benchmark of equality.

Undoubtedly, absolute justice exists, emanating from reason alone; but in order for it to be accepted among men, it has to be reciprocal. (SC, II.6.2)[15]

This again highlights Rousseau's concern with the *publicity* of the justification of political institutions. The criterion of success is the reasonable acceptability of the reasons offered in justifying the exercise of political power. We can also speak of "reciprocity of justification" in this context. This idea is also at the heart of the deliberative conceptions of democracy I explicate in the next chapter. As we shall see there, it also imposes limits on the kind of epistemic justification we can offer in support of democratic procedures. I outline in Chap. 5 how conciliatory democracy can meet the criterion.

The Epistemic Dimension of Democratic Procedures

So in order for any enacted legislation to be legitimate, that is, a genuine expression of the general will, it has to promote the fundamental, shared interests of citizens. As we have seen, another way of expressing this idea is to say that legitimate laws have to be publicly justifiable. One topic that concerns Rousseau is the designing of decision procedures which tend to produce outcomes meeting this criterion of legitimacy. The decision procedures ought to have a strong tendency to select the course of action which advances the fundamental, shared interests of citizens and does so without imposing unnecessary burdens on them (SC, II.4.4). Rousseau thought that, given certain background conditions, his preferred decision procedure, rule of a supermajority, has a plausible claim to possessing a significant tendency to track the general will. Because of this, he believed, the minority on the losing end faces pressure to defer to the judgment of the supermajority and regard their judgment as superior and not only as normatively but also as epistemically authoritative. We can thus observe that Rousseau advocates *a correctness theory of democratic decision-making*.

---

[15] In a typical move, Rousseau first seemingly grants religious premises only to then refute them decisively.

In the subsequent sections, I will expound the view that Rousseau regards the epistemic virtue of a procedure mainly as a consequence of the fact that it registers the level of agreement in a society. Hence, to what he ultimately assigns epistemic significance are not some mysterious properties of a procedure, about which he does not have much to say at all, but the citizens' judgments *as such*. The minority in a supermajoritarian decision procedure, then, does not face a demand of moral deference merely because of the fact that they lost but because they are part of a marginal minority which stands alone against the judgment of the overwhelming majority of citizens. This aspect of Rousseau's thought, that varying degrees of agreement ought to affect the credence levels of citizens because their judgments as such possess epistemic significance is the central insight and the most important link between his conception of democracy and the conciliatory conception of democracy. This also raises the question of how conciliatory democracy handles the issue of moral deference to a majority judgment (see Chap. 7; The Epistemic Authority of Democracy).

According to Rousseau, "[t]he first and the most important maxim of legitimate or popular government [...] is [...] in all things to follow the general will; *but in order to follow it, one has to know it*" (PE, 19; my emphasis). The task of the people as citizens is to enact legislation which qualifies as laws. In other words, they have to enact legislation which accords with the general will. In order to do so, however, they first have to identify the content of the general will and understand its bearings on particular legislative proposals.

Rousseau believes that certain institutional procedures can help them to do so. More specifically, he accords this role to voting procedures. Each person casts their vote according to what they believe the general will prescribes. The results of such democratic procedures subsequently reveal the general will. This procedural interpretation of the revelation of the general will ushers in a correctness theory of democracy. It is democratic because it requires the participation of all citizens in (some kind of) majoritarian voting procedure. The procedure has epistemic qualities because it potentially reveals the content of the general will. And if it does so, its results, that is, the substance of its outcomes, are democratic in their substance.[16] As I shall expound, his adherence to a correctness theory is connected to his sensitivity to the epistemic significance of citizens' judgments about the general will.[17]

Background Conditions Democratic procedures are fallible. They only *potentially* reveal the general will. In order for them to do so, certain background conditions have to hold. The first condition is that individual citizens cast their vote according to what they believe is the general will and not according to their private interest.[18] He thus states:

> When a law is proposed in the People's assembly, what they are being asked is not exactly whether they approve the proposal or reject it, but *whether it does or does not conform to the general will*, which is theirs; *everyone states his opinion about this by casting his ballot*, and the tally of the votes yields the declaration of the general will. (SC, IV.2.8; my emphasis)

Notice that Rousseau clearly presupposes access to a criterion of correctness, the true content of the general will, which is logically independentfrom and precedes the procedure. This point will reappear in the discussion of conceptions of deliberative democracy in Chap. 2. A further set of conditions is stated in a paragraph which begins thus:

> If, when an *adequately informed* people deliberates, the Citizens had no communication among themselves, the general will would always result from the number of small differences, and the deliberation would always be good. (SC, II.3.3; my emphasis)

---

[16] Rousseau would use the word republican instead of democratic (SC, II.6.9).

[17] Some have interpreted Rousseau as advocating a Condorcet-type theory which holds that if the reliability of individual reasoners surpasses the value of 0.5, the aggregation of their votes according to majority rule when given a binary choice results in a result which is almost certainly correct; cf. Grofman and Feld (1988). Jeremy Waldron, on the other hand, suggests that it is unlikely that Condorcet influenced Rousseau's thinking on this point; cf. Waldron et al. (1989).

[18] Rousseau's cognitive conception of voting stands therefore in opposition to minimal conceptions of democracy which conceive voting as the expression of the interests of individuals (see, e.g., Schumpeter ([1943] 2003)) and Downs (1957) both of whom I discuss in Chap. 5). If they were to vote according to their private interests, the outcome would reflect what Rousseau calls the will of all (*la volonté de tous*), which contrasts sharply with the general will (*la volonté générale*).

The second condition stated here is straightforward: citizens have to be adequately informed before they cast their vote. Presumably, the information citizens ought to have obtained prior to voting presumably is information about how a legislative proposal would affect their fundamental interests and those of others (although the latter part is taken care of by the generality of application of the general will). Rousseau is sometimes interpreted as being opposed to discourse or discussion among citizens. While the ideal of deliberative democracy, which ties political legitimacy in essential ways to public deliberation, was certainly alien to him, the exchange of information and reasoning among citizens is perfectly compatible with his theory. If citizens ought to reach a state of adequate information, as Rousseau says they should, it is even desirable. As will become evident, however, Rousseau uses the term "deliberation" to denote decision-making. Hence, it is not to be confused with the idea of deliberation present in contemporary conceptions of deliberative democracy.

Chapter 3 of Book II of SC is entitled *Whether the General Will Can Err* and commences with the following declaration:

> From the preceding it follows that the general will is always upright and always tends to the public utility: but it does not follow from it that the people's deliberations [i.e., decisions] are always equally upright. One always wants one's good, but one does not always see it: one can never corrupt the people, but one can often cause it to be mistaken, and only when it is, does it appear to want what is bad. (SC, II.3.1)

I will return to the conception of willing invoked in this quote later. As we shall see, it has important consequences for Rousseau's conception of sovereignty. What matters at this point is that this passage indicates that if the decisions taken by the people are to track the general will, the people has to possess *an undistorted conception of the common good*. Hence, the notion of an "adequately informed people" is more encompassing and includes not only adequate knowledge of the means to advance one's fundamental interests but also an adequate conception of the common good.

The third condition has already been mentioned. Recall the earlier stated quote "If, when an adequately informed people deliberates, the Citizens had *no communication* among themselves, [...]" (SC, II.3.3; my emphasis). One could understand this to mean that citizens ought not engage in political discussions with others and, for example, debate the merits of the proposal with each other. This, however, would significantly curtail their freedom of expression and effectively shut down public debate. Rousseau is quick to clarify that he has something quite different in mind. The paragraph continues with the explanation of the reason for the no communication condition:

> But when factions arise, small associations at the expense of the large association, the will of each one of these associations becomes general in relation to its members and particular in relation to the state; there can then no longer be said to be as many voters as there are men, but only as many as there are associations. The differences become less numerous and yield a less general result. Finally, when one of these associations is so large that it prevails over all the rest, the result you have is no longer a sum of small differences, but one single difference; then there is no longer a general will, and the opinion that prevails is nothing but a private opinion. (SC, II.3.3)

The real danger, then, is not communication but the existence of factions that pursue their own general will, which consists in the particular interests shared by its members, at the expense of the general will of the people as a whole, which consists in the fundamental interests shared by all members of society. Nowhere does Rousseau criticize public discussion properly carried out and there are various remarks that prove that he very much endorsed it. In fact, he takes the right to public discussion to be a constitutive part of the political freedom of the people. To quote just one example: "I could offer quite a few reflections here on the simple right to vote in every act of sovereignty; a right of which nothing can deprive Citizens; and on *the right of voicing opinions, proposing, dividing, discussing [motions], which the Government always takes great care to allow only to its own members*; but this important matter would require a separate book, and I cannot say everything in this one" (SC, IV.1.7; my emphasis). The no communication condition, therefore, is really a *no faction condition*.[19] While the existence of various smaller factions might bring about only moderate harm, the ultimate danger for the state is that one such faction becomes so strong that its general will can overpower and usurp the general will of society. Rousseau states that "[i]t is important, then, that in order to have the general will expressed, there be no partial society in the State, and *every Citizen state only his own opinion*" (SC, II.3.4; my emphasis).[20]

To summarize: necessary conditions for the democratic procedure to fulfill its epistemic role are that each citizen cast their votes according to their *independent, adequately informed*, and *sincere* opinion of the requirements of the general will with respect to a given legislative proposal.[21]

The Epistemic Dimension of the Procedure Explained Next, and presuming that the above conditions are met, we have to understand the mechanics of the procedure itself. To what does it owe its epistemic qualities, that is, how does it help us to discern the general will? One clue has already been given with the reasoning behind the no faction condition. If the adequate information and no faction conditions are met, "the general will would always result *from the number of small differences*, and the deliberation would always be good" (SC, II.3.3). When factions do arise, however, "[t]he differences become less numerous and yield a less general result"

---

[19] I will come back to the epistemic significance of the fact that citizens arrived at judgments that figure in political disagreement independently in Chap. 3 where I discuss what I call the *independent reasoning condition*. This is a different sense in which a no faction condition holds for democratic procedures to unfold their epistemic potential.

[20] Recall James Madison's definition of a faction: "By a faction I understand a number of citizens, whether amounting to a majority or a minority of the whole, *who are united and actuated by some common impulse of passion, or of interest, adverse to the rights of other citizens*, or to the permanent and aggregate interests of the community" (The Federalist Papers No. 10, in: Hamilton et al. 2003: p. 123). Madison thought the only way to solve the problem of factions is to mitigate their influence on the political order of society. Rousseau took a different path and stressed homogeneity and equality of circumstance to eradicate *the causes* of the formation of factions.

[21] Rousseau criticizes the influence of demagogues who are not sincere in their public opinions: "Thus do the most corrupt men invariably render some sort of homage to the public faith; this [...] is how even brigands, the enemies of virtue in the large society, worship its semblance in their dens" (PE, 17).

(SC, II.3.3). It is out of differences, then, that the general will emerges. In an enigmatic remark preceding these quotes, Rousseau remarks:

> There is often a considerable difference between the will of all and the general will: the latter looks only to the common interest, the former looks to private interest, and is nothing but a sum of particular wills; but if, from these same wills, one takes away *the pluses and the minuses which cancel each other out*, what is left as the sum of the differences is the general will. (SC, II.3.2; my emphasis)

How is this to be understood? One possible interpretation is that the differences in private interests cancel each other out when they are sufficiently numerous and opposed to each other so that no one could impose their private interests or preferences on others through a democratic procedure. The only interests that the procedure tends to are those that are widely shared. This would require supermajoritarian procedures, which Rousseau supports at various instances. He thus states that

> the more important and serious the deliberations are, the more nearly unanimous should be the opinion that prevails; […] the more rapidly the business at hand has to be resolved, the narrower should be the prescribed difference in weighting opinions; in deliberations which have to be concluded straightaway a majority should suffice. The first of these maxims appears better suited to Laws, the second to business. (SC, IV.2.11)

This interpretation reads Rousseau as writing about citizens who deliberately try to impose their private interests on other citizens. Supermajoritarian procedures and the rule of law are the safeguards that protect the freedom of all from the private wills of others.

However, supermajoritarian procedures also serve another function. Recall Rousseau's earlier quoted remark that votes ought not to be cast according to one's private interests but according to one's opinion regarding the common good (SC, IV.2.8). In this scenario, supermajoritarian procedures do not merely safeguard the freedom of citizens because they block attempts to abuse political power. Instead, they constitute epistemic filters through which the judgments of citizens about the general will have to pass. Only the surviving judgments can have a claim to be true expressions of the general will.

Self-Regarding Interests and the Virtue of Intellectual Humility In this scenario, the private interests of citizens do not figure in their votes with immediacy. Instead, they are present *in the judgments about the general will's content*, which they potentially distort.[22] Rousseau stresses that judging the content of the general will, one has "above all clearly to distinguish it from the particular will beginning with oneself" (PE, 19) and that this distinction "is always very difficult to draw and on which only the most sublime virtue can shed ad'equate light" (ibid.).

Notice that he does not speak of our sincerity that is lacking because we are drawn toward our particular will, which has its source in our private interests. The problem is not that citizens are insincere but that virtuous citizens have to distinguish their particular will from their general will and that this distinction is "very difficult to draw" and to do so correctly requires a capacity to reliably distinguish the general will from one's particular wills. The reason our reliability is limited in this respect is that our private interests are bound to influence our judgment about the common good due to the subtle effects our selfish biases have on our practical reasoning. Importantly, citizens are self-reflectively aware that their reasoning can be distorted in this way and this knowledge about their own precarious epistemic position undermines to some degree their confidence in their own judgment. As Rousseau says, "he [the citizen] should be wary of his own reason" (PE, 6). It is this intellectual humility born out of a self-reflective awareness of one's fallibility that opens the door to an acceptance of a demand of moral deference, which I discuss below.[23]

Mediated through the results of their reasoning, then, their private interests are present in the votes of citizens. Also in this mediated form do they cancel each other out, because—at least in all matters of

---

[22] My interpretation expands on Iring Fetscher's; cf. Fetscher (1975): p. 128f.

[23] This reasoning, which draws on the precarious epistemic status of moral reasoners, furthermore reappears in the arguments leading up to the conciliatory conception of democracy (see Chap. 3). It is another important link between Rousseau's democratic theory and the arguments I shall make in these chapters.

importance—they need to pass the barriers of supermajoritarian rules of decision-making (see SC, IV.2.11 quoted above). Neither an individual citizen nor a small group of citizens would be able to consciously or unconsciously impose their particular will on others as any legislative proposal motivated directly or indirectly by private interests would fail the threshold of supermajoritarian decision-making. This holds even though there is no overt clash of private interests. The key is that no particular will *disguised as the judgment about the content of the general will* can win the day in a vote. The institutionalized requirement of near unanimity guarantees that there is sufficient overlap of what citizens believe the content of the general will to be and how it actually bears on the legislative proposal in question. As Rousseau states, "the agreement between all interests is formed by opposition to each one's interest" (SC, II.3.2, *fn*). The results of the procedure thus stand a good chance of revealing the general will.[24] The reasoning is obvious for the case of insincere citizens trying to impose their private wills on others. It is less clear, though, why near unanimity of opinions about the general will bolsters the majority's claim to be correct. This is exactly the point, however, where Rousseau brings one of his major insights, namely the epistemic significance of the citizens' political judgments, to bear on political philosophy.

As we shall see in Chap. 4, Rousseau is correct in the general observation motivating the requirement of near unanimity. When their judgments have epistemic significance, the number of persons disagreeing and agreeing with us ought to affect the level of confidence we place in our own judgments, and the more people agree with us, the more reason we have to believe that we indeed got it right. However, he is wrong in linking this observation to a requirement of near unanimity and consequently to supermajoritarian decision-making, which in fact distorts the virtue of democratic procedures to take numbers into account in the right way (see Chap. 5).

Let us first explicate Rousseau's arguments on these questions in full, however. Because of the epistemic significance attributed to the political judgments of citizens, assuming the background conditions explicated

---

[24] Thus interpreted, the procedure would display a tendency to avoid false positives at the cost of a correlated tendency to produce false negatives; cf. Gaus (2008).

above are met, the results of democratic procedures obtain a particular authority over subjects. First, they are authoritative in the political sense that the people as subjects owe obedience to the law. Second, they enjoy an epistemic authority over citizens. They ought to defer to the result of the decision procedure. Rousseau says as much when he notes the following:

> The Citizen consents to all the laws, even to those passed in spite of him, and even to those that punish him when he dares to violate any one of them. The constant will of all the members of the State is the general will; it is through it that they are citizens and free. When a law is proposed in the People's assembly, what they are being asked is not exactly whether they approve the proposal or reject it, but whether it does or does not conform to the general will, which is theirs; everyone states his opinion about this by casting his ballot, and the tally of the votes yields the declaration of the general will. Therefore *when the opinion contrary to my own prevails, it proves nothing more than that I made a mistake and that what I took to be the general will was not*. If my particular opinion had prevailed, I would have done something other than what I had willed, and it is then that I would not have been free. (SC, IV.2.8; my emphasis)

Deference, (Near) Unanimity, and Levels of Confidence That citizens ought to defer to the results of democratic decision-making procedures is a very strong claim about the latter's epistemic properties, and one might indeed wonder whether it is not too strong. From the perspective of citizens, this can certainly seem too demanding a requirement on their reasoning. However, I will later argue that as long as they understand the mechanics that produce the procedure's epistemic benefits, it might be a reasonable requirement nevertheless. More specifically, if the justification given does not draw on the reasons the victorious majority has for accepting the outcome, it can be accessible to and possible even for a persistent minority to accept the claim that the procedure track the right (or best) outcomes. I introduce the idea of dependent and independent reasons to explicate this idea in the next chapter (see Chap. 2; Dependent versus Independent Reasons). I also discuss in more detail the normative criterion of reasonable acceptability and the correlated idea of publicly accessible justifications in Chap. 2. As long as this condition of public accessibility is met, the minority could come to understand *why* they ought to defer.

Yet, why does Rousseau argue that decisions have to be reached with near unanimity of judgments in order for the procedure to reveal the general will? Discord, says Rousseau, is a sign that particular wills have gained a foothold in the public decision-making of a community and that the state is in decline (SC, IV.2.1). A modicum of disagreement among citizens, though, is tolerable and even a sign of a healthy, free citizenry as, "[a]t the other end of the cycle, unanimity returns. That is when the citizens, fallen into servitude, no longer have freedom of will" (SC, IV.2.3).

However, if near unanimity is in fact a condition *before* the procedure is carried out, then the procedure does not *reveal* the general will in any particularly strong sense. Instead, it simply *registers* the degree of agreement about the content of the general will to which citizens have *independent* access; or, in Rousseau's words, "the tally of the votes yields the [mere] declaration of the general will" (SC, IV.2.8; my emphasis). The procedure would thus only have the secondary role of pooling information about the general will, but this by itself would not have any epistemic merits apart from informing the citizens that their conception of the general will is shared by (almost) everyone and can thus count as genuine. What has epistemic significance, on the other hand, is the fact that you agree or disagree with a (nearly) unanimous judgment. This all by itself indicates strongly that you are either correct or mistaken. Note the fact that this interpretation lays to rest the idea that the procedure is in any way *constitutive* of the general will.

According to Rousseau, the reverse also holds: the less agreement the procedure reveals, the less reason we have to trust its results. From the point of view of democratic decision-making, then, the lower the majority required to pass a law, the more likely it is that individuals whose judgments are distorted by their private interests in similar ways can influence and distort the outcome. These outcomes no longer reliably track the general will. Thus, the lower the majoritarian requirement, the less robust are the procedure's epistemic merits. In the Rousseauian conception of a correctness theory of democracy, then, the prevalence of disagreement is an indicator that the evidence about the common good provided by the procedure's role of pooling and balancing judgments about the common good is weaker in relation to the procedure-independent evidence supporting the original judgment of individual citizens. Hence, the more disagreement there is, the lower is the pressure to defer to the opinion of the majority.

If this interpretation is correct, it shows that Rousseau was acutely aware of the epistemic significance of political judgments as indicators of the common good and of the epistemic significance of the degree of disagreement in a community. Democratic procedures, on the other hand, serve an epistemic role primarily because they register the degree of agreement on a given question. The higher the consensus, at least as long as it is not a full consensus, the more trust citizens can place in the procedures' outcomes and the more reason they have to defer to them. Later on, I will show that Rousseau was right in emphasizing the epistemic significance of political judgments (Chap. 4) and mistaken in treating disagreement exclusively as a problem for the epistemic trust citizens can place in democratic outcomes and as a sign of the degeneration of the public culture of societies (Chap. 3). Before we get there, however, let me first elucidate why political judgments have epistemic significance in Rousseau's account.

Procedure-Independent versus Procedure-Dependent Access to the General Will As the discussion so far indicates, citizens have to at least potentially have procedure-independent access to the content of the general will. Indeed, Rousseau thought that at least in some cases the general will could be known without the need for democratic procedures at all. He states as follows:

> So long as several men united [...] have but a single will, which is concerned with their common preservation, and the general welfare. Then all of the springs of the State are vigorous and simple, its maxims are clear and perspicuous, it has no confused, contradictory interests, *the common good is everywhere fully evident and requires only good sense to be perceived.* (SC IV.1.1; my emphasis)

When the common good is fully evident, it seems likely that adequately informed, independent, and sincere citizens all arrive at the same judgment about the general will and thus reach a (nearly) unanimous verdict. Hence, in such cases the procedure merely *confirms* what everybody had already known and is no longer required to *reveal* the general will in any sense other than simply making public the near unanimous agreement of judgments and enacting a legislative proposal in a procedurally legitimate way so that the general will finds its expression in law. Because the general will is fully evident to all reasonable citizens, furthermore, they count as *equal epistemic authorities,* that is, prima facie equally reliable judges of the rightness of political decisions according to a procedure-independent criterion of rightness (the content of the general will).

However, when the common good is indeed *fully evident* but the outcome of the vote deviates from the judgments of adequately informed, independent, and sincere citizens, these citizens could be justified in believing that the procedure is deficient in some way or other and consequently in criticizing the outcome based on their own, sincere judgment. As Rousseau points out, the rise of strong factions can result in an incongruity of the will of the majority and the general will (SC, II.3.3; also see the discussion of the no communication or no faction condition above). In such cases, because the procedure is not constitutive of the general will but can only reveal the extent of agreement on its bearing on issues at stake in decision-making, the judgments of individual citizens about the general will could potentially serve a critical function. Citizens could criticize the outcome of procedures and, subsequently, they could criticize the procedure itself as defective. This would undoubtedly put a dent into the common perception of Rousseau as an advocate of a strong correctness theory of democracy. However, Rousseau himself does not explore this implication of independent access to the general will, and we would thus be mistaken to ascribe a weaker view to him. His ascription of a rather weak role to epistemic procedures, along with the postulation of independent access to the general will could be read as implying that under certain conditions, citizens could potentially stand their ground even against a large majority of disagreeing citizens.

The fact that the common good is fully evident, however, need not have this consequence. It could also be that the common good is indeed sometimes fully evident but that citizens cannot know that it is. In this scenario, if looked at in isolation, a citizen could form a fully justified, true belief B about the common good based on the evidence E available to them. This is simply what it means for something to be fully evident. But at the same time, it could also be the case that B would not be justified if other aspects of their epistemic circumstances are taken into account. They might, for instance, have countervailing evidence E' defeating their justification for believing B on the basis of E. E' could defeat their justification for believing B on the basis of E in two ways. It could be a *rebutting defeater*, that is, it could be better evidence for *non-B* than E is for B. Or it could be an *undercutting defeater*, that is, evidence undermining the evidential connection between E and B. You might be justified in believing B on the basis of a testimony you have received, for instance. However, you might learn later that the person who gave the testimony is a pathological liar, was drugged, or for some other reason untrustworthy. This new information now undermines your justification for B based on the testimony. Evidence which is an undercutting defeater, then, is *higher-order evidence*, evidence about your evidence.[25]

An example of E' could be the near unanimous outcome of the democratic procedure all have participated in. In such a case, the countervailing evidence E' might be so strong that they would be under pressure to defer to the outcome of such procedures *even though* the common good is in fact fully evident and the procedures are in fact and unbeknownst to them deficient. The outcome of the vote would then constitute defeating but misleading evidence. Furthermore, it would still be an undercutting defeater because it gives you reason to believe that your original evidence E on which you based your original belief B did not justify B. It does so because the near unanimous judgment of the majority is based on the same original evidence E, the fully evident common good. Rousseau believes that the fact that the vast majority of citizens judged the matter differently than you is higher-order evidence, evidence about the evidential connection between E and B, which undermines this connection.

---

[25] See Pollock and Cruz (1986) for the distinction between rebutting and undercutting defeaters. See also Feldman (2005): p. 104 and Christensen (2010): p. 193ff.

Whether we really ought to think that disagreement with a near unanimous judgment can indeed defeat the justification for your original belief depends on our analysis of the epistemic significance of disagreement. Which are we to trust more, our own judgment or the outcome of the procedure, that is, the judgment of the majority? When we stand alone in our judgment against the judgment of a vast majority of citizens, Rousseau argued, this higher-order evidence E', revealed through the procedure, conclusively undermines the evidential connection between your first-order evidence E, your procedure-independent access to the common good, and your belief B about the content of the common good.

All this pertains to the case when a proposal passes the hurdle of supermajoritarian procedures, or, alternatively, if it is nearly unanimously rejected. But what if neither is the case? In that case, the procedure of course nevertheless reveals the degree of agreement among citizens. Rousseau thought, however, that if the degree of the disagreement is higher, that is, if the size of the majority in favor of or against a proposal decreases, the less evidence it provides either way on the question as to whether it conforms to the general or not.

The Epistemic Significance of Political Disagreement We can explain Rousseau's reasoning on this point in two ways. The first way would be to ascribe to him the *Total Evidence View* on disagreement between equal epistemic authorities on the general will. I will discuss this view in more detail in Chap. 4. For now it suffices to say that, according to this view, the rationality of your reaction to disagreement with persons whom you regard as equally reliable judges of an issue depends on your first-order evidence and your second-order evidence taken together, that is, the total evidence. For Rousseau, this was the procedure-independent evidence E about the common good relative to the procedure-dependent evidence E', that is, the degree of disagreement. What decides which reaction to disagreement your total evidence supports is the strength of your first-order evidence relative to that of your second-order evidence. As we have seen, Rousseau thought that E was generally weak evidence. We are not justified in regarding our judgments about the common good as very reliable. Supermajoritarian outcomes, on the other hand, constitute strong evidence about the common good. In this constellation, our total evidence, according to the Total Evidence View, recommends that we dramatically lower our confidence in our original belief B up to the point of deferring to the unanimous judgment of the overwhelming majority. The closer the result comes to a 50:50 split of votes, however, the weaker the procedure-dependent evidence becomes until it eventually stops being evidence either way. Hence, if we are part of a minority which loses by a narrow margin, we do not have to regard it as reason to lower the confidence in our original belief. In this case, the total evidence is predominately determined by our first-order evidence, our procedure-independent judgment about the common good. This does not imply, of course, that we have reason to be any more confident about it. As we have seen, Rousseau also postulated an upper limit, near unanimity, after which, when unanimity returns, the vote provides evidence that "citizens, fallen into servitude, no longer have freedom of will" (SC, IV.2.3). Unanimity, then, seems to have the same effect as widespread disagreement. The outcome of the vote falls short of constituting evidence. This is not an entailment of the Total Evidence View, however, and speaks more to the claim that only the existence of strong factions could explain a nearly unanimous judgment.

The second way to explain Rousseau's statements about the epistemic significance of political disagreement is by appeal to the *Equal Weight View* on disagreement between persons who regard each other as equally reliable judges of the common good. According to the Equal Weight View, as the name suggests, we ought to give equal weight to the judgments which figure in the disagreement at hand. In the case of clear majorities, the view thus suggests that we go along with the majority. If all judgments weigh equally, the aggregated judgment of the majority weighs more. Hence, in the case of supermajoritarian outcomes, this view suggests the same result as the Total Evidence View. Citizens who disagree ought to defer to the majority.

When majorities become narrower, however, these views come apart. While the Total Evidence View suggests an increase in relative weight of the first-order evidence, thus justifying sticking to one's guns, the Equal Weight View states that we ought to move toward a suspension of judgment about the common good. Notably, it does so without any reference to your first-order evidence. Instead, it argues that the second-order evidence, the *fact* of disagreement, undermines your first-order evidence no matter the *degree* of disagreement. This is an important point to which I will return in Chap. 4. For now, I want to simply note that according to the Equal Weight View, once we arrive at a 50:50 split in votes, citizens ought to remain agnostic about the issue at stake.

Prima facie, it seems that Rousseau did not hold this view. He argued, after all, that more widespread disagreement is not a reason to alter our confidence in B based on your original evidence E. This, we might think, points to an endorsement of the Total Evidence View. However, after introducing the epistemological principle dubbed "Independence" in Chap. 4, I will argue that Rousseau's conclusion is in fact compatible with the Equal Weight View and that the textual evidence furthermore supports ascribing the view to him. Importantly, Rousseau cites a sociological observation, namely "a state in decline" as an independent reason to discard the epistemic significance of more widespread disagreement (SC, IV.2.1).

In Dubiis Libertas In either case, Rousseau seems to have regarded our procedure-independent evidence E quite generally as too weak a source of support for our belief B and, crucially, as *insufficient to justify the exercise of political power*. Rousseau argues that the exercise of political power on the basis of B is only legitimate when our credence in B passes a certain threshold. For Rousseau, this threshold was extremely high. We have to be certain that B tracks the general will. Only if credence in B is reinforced through procedure-dependent evidence E' is acting on it fully justified and the exercise of political power legitimate. He thus states that "it can never be certain that something willed by a particular person is in conformity with the general will until it has been submitted to the free vote of the people" (SC, II.7.7) and, we should add, has passed the hurdle of supermajoritarian decision-making.

The reason for putting the threshold so high is that binding law, if it is not an expression of the general will, is a severe violation of our freedom, which Rousseau regards as the overriding good of citizens. No advantage that we might incur can justify the loss of freedom. Any law which is not an expression of the general will decreases the freedom of those subject to it. It follows that the most important task of institutional design is to ensure, as far as this is possible, that only those proposals can be passed into law which are expressions of the general will. The focus, then, lies on avoiding false positives, that is, laws which are *not* expressions of the general will.[26] Hence, before passing a proposal into law, we ought to be *certain* that it is an expression of the general will. Because our own independently reached judgments about the general will are unreliable, or at least not reliable enough to warrant certainty, we cannot legislate based on them alone. This is where the epistemic significance of political judgments of other citizens as equally reliable indicators of the general will comes in. Rousseau maintains that the only way to reach certainty is when a judgment is held nearly unanimously. This fact, the fact that the vast majority of citizens agrees with us, gives us reason to increase the credence in B. Conversely, when we disagree with their judgment, this fact gives us reason to drastically lower credence in our belief about the general will and eventually to defer to their judgment.

The Simplicity Assumption What makes near unanimity possible is that, under ideal conditions, the general will is fully evident to all citizens. Specifying these ideal conditions, Rousseau states that in a well-ordered society, citizens meet the following requirements: (1) their votes are determined by their sincere judgments about the justice of the public choices confronting them; and (2) they give motivational primacy to the common good. Let us call such citizens "reasonable." As we proceed through the chapters of this book, I will expand the conception of the reasonableness of citizens of a well-ordered society. For Rousseau, such reasonable citizens make for a well-ordered society, in which "the common good is everywhere fully evident and requires only good sense to be perceived" (SC IV.1.1) and which "needs very few Laws, and as it becomes necessary to promulgate new ones, this necessity is universally seen" (SC, IV.1.2). Thus, characteristic of the legal regulation of the political affairs of a well-ordered society is its simplicity. Crucially, it is *because* of this simplicity

---

[26] Apparently, Rousseau thought that false negatives, that is, proposals which *are* expressions of the general will but are *not* passed into law, do not interfere with the freedom of citizens, or that this is at least less worrysome.

of what the general will prescribes that the latter can be fully evident to sincere citizens fully committed to the common good in the first place.

Given the complexities of the regulation of modern societies we are familiar with, however, the idea that "very few laws" could suffice to advance the common good must strike us as wildly outdated. And if we thus drop the simplicity assumption, we consequently have to put in doubt the notion that the common good is fully evident to citizens of a well-ordered society and, consequently, that near unanimity is a hopelessly unrealistic ideal. If the common good is not fully evident to all, furthermore, an institutional requirement of supermajoritarian decision-making ensuring near unanimity would make legislation outright impossible. A further consequence is that if we stick to Rousseau's analysis of the epistemic significance of political disagreement and the demand of intellectual humility, we cannot reach the certainty we were hoping for in the belief that a given proposal is an expression of the general will.

Once we drop the simplicity assumption, we consequently face a choice between two options. First, we could maintain the requirement of near unanimity and accept that collective decision-making will become virtually impossible, or, second, we could give up the requirement and accept that our decision-making takes place under conditions of severe uncertainty (or even ignorance).

Yet, once we reject as unrealistic the assumption of simplicity of legal regulation under ideal conditions, all that citizens can do is to vote according to their sincere belief about the common good and accept that there is a significant degree of uncertainty that their decision-making ensures their freedom as independence.

Legitimacy without Procedures? In spite of all this, Rousseau thought that the justification provided by the available procedure-independent evidence is sometimes strong enough to justify organs of the state to act on their sincere belief about the general will's bearing on an issue *in the absence of procedural evidence* that they are correct in their assessment. Rousseau states that when the government, that is, the entity in charge of the administration of the abstract laws issued by the people acting as sovereign applies the law to particular cases, it has to take into account "an infinite number of details of policy and of economy" (PE, 23) and decide cases which the sovereign had not anticipated. Being obligated to follow the general will in all its actions, the government, just as citizens, "*in order to follow it, [...] has to know it*" (PE, 19; my emphasis). Rousseau now states:

> It will be all the less necessary to assemble it [the entire nation], as *it is not certain that its [the entire nation's] decision would be the expression of the general will*; as this method is impractical with a large people, and is rarely necessary when the government is well intentioned: for the chiefs know well enough that the general will is always on the side most favorable to the public interest, that is to say, the most equitable; so that one need only be just in order to be sure of following the general will. (PE, 23; my emphasis)

This indicates that the general will can indeed be known by those administrating the law, or at least what it demands when the law is applied to unforeseen cases, without reference to procedures. Yet this is put into doubt again by other remarks. Consider this one:

> It seems to me that the *evidence* can be in the natural and political laws *only when they are considered in abstraction*. In any particular government, which is a composite of so many diverse elements, *this evidence necessarily disappears*. (LtoM, 1; my emphasis throughout)

Citizens, it seems then, only have independent epistemic access to the content of the general if it is "considered in abstraction."[27] The quote furthermore seems to imply that the business of the government, on the other hand, is so complex that any justification for a belief about the implications of the general will for fine-grained policy-making is undermined. I believe that there is indeed something to be said for an argument along these lines, and I will consider how it bears on our (epistemic) respect for the judgments of others as they figure in their vote (see Chap. 3; The Argument from Institutional Expertise). I will argue that democratic institutions and most notably political parties in

---

[27] This epistemic constraint provides a further reason for the form of the general will. Although, this reason certainly does not feature prominently in Rousseau's arguments.

a multiparty system have a significant epistemic role which consists in furnishing the abstract-value judgments of citizens in *sufficiently coherent* and *sufficiently specific* conceptions of justice, thus translating them into detailed and interlocking policy proposals. In Chaps. 5 and 6, finally, I will take up this idea and outline an argument for democracy which takes the constructive role of political parties seriously and thus treats political parties as an integral part of a civic conception of democracy.

The Normative Dimension of Democratic Procedures

In the opening paragraphs of this chapter, I have discussed the substantive aspects of Rousseau's conception of democracy, by which I mean the requirements of the general will's form and content. I then discussed his epistemic conception of democracy. Now, I turn to the normative dimension he accords to democratic procedures.

Sovereignty as the Epistemic and Normative Authority of the People
Rousseau famously argued that the will of the people cannot be represented. And because sovereignty is the exercise of the general will *of the people*, a people are only sovereign as long as it is they who make the laws. He took this to imply that sovereignty is incompatible with representative legislative institutions. Indeed, he issued drastic warnings that the only institutions through which a people can remain sovereign are direct democratic (SC, III.15). For the purposes of this discussion, I leave the question of representation and direct democracy aside, and I thus proceed to discuss an important question related to the people's exclusive right to exercise the general will.[28]

---

[28] I might only note here that I believe that Rousseau is mistaken in his criticism of representative institutions even according to his own assumptions. We have already learned that the general will is the *constant* will of the people, that is, what they would will if they had an enlightened understanding of their fundamental, shared interests and the means to promote them. If we assume that representative institutions have epistemic advantages over the belief-forming process of individual citizens would lack, we can see that the counterfactual test for the will of the people, their general will, leads us to

As we have just heard, the democratic enactment of laws is part of their legitimacy. I have shown earlier that, according to Rousseau, for them to count as genuine acts of the general will, they have to share its threefold generality expressed in both form and content. Hence, the conception of legitimacy that emerges from Rousseau's conception of sovereignty and the general will is both procedural and substantive. Only those laws are legitimate which are the outcome of democratic procedures and satisfy the three conditions of generality of both form and content. Rousseau thus defends a conception of complex legitimacy which mixes procedural and substantive criteria of legitimacy.[29]

The role of democratic procedures in this is ambivalent, however. I have shown earlier that Rousseau endorsed a correctness theory of democracy which ascribes an epistemic role to democratic procedures, namely the revelation of the degree of agreement among citizens. The requirement of a supermajority is nothing but an institutional safeguard that the decision procedure avoids false positives, that is, laws which bind citizens even though they do not correspond to the general will, and hence are illegitimate in their substance. This is in line with the primary aim of Rousseau's political philosophy to ensure that citizens only obey laws that they have willed themselves and which accord with their constant will, which is the general will.

We have now learned that the procedure also has a normative dimension because through it a people exercises its sovereignty. But how do the epistemic and normative dimensions of democratic procedures interact in Rousseau's conception of legitimacy and sovereignty? And why is it not enough that political power is wielded in accordance with the general will but instead has to be made efficacious through an actual act of willing on part of the citizens? In other words, how does procedural legitimacy add to the substantive legitimacy of decisions which accord with the general will?

---

endorse these institutions. Representatives might have a better understanding of the means to promote the fundamental, shared interests of citizens than they do themselves. Epistemic benefits of representative institutions arise from the discussions in legislative assemblies among representatives of different groups or by the manifold ways in which political parties take expert knowledge into account in their formulation of proposals of public policy and institutional reform (see Chap. 3; The Argument from Institutional Expertise; also Chap. 6; The Fundamental Role of Political Parties).

[29] Charles Beitz (1989) employs the term "complex legitimacy" to describe such conceptions of legitimacy.

The key to this mystery is, I believe, Rousseau's statement that the Sovereign, "*who is alone judge*" (SC, II.4.3; my emphasis) on these matters, determines what part of "his power, his goods, his [civil] freedom" (ibid.) a member of society has to sacrifice in their service to the common good. The role of sovereign as judge has obvious normative connotations. The sovereign *decides* the issue. On the other hand, the role of a judge can also serve an epistemic function. The sovereign judges as in *making a judgment* regarding the question at hand and this judgment cannot only be *normatively* but also *epistemically* authoritative. According to this interpretation of the role of a judge, the sovereign, who is nothing but the citizens taken collectively, enjoys an epistemic authority over what the general will requires of the members of society. Furthermore, because "judging what is foreign to us, we have no true principle of equity to guide us" (SC, II.4.5), nobody can act as a stand-in for the actual citizens when it comes to determining their common good. In addition, because in a well-ordered society the common good is fully evident to all citizens, citizens count as equal epistemic authorities regarding the content of their general will (SC, IV.1.1; see also Procedure-Independent versus Procedure-Dependent Access to the General Will above). In other words, citizens regard each other as equally reliable judges of the content of the general will. Moreover, this standing as equal epistemic authorities provides the foundation for their standing as *equal normative authorities* with an equal right to take the result of their deliberations as prima facie reasons for action and, subsequently, to participate as equals in the process of collective decision-making.

Because of how the epistemic and normative dimensions of democratic procedures interact, they are not in opposition but instead two sides of the same coin. Citizens as equal normative authorities have the exclusive right to pass binding laws. They enjoy this right (at least in part) because they are equal epistemic authorities. The epistemic qualities of democratic procedures aim to reveal the conception of the common good that is undistorted by the selfish biases of citizens. The form of law and a sufficient equality of circumstances, finally, ensure that the outcomes of democratic decision procedures take on the generality required for them to count as acts of the general will of all members of society. This is the solution Rousseau offers for the meta-problem of democratic theory, namely how to make the normative and the epistemic dimensions of democratic procedures converge.

Part of this conception of sovereignty as the equal epistemic and normative authority of citizens expressing itself in the form of law is that there are no pre-political limits on the legitimate exercise of political power apart from those internal to the conception of sovereignty itself. These internal limits are a function of the fundamental interests that go into the social contract and the general reciprocity that is its formal element:

> What, then, is, properly, an act of sovereignty? It is not a convention of the superior with the inferior, but a convention of the body with each one of its members: A convention which is legitimate because it is based on the social contract, equitable because it is common to all, and secure because the public force and the supreme power are its guarantors. So long as subjects are subjected only to conventions such as these, they obey no one, but only their own will; and to ask how far the respective rights of Sovereign and Citizens extend is to ask how far the Citizens can commit themselves to one another, each to all, and all to each. (SC, II.4.8)

The Lawgiver In addition to this, Rousseau introduces the figure of the lawgiver. The task of the lawgiver is the original constitution of the people, that is, of the sovereign and the original legislation of the fundamental laws of the polity enabling the people to exercise their sovereignty. The acts of original constitution and legislation are not themselves acts of sovereignty, yet Rousseau thought that they are nevertheless legitimate because they derive from the lawgiver's peculiar authority which "is specific and superior, having nothing in common with human authority" (SC, II.7.4).

Speaking of his favored historical example of a wise lawgiver, Rousseau notes that "[w]hen Lycurgus gave laws to his country, he began by abdicating the throne" (SC, II.7.5). And this is an act of political wisdom because if he had done otherwise, his particular interests as an individual would have impaired "the sanctity of the work" (SC, II.7.4). However, referring to this act of abdication after the legislation of the fundamental laws governing society also makes a philosophical point. The point is that "[h]e who frames the laws [...] has not, or should not have, any rights of making law; the people cannot, even if it wished to, divest itself of these incommunicable rights" (SC, II.7.7). The incommunicable rights of the people, however, do not extend to the fundamental laws which make their exercise possible in the first place.[30]

We can read the role of the lawgiver, furthermore, as a reflection on the role and proper self-understanding of political philosophy. How does philosophers who "legislates" ex cathedra the necessary conditions of political legitimacy, for instance, position themselves vis-à-vis the people's sovereignty to make their own laws? This fundamental question for political philosophy shall play its part in the discussion of deliberative democracy in the subsequent chapter.[31] As we shall see, the political judgments of citizens gain additional normative weight in conceptions of deliberative democracy.

References

Beitz, C. R. (1989). *Political Equality*. Princeton, NJ: Princeton University Press.
Bloom, A. (1997). Rousseau's Critique of Liberal Constitutionalism. In C. Orwin & N. Tarcov (Eds.), *The Legacy of Rousseau* (pp. 143–167). Chicago: University of Chicago Press.

---

[30] This thought already points to Habermas's thesis of the co-originality of human rights and the rights of citizens to exercise their political autonomy. Habermas describes the former as enabling conditions for the exercise of political autonomy through the medium of law; cf. Habermas (1996): Chap. 3.1 and Habermas (1998): Chap. 10.

[31] The lawgiver, it should be noted, enters the picture not only as an external source of authority. Rousseau was deeply pessimistic about the prospect of reaching the harmonious social and political circumstances outlined in his various works. He thought that the corruption of the human mind in the societies of his time was an almost insurmountable obstacle on the way to a social world in which everybody could live according to their true nature and unfold their potential for virtue. He was thus forced to look for an outside force of intervention, a deus ex machina, to turn the ship around and set humankind on the path to an existence in harmony with its true nature. This figure is the lawgiver. It is the rare wise statesman who has gained deeper insights into these matters and who, when circumstances are right, takes the opportunity to reform the social and political institutions of their society (SC, II.7.1). This top-down transformation of society affects the psyche of citizens, making them more virtuous, capable of recognizing their true interests and reliably acting on them, and providing the motivational reinforcements of love of fatherland and a civil religion (SC, II.7.3). This is the political function of the lawgiver.

Cassirer, E. (1963). *Question of Jean-Jacques Rousseau* (P. Gay, Trans.). Indianapolis, IN: Indiana University Press.

Christensen, D. (2010). Higher-Order Evidence. *Philosophy and Phenomenological Research, 81*(1), 185–215.

Cohen, J. (2010). *Rousseau. A Free Community of Equals*. Oxford: Oxford University Press.

Downs, A. (1957). *An Economic Theory of Democracy*. New York: Harper and Row.

Durkheim, E. (1960). *Montesquieu and Rousseau*. Ann Arbor, MI: University of Michigan Press.

Estlund, D., Waldron, J., Grofman, B., Feld, S.L. (1989). Democratic Theory and the Public Interest: Condorcet and Rousseau Revisited, *The American Political Science Review, 83*(4), 1317–1340.

Feldman, R. (2005). Respecting the Evidence. *Philosophical Perspectives, 19*(1), 95–119.

Fetscher, I. (1975). *Rousseaus politische Philosophie: Zur Geschichte des demokratischen Freiheitsbegriffs*. Frankfurt a.M.: Suhrkamp Verlag.

Freeman, S. (2007). *Rawls*. London: Routledge.

Gaus, G. F. (2003). Liberal Neutrality: A Compelling and Radical Principle. In G. Klosko & S. Wall (Eds.), *Perfectionism and Neutrality* (pp. 137–165). Lanham, MD: Rowman & Littlefield.

Gaus, G. F. (2008). The (Severe) Limits of Deliberative Democracy as the Basis for Political Choice. *Theoria: A Journal of Social and Political Theory, 117*, 26–53.

Gauthier, D. (1995). Public Reason. *Social Philosophy and Policy, 12*(Winter), 19–42.

Grofman, B., & Feld, S. L. (1988). Rousseau's General Will: A Condorcetian Perspective. *American Political Science Review, 82*, 567–576.

Habermas, J. (1996). *Between Facts and Norms: Contributions to a Discourse Theory of Law and Democracy* (W. Rehg, Trans.). Cambridge, MA: MIT Press. This work originally appeared in German under the title *Faktizität und Geltung. Beiträge zur Diskurstheorie des Rechts und des demokratischen Rechtsstaats*, Suhrkamp Verlag, Frankfurt am Main, Germany, 1992.

Habermas, J. (1998). In C. Cronin & P. De Greiff (Eds.), *The Inclusion of the Other: Studies in Political Theory*. Cambridge, MA: The MIT Press. This work originally appeared in German under the title *Die Einbeziehung des anderen. Studien zur politischen Theorie*. Frankfurt am Main, Germany: Suhrkamp Verlag, 1996.

Hamilton, A., Madison, J., & Jay, J. (2003). The Federalist. In T. Ball (Ed.), *Hamilton, Madison and Jay: The Federalist with Letters of "Brutus"* (pp. 1–433). Cambridge: Cambridge University Press.

Herb, K. (1989). *Rousseaus Theorie legitimer Herrschaft. Voraussetzungen und Begründungen.* Würzburg: Königshausen und Neumann.

Maus, I. (1996). Liberties and Popular Sovereignty: On Jürgen Habermas's Reconstruction of the System of Rights. *Cardozo Law Review, 17*(4–5), 825–882. This work originally appeared in German under the title *Freiheitsrechte und Volkssouveränität. Zu Jürgen Habermas' Rekonstruktion des Systems der Rechte*. Rechtstheorie, Jg. 26, H. 4, 1995, pp. 507–562.

Neuhouser, F. (2008). *Rousseau's Theodicy of Self-Love: Evil, Rationality, and the Drive for Recognition.* Oxford: Oxford University Press.

Pollock, J. L., & Cruz, J. (1986). *Contemporary Theories of Knowledge.* Oxford: Rowman & Littlefield.

Rawls, J. (1996). *Political Liberalism* (2nd ed.). New York: Columbia University Press.

Rousseau, J.-J. (1994). *Discourse on Political Economy and The Social Contract* (C. Betts, Trans.). Oxford: Oxford University Press.

Schumpeter, J. A. ([1943] 2003). *Capitalism, Socialism, and Democracy.* London: Routledge.

Waldron, J. (1987). Theoretical Foundations of Liberalism. *The Philosophical Quarterly, 37*(147), 127–150.

2

Deliberative Democracy and the Normative Authority of Citizens

I have introduced Rousseau's political philosophy in the preceding chapter because it is the natural point of reference and most important source of inspiration in the history of philosophy for the conception of conciliatory democracy I advance in this book. Naturally, then, I believe that we can still learn a great deal from his ideas today. As I will show in the chapters to come (esp. Chaps. 3 and 4), this holds specifically for his central insight that the judgments of citizens can have epistemic significance as equally reliable indicators of the common good, and the way this connects to the epistemic role of democratic procedures.

    I now want to turn the attention away from this philosopher of old toward contemporary political philosophy and to one strand in democratic theory in particular, namely the school of deliberative democracy. While doing so, we will not lose touch with Rousseau completely, however. One reason for focusing on the idea of deliberative democracy in contemporary political philosophy is that it is in important respects continuous with Rousseau's political philosophy and contributes an additional layer to our understanding of the normative weight of political judgments. Hence, it will be interesting to see how contemporary political philosophers carry over to modern times ideas from the eighteenth century and build on them. Moreover, the

© The Author(s) 2017
M. Ebeling, *Conciliatory Democracy*,
DOI 10.1057/978-1-137-57743-6_2

argument for the conception of conciliatory democracy draws on these insights of deliberative democrats about the normative criteria for political legitimacy; and even though I do not myself argue for the normative premises of deliberative democracy—apart from revisiting arguments others have made I use them as building blocks in my overall argument for conciliatory democracy. One could say, then, that the conciliatory conception of democracy is continuous with deliberative conceptions in its basic normative orientation. Where it differs is in reinserting the epistemic significance of political judgments and the epistemic role of procedures into this shared normative framework. Hence, it reintroduces neglected Rousseauian ideas into democratic theory, albeit now in a very different form.

In this chapter, I thus start by discussing the broader strand of theories of deliberative democracy and their shared normative commitments. The focus of my discussion lies on the interplay of a commitment to the actual deliberation of citizens and an acknowledgment of the fact of disagreement between them. I will explore how far the normative commitments can carry us toward a comprehensive theory of democracy, by which I mean a theory comprising both deliberation *and* decision-making in the face of the inevitable disagreement between citizens sincerely advocating their view of the common good in public deliberation. What the discussion will show is that the legitimacy of decision procedures has to have an independent footing in the normative framework of democracy. In this sense, deliberative democracy cannot be deliberative all the way down. Even when we concede this point, however, the normative framework does still not lend itself to specifying one among a number of possible decision procedures. It is at this point that epistemic considerations become pertinent. In particular, the question will take center stage whether the claim that decision procedures track the right or most reasonable decisions, or track *bestness* in this sense, can be justified to all citizens who are in reasonable disagreement about what the right outcome actually is. In my discussion of such attempts, I show, on the one hand, how we should not go about answering his question. On the other hand, I develop positive criteria for such a claim, and the corresponding demand of moral deference, to be justifiable to all reasonable citizens. Before getting there, however, I will take a step back and elucidate the points of contact between Rousseau's political philosophy and the idea of deliberative democracy and where they part ways.

A Shared Fund of Ideas Deliberative Democrats and Rousseau draw from a shared fund of ideas. First among them is the idea that legitimacy is tied to justice, or the common good (and not peace as, for example, Hobbesians would have it). The exercise of political power therefore cannot be arbitrary but has to aim at justice or the common good. In addition, it has to do so in a way that is intelligible to citizens. This includes the constraints that the conception of the common good has to be public in a certain way and that citizens can see justice being done, or at least see that the exercise of political power is acceptable from a point of view of rational and reasonable citizens. Regarding the second constraint, Rousseau thought that the procedure-independent access to the general will and the fact that a particular conception of it has passed the bar of supermajoritarian procedures suffices to reassure citizens of this fact. Where the general will is "fully evident" (SC, IV.1.1) it should indeed be easy to see when it is followed. To fulfill the first constraint, the justification of the exercise of political power cannot draw on premises that are beyond the reach of the common reason of citizens. This excludes, for example, religious justifications (SC, II.6.2). It is only met, according to Rousseau, when the exercise of political power aims at a conception of the common good that establishes reciprocity of advantage, that is, it advances the interests of citizens according to an appropriate benchmark of equality (see Chap. 1; Justice as Reciprocity). For Rousseau, this leads to a conception of the general will on the basis of the fundamental, shared interests of each and all citizens, a conception with implications evident to all rational citizens. Accordingly, when citizens, their representatives, or other officials of the state exercise political power, they ought to do so according to their sincere conception of the common good in the case of the first two groups, and according to how it found its expression in democratic legislation in the case of the latter (SC, V.2.8 and PE, 23).[1]

Deliberative democrats share Rousseau's commitments to the twofold publicity of the legitimate exercise of political power. As we shall see, however, they believe that these are harder to live up to. One demand that deliberative democrats add is that citizens (and their representatives)

---

[1] This demand presumes that these actors have an effective sense of justice, that is, they can be motivated by moral reasons.

ought to be willing to justify their exercise of political power in an ongoing process of public deliberation.[2] According to them, public deliberation serves two purposes: it generates reasonable conceptions of the common good and it makes the exercise of political power intelligible to citizens. They can regard it as rational because they understand that it conforms to reasons which are reasonably acceptable.

In line with this common good orientation of citizens is the rejection of models of democracy which conceive the primary task of democratic procedures as aggregating the self-regarding interests of citizens. As Rousseau would put it, these particular wills are to be excluded from politics and replaced by the general will of all citizens. In other words, the common good ought to replace the good of some in the regulation of political affairs. I discuss the opposition of deliberative democrats to such "aggregative" conceptions of democracy in more detail in Chap. 6.

The Points of Departure One point at which Rousseau and deliberative democrats part ways concerns two background assumptions of Rousseau's political philosophy which for him go hand in hand. It is the assumption that a well-ordered society is characterized by a social and legal simplicity which makes it possible that to adequately informed, independent, and sincere citizens "the common good is everywhere fully evident and [that it] requires only good sense to be perceived" (SC 4.1.1). Recall that a society is well-ordered, according to Rousseau, when its citizens are reasonable in the sense that (1) their votes are determined by their sincere judgments about the justice of the public choices confronting them; and (2) they give motivational primacy to the common good (see Chap. 1; The Simplicity Assumption). Deliberative democrats, however, are well aware of the complexity of reasoning about justice and the common good in modern, pluralistic societies (see also Chap. 3; The Argument from Multidimensional Complexity). Therefore, they are willing to accommodate the fact that even adequately informed, independent, and the most sincere citizens are likely to disagree on many political questions.[3] Unlike Rousseau, who was not in principle opposed to public debate but nev-

---

[2] Deliberation here means public debate with the aim of reaching a decision.

[3] It is noteworthy in this context that adequately informed does not mean fully informed. There are cognitive and structural limits to the information at the disposal of each citizen even under condi-

ertheless thought that "long debates, dissensions, and tumult betoken the ascendance of private interests and the decline of the state" (SC IV.2.1), they cherish ongoing processes of public deliberation as a sign of a healthy democratic society.

Connected to this is another and crucial assumption of Rousseau's political philosophy which deliberative democrats reject. It is the idea that decision procedures play a role in unveiling the common good. As I have argued in the preceding chapter, Rousseau thought that democratic decision procedures can play an epistemic role because they register the extent of agreement among citizens. The fact that one agrees with a vast majority of citizens can be a reason to raise the confidence one has in one's judgment about the common good. Conversely, the fact that one *dis*agrees with a vast majority of citizens is a reason to lower one's confidence in one's belief and even to defer to the judgment of the majority. Ultimately, it is thus the epistemic significance of agreement and disagreement among citizens which explains the epistemic role of decision rules (see Chap. 1; The Epistemic Dimension of the Procedure Explained). In the background of this presumed link stands Rousseau's belief that more than a modicum of disagreement is a reason to believe that citizens are not being reasonable because to adequately informed, independent, and sincere citizens, the common good is always fully evident (see Chap. 1; Procedure-Independent versus Procedure-Dependent Access to the General Will). So one reason deliberative democrats have for rejecting the epistemic role Rousseau ascribed to democratic decision procedures is the observation that reasonable citizens can, and usually do, disagree about the common good. Furthermore, this disagreement, they take it, is no reason to doubt their sincere belief that their conception of the common good is the most reasonable. Hence, for them, disagreement does not carry epistemic significance of the sort Rousseau ascribes to it.[4] Consequently, a demand to defer to the majority's judgment is unjustified. This point is generalizable as deliberative democrats—with

---

tions of ideal deliberation (see the local knowledge argument and the argument from complexity in the next chapter).

[4] Reasonable disagreement does have epistemic significance in another sense. As it features in Rawls's burdens of judgment argument, for instance, it opens the door for the toleration of reasonable comprehensive doctrines different from one's own. Cf. Rawls (1996): pp. 56ff.

some rare exceptions noted below—in general tend to deny that (post-deliberative) decision procedures have an epistemic function and argue for them primarily on normative grounds. To explain exactly how they do so makes it necessary to expose the normative foundations of deliberative democracy.

The Normative Dimension of Deliberative Democracy

Another crucial point where most deliberative democrats depart from Rousseau is in the idea that rational and reasonable citizens would come to agree on a conception of the common good or could draw on a preexisting consensus on the values and norms regulating their social life. In pluralistic societies, the appeal to fundamental, shared interests will not be convincing to all citizens reasoning sincerely about the common good. Disagreement about these questions is reasonable and for a justification of the exercise of political power to be accessible to all, it cannot presume agreement where the sincere exercise of reason makes disagreement reasonable.[5]

This idea is expressed in different forms in deliberative democracy. John Rawls, for instance, invokes what he calls "the burdens of judgment" to explain why disagreement is reasonable and the inevitable outcome of the free use of reason under free institutions.[6] In light of this, Rawls thinks that the reservoir of reasons from which a justification of the exercise of political power could draw has shrunk significantly. The exercise of political power has to be justified in terms of political conceptions of justice which are neutral between reasonably contested comprehensive doctrines and provide the content of the public reason of the citizens of liberal

---

[5] If we take into view the ethical commitments to a particular community which Rousseau thought were preconditions for the possibility of a society effectively regulated by a general will over time, the rejection extends to this form of a pre-political consensus as well.

[6] Rawls provides an (incomplete) list of these sources for reasonable disagreement between comprehensive doctrines stretching from difficulties in accessing complex evidence, over the balancing of the relative importance of relevant considerations, to the conditionality of our judgment in view of our total experience that taken together explain why we disagree so often on important matters even when we conscientiously reason with one another about practical matters (which, according to Rawls, makes the resulting pluralism of doctrines reasonable); cf. Rawls (1996): p. 56.

societies. It thus has to apply the principle of toleration to philosophy itself and find a basis of justification that is "political, not metaphysical."[7] Jürgen Habermas, on the other hand, delivers a sociologically informed thesis about the rationalization of the lifeworld in modernity which dissolves a consensus on shared norms regulating the social life of premodern societies.[8] For him, it is the task of citizens to reason their way to a shared understanding of norms which they can regard as valid because they are supported by what they see as the best reasons. Democracy is first and foremost about the public use of reason in an effort to coordinate social life according to valid norms. The role of political philosophy in this picture is to explicate the philosophical presuppositions of such rational discourses and the legal framework enabling citizens to exercise their political autonomy in rational procedures of law-making, which then usher in legitimate law.[9] However, besides committing itself to this task, a "postmetaphysical" philosophy should resign from the role of a Rousseauian lawgiver in the philosophical sense.[10]

At this point, it might be useful to foreshadow the way in which I shall approach this issue. I shall suggest that regardless of what might be the metaphysical truth about the existence of fundamental, shared interests, the reflective engagement of reasonable citizens of a well-ordered society with questions of justice and the common good conditioned by a framework of shared high-confidence beliefs. I call this framework their *"Democratic Public Reason"* (see Chap. 4). Its content includes the basic settled judgments we find in modern democratic thought, among them the idea of universal human rights. I take it that an ordinary assumption about the role of human rights, furthermore, is inter alia to protect certain fundamental, shared human interests. Though I do not explore this issue in this book, it might promote the understanding of some readers when

---

[7] Cf. Rawls (1996): p. 10.
[8] The roots of the rationalization of the lifeworld thesis lie in the Webberian analysis of modernity as a process and result of the rationalization and "disenchantment" of the world; cf. Weber (1978). Habermas expands on this analysis and injects into it the concept of "communicative reason." For Habermas the lifeworld remains a reservoir of shared meaning which is in constant need of replenishing itself through what he calls "communicative action," that is, non-strategic action which aims at establishing freely agreed-upon action norms. Cf. Habermas (1984, 1998). See also the entry "The Rationalisation of the Lifeworld" in Edgar (2006): pp. 127–130.
[9] Cf. Habermas (1992a, 1996): Chap. 3.1, and Habermas (1998): Chap. 10.
[10] Cf. Habermas (1992b).

I say that the way I conceive Democratic Public Reason as the epistemic framework of the reasonable citizens of a well-ordered society owes a lot to Wittgenstein's treatment of the role of certain high-confidence convictions in *On Certainty*.[11] Among other things, Wittgenstein argues, in short, that the question of truth is a secondary one and according to some readings even devoid of meaning. If we analyze our epistemic circumstances correctly, we will come to understand that certainty is a precondition for the concept of truth and that the question of truth is only meaningful when asked from a standpoint internal to a given epistemic framework.

The way Habermas and Rawls approach the issue is ordinarily dubbed "reconstructive" as it aims to reconstruct the political morality of the reasonable citizens of modern democracy. Rawls thus refers to "the public culture itself as the shared fund of implicitly recognized basic ideas and principles."[12] Habermas, on the other hand, approaches the reconstructive project in a different manner and engages, depending on the subject of his investigation, with philosophy of language, sociological theories of modernity, and the philosophy of law. Such reconstruction is not an aim in itself and, as a philosophical project, not a descriptive one. The ambitious aim of a reconstructive approach, an aim which Rawls and Habermas share, is to illuminate the self-understanding of a class of moral agents and to clarify and attempt to harmonize (as far as this is possible) their normative commitments and social practices.[13]

The peculiar significance we give to political disagreement tells us something important. It tells us something about our respect for others and their judgments as political equals. One way of discerning how this type of respect figures in our assessment of democratic disagreement is to take into view how John Rawls conceptualizes oppression.[14] According to him, oppression exists in a given society on the following condition:

---

[11] Cf. Wittgenstein (1998).

[12] Rawls (1996): p. 8.

[13] This might include pointing out irreconcilable elements and "pathologies" of modernity, which figure more prominently in Habermas's work, and it is precisely fear of internal inconsistencies in the modern liberal view of the social world which motivates Rawls's *Political Liberalism*.

[14] Insofar as Rawls tries to spell out the self-understanding of democratic citizens, "we," "us," and "our" can be read as an attempt to capture this self-understanding. The reference to "we," "us," and "our" is thus meant to refer to persons who share the two commitments spelled out presently.

A continuing shared understanding on one comprehensive religious, philosophical, or moral doctrine can be maintained only by the oppressive use of state power. If we think of political society as a community united in affirming one and the same comprehensive doctrine, then the oppressive use of state power is necessary for political community.[15]

In other words, oppression exists when *disagreement* about "comprehensive religious, philosophical, or moral doctrines" is not allowed to translate itself into a plurality of ways of ordering the lives of individuals, and this plurality is instead suppressed by the use of state power.[16]

The broader and in a way more significant consequence which Rawls drew from the objective to avoid oppression concerns the *justification* of the exercise of political power according to this criterion. Rawls famously invokes the liberal principle of legitimacy, according to which

> our exercise of political power is proper and hence justifiable only when it is exercised in accordance with a constitution the essentials of which all citizens may reasonably be expected to endorse in the light of principles and ideals acceptable to them as reasonable and rational.[17]

Hence, political disagreement gains a new normative significance in political philosophy through the way it affects the justifiability of the exercise of political power in terms of reasons that are reasonably acceptable.

We could say that a particular kind of normative authority pertains to citizens in this picture. Their normative outlook on the world, that is, their conceptions of the good and the right, are the limiting forces of a conception of justice capable of grounding the claim to legitimacy of the exercise of political power. Only if such a conception can be reasonably acceptable to all reasonable citizens can it give rise to legitimate political institutions and forms of exercising political power. A further way in which normative authority pertains to citizens is their equal right to take the results of their

---

[15] Rawls (1996): p. 37.
[16] A stickler might note that Rawls uses the definiendum ("oppression") in the definiens ("oppressive use of state power"). What Rawls wants to say is still easily understood (which is why the stickler is indeed a stickler).
[17] Rawls (1996): p. 217.

deliberations as prima facie reasons for action in a restricted domain. At least in their private lives, we grant those we disagree with the right to act as *they* see fit without imposing on them a way to lead their lives that *we* see fit.[18] The criterion of reasonable acceptability is also taken to underwrite a claim to political equality, which extends this right to the political domain. In deciding the common course of action, reasonable citizens ought to be granted the right to take the result of their deliberations as prima facie reasons for action. Along this normative dimension of the significance of political disagreement, we can thus detect a widely shared normative commitment to treat other reasonable citizens as *equal normative authorities*, that is, as persons with an equal right to take the result of their deliberations as prima facie reasons for action.[19]

Importantly, in this picture, the commitment to treat others as equal normative authorities is *not* grounded in a deeper commitment to treat citizens as equal epistemic authorities, that is, as prima facie equally reliable judges of the rightness of political decisions. Recall Rousseau's argument that equal normative authority pertains to citizens (at least in part) because "judging what is foreign to us, we have no true principle of equity to guide us" (SC, II.4.5) and because in a well-ordered society "the common good is everywhere fully evident [to its citizens] and requires only good sense to be perceived" (SC IV.1.1). As I have argued in the preceding chapter, for Rousseau, it is this status as equal epistemic authorities which grounds

---

[18] Of course, Rawls is not the only one who cherished a plurality of individual lifestyles and a protected private sphere in which individuals could safely pursue their private interests. Rather, he stood paradigmatically for the overwhelming majority of contemporary political theorists who share this attitude with many important historical figures of political thought, among them Rousseau, who argues that citizens ought to enjoy not only political and moral but also *civil* freedom. Other examples are Locke, Kant, Mill, and Hegel among many others. A more ancient example of this attitude is the emphasis Thukydides places on the protected private sphere of Athenian citizens in his funeral speech—a fact, he says, Athenians take pride in.

[19] In an argument for freedom of conscience, Jeremy Gaus similarly emphasizes the epistemic dimension of the manifestation of our attitude of equal respect in political circumstances: "To respect a person's reason and his freedom of thought is to grant to him a right to think as he pleases in the sense not only of external moral rights, but a claim that *his* deliberations properly determine what *he* ought to believe. When someone says he has a right to his opinion, he is not merely claiming that no one can legitimately force him to abandon it; he is insisting that his opinions properly track his own deliberations. That is, freedom of thought supposes the right to believe that which one has deliberated on and has determined to be well founded. Alternatively, as I shall say to stress its epistemic aspect, one has some warrant to believe that to which one's deliberations lead. I shall call this *respect for the people's deliberations*" (Gaus 2003: p. 151).

their standing as equal normative authorities in the domain of politics and their corresponding right to participate as equals in political decision-making (see Chap. 1; Sovereignty as the Epistemic and Normative Authority of the People). In the current framework, on the other hand, the equal normative authority of citizens is independent from a claim to count as equal epistemic authorities. The idea of an equal normative authority of citizens has epistemic import, however, in the way it affects the justifiability of the exercise of political power.

From Justifiability to Deliberation In deliberative conceptions of democracy, the normative authority of citizens does not only concern the limits it imposes on the justifiability of the exercise of political power. It extends to the way justifications of such exercise are delivered. The best way to capture the fundamental concern of the deliberative strand of political theory is the idea of *justification through the public use of reason*. It implies that public reason in the real sense of the word "public" is not the reasoning of armchair philosophers but the product of the actual processes of reasoning among citizens, not only a correlate of a conception of justifiability but of actual practices of justification among citizens.[20] Habermas thus leveled the following critique against Rousseau:

> [T]he claim that a norm lies equally in the interest of everyone has the sense of rational acceptability: all those possibly affected should be able to accept the norm on the basis of good reasons. But this can become clear only under the pragmatic conditions of rational discourses in which the only thing that counts is the compelling force of the better argument based on the relevant information.[21]

Habermas and like-minded theorists thus approach the problem of disagreement in a particular way. It is not for philosophers to devise theories which overcome it. Instead, it is through the workings of public discourse that citizens come to justify their political arrangements vis-à-vis other

---

[20] This thought also expresses the opposition some deliberative democrats express against Rawls's conception of public reason as a component idea of his conception of political liberalism which specifies important aspects of the content of public reason.
[21] Habermas (1996): p. 103.

citizens. Paraphrasing Rawls, we could call this idea the application of the idea of democracy to philosophy itself.[22] This democratization of political philosophy itself changes in important ways how we ought to conceive political legitimacy. If legitimacy presupposes justifiability and justifiability in turn presupposes actual deliberation among citizens, legitimacy has to be conceived as presupposing actual public deliberation. This internal relation between legitimacy, justifiability, and public deliberation is a complicated one and I will therefore need to spell it out in more detail.

The Deliberative Standard of Legitimacy Adherents of deliberative conceptions of democracy, I shall call them "deliberative democrats" for shorthand, believe that the legitimacy of laws and institutions presupposes public deliberation. The cornerstone of the deliberative standard of legitimacy is thus the interplay between the ideal of public justifiability and the actual public deliberation among citizens which gives reality to the ideal. We find many statements of this general idea in the literature. For instance, we are told that "broadly defined, deliberative democracy refers to the idea that legitimate lawmaking arises from the public deliberation of citizens."[23] It is an idea that has been with theories of deliberative democracy from the outset and which has lost nothing of the appeal it exerts on their advocates.[24] I shall call it *the deliberative standard of legitimacy* (DSL). In the literature, we find two ways in which this general conception of legitimacy is spelled out.

The Consensus Conception of DSL The first is what we might call *the consensus conception of DSL*. One locus classicus is Joshua Cohen's essay *Deliberation and Democratic Legitimacy*.[25] In the essay, he explicates in detail how this broadly defined conception of legitimacy as public justification in public deliberation translates into DSL. Cohen explains that citizens of a deliberative democracy share "a commitment to coordinating their activities

---

[22] Cf. *fn* 57 *supra*.
[23] Bohman and Rehg (1997): p. ix.
[24] Elsewhere, we find the claim that "Because it comes at the close of a deliberative process in which everyone was able to take part, [...] the result carries legitimacy" (Manin (1987): p. 359).
[25] Cf. Cohen (1989).

within institutions that make deliberation possible and according to norms that they arrive at through their deliberation. For them, free deliberation among equals is the basis of legitimacy."[26] He then goes on to develop an *ideal deliberative procedure*, which he employs to capture the principle that "outcomes are democratically legitimate if and only if they could be the object of a free and reasoned agreement among equals."[27] Part of it is the idea that "participants regard themselves as bound only by the results of their deliberation and by the preconditions for that deliberation. Their consideration of proposals is not constrained by the authority of prior norms or requirements."[28] In another classic essay, Seyla Benhabib argues that the validity of norms depends on the acceptance of all those affected in an idealized process of deliberation.[29]

Cohen's consensus-formulation of DSL bears strong traces of Habermas's discourse ethics according to which the validity of moral norms depends on the consensual consent of impartial reasoners in an ideal discursive setting.[30] Habermas's own conception of political legitimacy, however, is much more complex than his conception of moral validity.[31] As I alluded to above, his theory of law and its internal relation to democracy rests on the assumption that law is the medium through which citizens aim to coordinate their actions according to valid norms. This theory is embedded in a sociological thesis about the disintegration of a shared background consensus on values under the conditions of modernity and the ensuing pluralism of worldviews through which citizens interpret their social world.[32] In spite of this impressive complexity of his approach and Habermas's acute awareness of the disintegrating effects of processes of rationalization in the sociological sense, the normative core of the theory maintains the necessary connection

---

[26] Cohen (1989): p. 3.
[27] Cohen (1989): p. 4.
[28] Cohen (1989): p. 4.
[29] Cf. Benhabib (1996): p. 70.
[30] Cf. Habermas (1992a): p. 93; The Habermasian program of discourse ethics is to give an interpretation to Kant's conception of the universalizability of moral norms that is adequate to "postmetaphysical" thought and the conditions of modernity.
[31] Cf. Habermas (1996).
[32] See also *fn 9 supra*.

between normative validity and consensus. Law enters his thinking primarily, on the one hand, as a medium through which citizens achieve the necessary coordination of their actions according to norms which are backed by the enforcing mechanisms of the modern state. Law thus confronts citizens in its facticity, that is, as external constraints on their actions. On the other hand, law is an expression of a process of the rational will-formation of citizens who attempt to regulate their social life according to valid norms, hence its normativity. Importantly, these norms have to be validated in actual discourses among reasonable citizens. However, "[e]ven if Habermas' model makes considerable concessions to the complexity and plurality of actual, situated deliberation, *at the ideal level* it concedes nothing. [...] To put it another way, real plurality is 'transubstantiated' into idealized unanimity, and thereby rationalized."[33] In fact, Habermas holds a particularly strong view of the consensus conception, arguing that a consensus "must rest on *identical* reasons that are able to convince parties in the same way."[34]

Hence, deliberative democrats of the Habermas–Cohen–Benhabib variant endorse *the consensus conception of DSL*. It reads thus:

(1) A law L or a set of institutions I has legitimate authority over those to whom they apply if and only if they would be the object of a free and reasoned agreement among reasonable citizens in an ideal discourse.

What makes the standard a component of a deliberative theory of democracy is the additional condition:

(2) There is no deliberation-independent (access to a) criterion determining what L or I could be the object of a free and reasoned agreement among equals.

Part (2) of the consensus conception of DSL is a bit tricky. In one sense, there is a way in which the content of (1) is not deliberation-dependent. Citizens might appeal to what they believe would be the object of a free

---

[33] Rehg and Bohman (1996): p. 91; emphasis in the original.
[34] Habermas (1996): p. 166; my emphasis.

and reasoned agreement among reasonable citizens in an ideal discourse. The standard can thus certainly be conceived as logically independent from actual deliberation.[35] However, the reason I believe this does not contradict part (2) of DSL is because any such claim will eventually have to be validated in actual deliberative practices. In the final instance, when it comes to our access to its substantive content, the criterion is thus not deliberation-independent. We shall see presently that this strong form of deliberation-dependence leads to some awkward consequences.

The Epistemic Circularity of the Consensus Conception of DSL According to the consensus conception, then, the content of part (1) of DSL has to be spelled out through an actual deliberative effort of citizens. We can now ask ourselves: what do these real deliberators *reason about*? The answer is: about justice, of course! But what is justice? Or in other words, what makes a reason a good reason to invoke in support of your justice claim, that is, what is the standard of correctness? The answer is: what ideal deliberators would accept as a reason in the ideal deliberative situation.[36] But this reply is a very puzzling one indeed. For how do we *know* what ideal deliberators would accept as a reason in the ideal situation? The answer is: it is approximately what we, the actual deliberators, happen to agree on in our real deliberative situation. The question of access to the substantive content of part (1) of DSL, which we might conceive as logically independent from actual deliberative processes, leads us back to the actual deliberation and subsequently to our disagreement. This exposes the *epistemic* circularity of a thoroughly deliberation-dependent standard of legitimate authority. The problem of deliberation-dependence, then, is an epistemic one. We plainly lack cognitive access to the substantive content of the ideal that is to govern our deliberative pursuits. For when we ask ourselves what ideal deliberators would agree on in the ideal deliberative situation we are referred back to our deliberative practice, which is the only plausible indicator of how

---

[35] Cf. Estlund (1997): p. 180.
[36] Compare, for example, Habermas (1996): p. 322f., where he describes the "thought experiment" actual deliberators undertake when assessing their actual deliberative practice in light of a context-transcending ideal of that practice.

the ideal could be spelled out. The standard of correctness offered by Habermas therefore suffers from *epistemic circularity*.

We could of course try to abstract from the particularity of our perspective that we bring to the table when we engage in reasoned discussion and encounter persistent disagreement. However,

> [h]ere has arisen the great dilemma pointed out by Habermas's critics. If we imagine that under ideal conditions others continue to hold their own view of the world, and that that view is significantly different from our own (imagine them to be the Bororo, or Tutankhamen and Li Po), we cannot expect that they could come to agree with us about the justification of some substantial claims of ours. And if, as Habermas seems to prefer, we imagine the supposedly ideal conditions as detached from our general view of the world as well as from theirs, we have no good notion of what would take place, if anything, and it is certainly unclear what sense there would be to saying that it is with the Bororo that we would be conversing. The quandary can be avoided, however, if the ideal conditions in which someone supposes his claim would be vindicated to others are understood as including what he considers to be the correct general view of the world and of ways of acquiring knowledge about it.[37]

Hence, the only epistemic route from actual to ideal deliberation leads us to an (if at all) only very slightly idealized version of our actual deliberative practice. If this is true and if it is also the case that our actual deliberative practice is beset with deep disagreement about many questions concerning matters of justice, even the idea of an ideal deliberation will provide a philosophical key to the question of legitimate political authority given DSL. We need not go as far as the Borobo, Tutankhamen, or Li Po but can find the same problems much closer to home.

The Reasonable-Acceptability Conception of DSL An alternative formulation of DSL often found in the literature is the *reasonable-acceptability conception*, or alternatively, *the no-reasonable-rejectability conception*. Its distinctive advantage over the consensus conception is that it does not presuppose or aim at the kind of thick consensus at the heart of the latter.

---

[37] Larmore (1987): p. 57f.; citation in the original omitted.

It merely requires that citizens could reasonably accept/not reasonably reject, a justification offered for a law or set of institutions. It reads thus:

(1) A law L or a set of institutions I has legitimate authority over those to whom they apply if and only if it can be justified in terms of reasons all (can or) could reasonably accept/not reasonably reject.[38]

At a general level, the idea of reasonable acceptability expresses the thought that not any kind of reason is a good reason in the context of public justification. Or, put differently, not every reason serves to justify the exercise of political power thus rendering it legitimate. Another way of expressing this is that reasonably acceptable reasons have to be *public* and, in order to be public, they have to be *accessible* to all reasonable citizens motivated to find a mutually acceptable justification of the exercise of political power. Rousseau took up this idea of *publicity as accessibility* in imposing two constraints on a justification of the exercise of political power. First, it cannot draw on sectarian doctrines which place the source of legitimacy in a sphere beyond the reach of the common reason of citizens. He thus excluded religious justifications and put reciprocity at the heart of a public conception of justice (see Chap. 1; Justice as Reciprocity). In addition, he argued that a public conception of justice cannot refer to the particular wills (or interests) of some but only to the fundamental and shared interests of all, the general will, thus making the reasons for the exercise of political power derive from the common reason of citizens (see Chap. 1; The General Will as a Conception of Public Reason). Deliberative democrats express the idea of publicity as accessibility in very similar ways. They agree that the justification has to stand its ground in the light of the reason of those over whom power is wielded. Only to them, a public justification has to be public in the additional sense that it is the product of citizens deliberating in public. They thus leave behind the firm ground on which Rousseau, in his assertive Enlightenment philosophy, was still able to erect his solution to the problem of legitimacy. In order to be accessible to the citizens of post-Enlightenment societies, a

---

[38] I shall neglect the reasonably acceptable/not reasonably rejectable distinction for the purposes of this chapter. See Scanlon (1998): Chap. 5 for a discussion of the issue. See Bohman and Richardson (2009) for a critique of the "reasons that all can accept" version.

justification of the exercise of political power has to navigate the currents of value-pluralism and reasonable disagreement.

What is common to Rousseau and deliberative democrats is that a public justification of the exercise of political power has to refer to the common good and cannot derive from sectarian doctrines. Hence, mutually acceptable reasons are moral reasons not impervious to the common reason of citizens. Political liberals are likely to add the criterion of neutrality, which imposes the additional constraint that reasonably acceptable reasons have to be neutral with respect to reasonably contested conceptions of the good or comprehensive doctrines.[39] The idea of reasonable acceptability, then, aims at reciprocity of justification: publicly justifying reasons have to be in principle accessible to other reasonable citizens who are equally committed to publicly justifying the exercise of political power. But again, what makes the standard a component of a deliberative theory of democracy is the following additional condition:

(2) There is no deliberation-independent criterion for determining the reasonable acceptability of reasons.

Importantly, as (2) in both versions of DSL suggests, deliberative democrats do not conceive DSL as specifying substantive criteria of legitimate authority in the abstract. This is not to say that all limit their theories to procedural values. Some might agree with Seyla Benhabib who argues that "[a]greements in societies living with value-pluralism are to be sought for not at the level of substantive beliefs but at that of procedures, processes, and practices for attaining and revising beliefs," which makes "[p]roceduralism [...] a rational answer to persisting value conflicts at the substantive level."[40] (We will come back to the question of proceduralism in the second part of this chapter.) Others, however, might concur with Gutman and Thompson who reject the procedural/substantive divide arguing instead that the underlying ideal of free and equal personhood justifies substantive and procedural criteria.[41] The emphasis, then,

---

[39] For some proponents of political liberalism see Rawls (1996), Ackerman (1980, 1994), and Larmore (1987, 1999).
[40] Benhabib (1996): p. 73.
[41] Cf. Gutman and Thompson (2004): p. 102 ff.

is to be placed on *in the abstract*. What deliberative democrats agree on is that the validity of such criteria is essentially tied to *actual* processes of deliberation.

Hence, the criteria of legitimacy have to be borne out by actual processes of deliberation. We can read "borne out" in two ways. One version makes a constructivist turn and argues that (reasons justifying) these criteria are constructed in the process of deliberation. The other version takes the epistemic route and views deliberation as a process of discovery which unveils the (reasons justifying) criteria of legitimate authority. On the one hand, this uncovers a deeply democratic idea of political philosophy itself as these theorists forgo the standpoint of an outsider who can play the Rousseauian lawgiver and unilaterally "legislate" criteria of legitimacy.[42] On the other hand, it leaves us with an awkward sense of emptiness as we engage with political philosophy in the hope of deriving these criteria from somewhere else than the deliberation with people with whom we disagree. I will return to this point below (see section DSL and the Sense of Emptiness below).

The Push Toward Procedural Legitimacy and the Limits of DSL Notice that an endorsement of DSL pushes deliberative democrats toward tying legitimacy to procedures in two ways. First, they proceduralize the shared reason of citizens itself. Legitimacy as public justifiability is tied to procedures of actual public deliberation. Second, deliberative democrats largely refrain from claims about the substantive legitimacy of decisions.[43] Excluded from this are claims about the legitimacy of certain institutions, however. Those institutions which enable deliberative will-formation count as legitimate and their legitimacy does not depend on, and some also claim that it does not limit, the autonomous public use of the reason of citizens.[44] Furthermore, they impose formal constraints, such as gen-

---

[42] See Habermas's infamous critique of Rawls in his Habermas (1995). See also Forst (2012): Chap. 7, where he develops the idea of "the rule of reasons" as in opposition to the ideas of "the rule of values" and "the rule of principles," and Gutman and Thompson (2004).

[43] Gutman and Thompson (1996) and (2004) are an exception.

[44] Cf., for example, Habermas (1996): Chap. 3 and Cohen (1998): p. 193. Joshua Cohen argues that a "principle of deliberative inclusion" can motivate the inclusion of negative liberties which do not stand in direct relation to the autonomous exercise of political power in the "a priori" institutional structure of deliberative democracy. As already mentioned, Gutman and Thompson also go

erality and reasonable acceptability, on the substantive justifications of decisions, and these features do impact what can count as substantively legitimate. In fact, they are specifically designed to take certain options off the table. Obvious examples are laws which can only be justified with reference to contested conceptions of the good[45] or only communally shared values which derive from a shared background in ethical orientation.[46] Neutrality of justification, then, does not engender neutrality of effects. Other tangible examples are justifications which invoke race as a decisive factor. If such morally arbitrary distinctions are used to justify exclusion or a disregard for the interests of individuals or groups, their standing as equals is clearly violated. And if religious fundamentalists insist on relying on revelation to justify the promotion of their faith through public institutions, they fail to provide reasons which are not impervious to reason or not provisional (see also section The Principle of Provisionality below). Apart from these clear-cut cases, however, deliberative democrats have a hands-off attitude toward criteria of substantive legitimacy. It is a mark of a political philosophy which, paraphrasing Rawls, applies the ideal of democracy to philosophy itself to leave these questions to the citizens' public use of public reason.

As a consequence, another question is brought to the fore. If substantive standards are elusive, then how do we assess the legitimacy of decisions in procedural terms? It is important to keep in mind that decision procedures are not among the *presuppositions* of the rational will-formation of citizens. One might conceive them as a presupposition of a rational and *efficacious* will-formation. This assumes, however, that decision procedures bear some intrinsic connection to the *rationality* of the process of will-formation. Hence, deliberative democrats cannot take the question off the table in the same way they can with rights to freedom of expression and freedom of conscience, for instance, which are both

---

beyond the presuppositions of discourse and draw on a richer ideal of free and equal personhood; cf. Gutman and Thompson (2004): p. 24. Rainer Forst develops the idea of a "basic structure of justification" in Forst (2012): esp. Chap. 8. However, he argues that the criteria of reciprocity and universality of justifying reasons are at the same time substantive and procedural and procedure-dependent and procedure-independent.

[45] Cf. Rawls (1996): Lecture VI: The Idea of Public Reason.
[46] Cf. Habermas (1998): Chap. 9 and Forst (2002: Chap. 5, 2012: Chap. 7).

obvious presuppositions of an adequate deliberative process.[47] Notice also that to answer this question of procedural legitimacy, it does not suffice to refer back to procedures of deliberation. The crux with deliberation is that it leads to disagreement. Not only is this a feature of deliberation under the non-ideal conditions of actual deliberation but, as I will show in the next chapter, it is a feature of (decentered) deliberation even in ideal circumstances (see Chap. 3; The (Un)Reasonableness of Political Disagreement). The question of procedural legitimacy, then, is a question about the legitimacy of decision procedures which we adopt in the face of such deliberative disagreement. At this point, deliberative democrats have to let go of something very dear to them. This is part (2) of DSL, which, depending on the conception of DSL, reads either that there is no deliberation-independent (access to a) criterion determining what L or I could be the object of a free and reasoned agreement among equals, or as there is no deliberation-independent (access to a) criterion for determining the reasonable acceptability of reasons. At the level of the legitimacy of decision procedures, it does not do to refer us back to deliberation or to the presuppositions of deliberative conceptions of democracy. It is thus here, I believe, that philosophers must be Rousseauian lawgivers in the philosophical sense.

A point of caution is in order. Some people might object to how I conceive conceptions of deliberative democracy for they might see themselves as advancing such a conception while rejecting DSL.[48] Furthermore, they claim that having come of age, deliberative democracy has shed some of the opposition to voting and bargaining from its early days and learned to deal with deep disagreement and ongoing conflicts even in ideal circumstances.[49] Hence, they might assert that I unduly limit the scope of the idea of deliberative democracy. There surely is some warrant to this objection as the school of deliberative democracy has had a much broader impact than what I seem to allow for here. However, I try to differentiate between a narrower core of deliberative

---

[47] Deliberative democrats ordinarily also count other aspects like a sufficient provision of health care, education, and a baseline of material well-being among the presuppositions of deliberative democracy.
[48] Cf. Bohman and Richardson (2009).
[49] Cf. Bohman (1998).

democracy which ties deliberation to political legitimacy and a wider movement which gives an important role to deliberation in the political process of reaching decisions. "Core deliberative democrats" maintain that deliberation is the practice that enables us to arrive at decisions justified in terms of reasons that meet DSL: "Deliberative democracy [...] is thus any one of a family of views according to which the public deliberation of free and equal citizens is the core of legitimate political decision making and self-government."[50] They claim that "whatever form it [deliberative democracy] takes it must refer to the ideal of public reason, to the requirement that legitimate decisions be ones that 'everyone could accept' or at least 'not reasonably reject'."[51] "Core deliberative democrats" maintain, furthermore, that deliberation is the practice that—in one way or another—enables us to arrive at decisions justified in terms of reasons that meet either of the criteria inherent in DSL. While I engage with this dogmatic core—in an innocent sense of dogmatism—I shall cite and discuss an example of the latter below.[52]

The Ideal of Deliberation and the Moment of Decision As I have elaborated above, the ideal of deliberative democracy is that of trial by discussion. More specifically, it is the idea that the exercise of political power ought to be tied to public reason and, even more specifically, to the public reason of the deliberating public. The ideal of deliberative democracy, in other words, is that of a public use of public reason. It is a very attractive ideal and one of its prominent supporters, Amartya Sen, points out that it is an ideal that is not locally confined to European societies. He argues that whatever the idea of democracy as the practice of elections might be, this alternative vision of "democracy in terms of public reason"[53] is truly cosmopolitan, and that we encounter it in many cultures and across time. Sen cites a few historical examples to corroborate this claim including the following:

---

[50] Bohman (1998): 401.
[51] Bohman (1998): 401 f.
[52] What Bohman refers to as "the coming of age of deliberative democracy", one can read as a departure from this core commitment.
[53] Sen (2009): p. 330.

> [I]n early seventh-century Japan the Buddhist Prince Shotoku, who was Regent to his mother, Empress Suiko, produced the so-called "constitution of seventeen articles," in 604 AD. The constitution insisted, much in the spirit of the Magna Carta, signed six centuries later in 1215 AD: "Decisions on important matters should not be made by one person alone. They should be discussed with many." Some commentators have seen in this seventh-century Buddhism-inspired constitution, Japan's "first step of gradual development toward democracy."[54]

This quote does indeed demonstrate that the ideal of deliberation is more widely shared than one might have thought. However, it also demonstrates very clearly that it does not translate into a wholesale commitment to democracy, which *also* includes a set of decision-making institutions embodying the ideal of political equality. The referred-to commentators might be correct in describing the constitution as "a first step of gradual development toward democracy." More so than Sen himself seems to be, however, they are aware of the fact that the commitment to an ideal of deliberation can be nothing more than "a first step" toward democracy. Citing the example as an example of "democracy in terms of public reason," Sen simply neglects that, in the end, it will be the king who decides what will be done. While reasoned debate had its moment, the time has come to make a decision in spite of persistent disagreement. Because of this, the ideal of deliberative democracy cannot be the whole story of democracy. We will have to supplement it with a further aspect of democracy. This is the moment of decision. On this part of the story, however, deliberative democrats have surprisingly little to say. Maybe this should not surprise us very much at all. As the idea of public justifiability in public deliberation indicates, it was their declared aim to shift the focus of democratic theory *away* from decision procedures. Their lack of things to say on the subject might then just be a logical consequence of their approach. However, at least in this respect, one can just as well see them as victims of their own success. After all, a theory of democracy should be able to tell both sides of the story.

---

[54] Sen (2009): p. 331; I have omitted references cited in the original.

DSL and the Sense of Emptiness Deliberative democrats realize, of course, that under real-world conditions, deliberation will have to be brought to a "violent" end. Thus, they do recognize the need for decision procedures. Alluding to the constraints of limited time and resources in decision-making is enough for Habermas to declare that "[p]olitical deliberations [...] must be concluded by majority decision in view of the pressures to decide."[55] They recognize the moment of decision and for this reason make some attempts to derive a story about the other side of democracy from their respective theories. At the very least, they try to show that the two sides of democracy, deliberation and decision-making, are compatible. Thus, Joshua Cohen states that

> different views will have different interpretations of the acceptable reasons and of how different reasons are to be weighted—for example, reasons of equality and of aggregate well-being. As a result, even an ideal deliberative procedure will not, in general, issue in consensus. But even if there is such disagreement, and a need to submit the decision to majority rule, still, participants in the ideal case will need to appeal to considerations that are quite generally recognized as having considerable weight and as a suitable basis for collective choice, even among people who disagree about the right result: agreement on political values is not agreement on the proper combination of them. But when people do appeal to considerations that are quite generally recognized as having considerable weight, then the fact that a proposal has majority support will itself commonly count as a reason for endorsing it.[56]

Elsewhere, Cohen again emphasizes that "discussion, even when it is founded on reasons, may not—and often does not—issue in consensus. No account of deliberative democracy has ever suggested otherwise."[57] And because of this, Cohen—a deliberative democrat par excellence—maintains that "collective decisions will always be made through voting, under *some* form of majority rule."[58] Tellingly, however, Cohen does not

---

[55] Habermas (1996): 306.
[56] Cohen (1998): p. 197.
[57] Cohen (2009): p. 250.
[58] Ibid.

specify *which* form of majority rule that will be and provides no non-instrumental argument *why* it should be majority rule at all. Without such an argument his statement remains at the level of an assertion, a fact underlined by the ambivalence of the future tense in his formulations. Cohen's statements are particularly telling because they do the opposite of what their author intended. Instead of laying to rest our worries about the implications of DSL for the procedural legitimacy of democratic decision-making, they lay bare the fact that the connection deliberative democrats see between the two might be a feat of their imagination rather than of philosophical argument.[59] I shall demonstrate that DSL does have implications for the procedural legitimacy of decision procedures. It takes substantial philosophical work to tease them out, however, certainly more than Cohen is willing to invest.

Deliberation as the Final Court of Appeal? What would such an argument have to look like? As I have already indicated, it is not an advisable move to conceive the validity of criteria of procedural legitimacy as itself presupposing procedures of deliberation. I now illustrate why this is so.

Few deliberative democrats have given as much thought to *Democracy and Disagreement*—the title of their important contribution to the debate—as Amy Gutman and Dennis Thompson. It will therefore be useful to see how they negotiate the looming threat of disagreement for deliberative democrats.

In their effort to counter this threat, Gutman and Thompson try to take the idea of deliberative democracy very far indeed. They agree that deliberation will uncover deep disagreement about many moral issues without necessarily resolving it.[60] At the same time, they maintain that deliberation is the final court of appeal for citizens in disagreement and philosophers reflecting on it alike. They claim that "compared to the

---

[59] Another example is Rawls, who *simply tells his readers* that "when, on a constitutional essential or matter of basic justice, all appropriate government officials act from and follow public reason, and when all reasonable citizens think of themselves ideally as if they were legislators following public reason, *the legal enactment expressing the opinion of the majority is legitimate law*" (Rawls 1997: p. 769; my emphasis).

[60] However, deliberation might help to minimize it. Gutman and Thompson thus suggest that citizens practice an "economy of disagreement." Cf. Gutman and Thompson (1996): p. 84ff.

purer theories, deliberative democracy more fully faces up to the potential conflicts between moral and political deliberation. It does not provide a simple resolution, but instead relies on deliberation itself to deal with the conflicts as they arise."[61] In a nutshell, then, their answer to deliberative disagreement is this: more deliberation.

The Principle of Provisionality Underlying this vertiginous move into a spiral of deliberation is a fear characteristic of deliberative democrats "to usurp legitimate democratic authority if they put forward, without benefit of democratic deliberation, [procedural and/or substantive principles] as morally and politically authoritative."[62] To give their theory the desired thoroughly deliberative bend, they introduce the principles of moral and political provisionality.[63] By moral provisionality they refer to the alterability of principles through further moral argument. Political provisionality, on the other hand, denotes the idea that principles are alterable subject to further political argument. Philosophers reflecting on questions of normative legitimacy, deliberation, disagreement, and democracy can hardly do without grounding their theories on moral principles, of course. However, according to Gutman and Thompson's idea of provisionality, they should treat these principles as morally provisional and consider them as "normative hypotheses about political morality"[64] whose "confirmation, refutation, or revision calls for public deliberation in the democratic process."[65] Because of their self-reflective stance, philosophers (or any other citizens engaged in similar reflections) who take into account the imperfections of their own process of reasoning are acquitted from the charge of usurping the legitimate authority of citizens.[66] Or, in their words, "[b]ecause deliberative principles must be justified in an actual deliberative process in which citizens or their

---

[61] Gutman and Thompson (2004): p. 121.
[62] Gutman and Thompson (2004): p. 25.
[63] Gutman and Thompson (2004): p. 111.
[64] Gutman and Thompson (2004): p. 122.
[65] Ibid.
[66] Cf. ibid.

2 Deliberative Democracy and the Normative Authority... 63

accountable representatives take part, the political authority of democratic citizens is to a significant degree respected."[67]

Here, we again encounter the respect for the ideal of democratic self-legislation that makes deliberative democracy such an appealing approach.[68] It is the appeal of applying the ideal of democracy to philosophy itself. What, then, is wrong with this reply to disagreement? The problem is plainly that it does not generate a theory of legitimate political decision-making, which is, of course, what we wanted in the first place. Philosophers just as citizens can respect disagreement all they want but at *some* point they have to throw out some normative anchors which ground their moral response to disagreement on practical reasoning in a way that does not refer us back to the disagreement we face in deliberation. Provisionality of moral principles is not even necessarily the wrong idea in this context. In a sense, it is even a trivial one. We should treat any judgment we make as provisional in the sense that we are willing to revise it when we become aware of good reasons for doing so. Put this way and the principle simply describes a basic requirement of rationality. However, it not make sense to conceive *political legitimacy* in this forward-looking manner. Philosophers aim at a theory of legitimacy that provides an evaluation of the legitimacy of political decisions here and now, based on what we believe are the best reasons *even when* they are contested in the messy process of public discourse and *even when*, as most would surely do, they accept the proviso that they ought to change their theory if they become aware of better reasons. Hence, instead of making the principles invoked by philosophers provisional in the sense that their validity depends on future deliberation, a quest for legitimacy at any point in the deliberative process (read: when they encounter disagreement) has to conceive the role of legitimacy in the exactly opposite fashion. They have to provisionally *withdraw* the validity claim of principles from the contestation they experience in discourse. Otherwise, a theory of legitimacy cannot get off the ground.[69]

---

[67] Gutman and Thompson (2004): 117.
[68] Habermas invokes the "radical democratic embers of the original position" in his critique of Rawls; cf. *fn 89 supra*.
[69] See also Chrisitano's critique of Waldron's theory of democratic legitimacy based on a thoroughgoing respect for judgments in Christiano (2009). This point differs from the problem Frank

Provisionality and Majority Rule Gutman and Thompson's position is a good example of the paradoxes their view entails. In view of persistent disagreement, they very willingly acknowledge that decision procedures are necessary components of a theory of democracy. At one instance, they state quite nonchalantly that "[a]t some point, the deliberation temporarily ceases, and the leaders make a decision."[70] However, for a theory of democracy it is not enough to say that leaders make a decision—and Gutman and Thompson do not stop at that. They believe that decisions should be made according to the principle of majority rule. This is because, as they claim, "no one has yet proposed a decision-making procedure that is *generally* more justified than majority rule (and its variations)."[71] Presumably, then, they would say that there are constraints to how leaders can make their decisions if those are to count as legitimate and to how leaders became leaders in the first place. There might be various alternative decision-making procedures satisfying these constraints, and among these reasonable alternatives, no other decision rule is generally more justified than majority rule. Notice that, so far, this fits nicely with the no-reasonable-rejectability conception of DSL. We have a set of alternatives that are equally reasonable; hence, no one can reject any alternative on the grounds that there is an alternative which is superior with regard to the relevant conception of reasonableness.[72] Thus, no one can reasonably reject any alternative. It follows that democrats are on safe grounds when they endorse majority rule as a legitimate way of making decisions.[73] However, just a few paragraphs below, Gutman and Thompson claim that "[t]o decide whether majority rule or some other procedure is justified, citizens

---

Michelman identifies in theories advocating such an ideal of "deep democracy" (his term). While he is concerned with the conceptual impossibility *of the deliberate pursuit* of the ideal of deep democracy, my analysis concerns the conceptual impossibility of the ideal itself; cf. Michelman (1997).

[70] Gutman and Thompson (2004): p. 12.

[71] Gutman and Thompson (1996): p. 31.

[72] It might be held to be superior on other grounds which are excluded from the justificatory contexts due to the requirement of publicity.

[73] I suspect that Gutman and Thompson want to make the stronger claim that majority rule is in fact generally the *most* justified decision-making procedure. However, because they do not state this explicitly, I refrain from ascribing to them this stronger claim. In either case, to make my point it suffices to show that even the acceptance of the weaker claim has the same deleterious consequences.

have to deliberate about the substantive value of alternative procedures."[74] The reader is left behind confused, for Gutman and Thompson claim to believe both that

- majority rule is a justified decision-making procedure (or: no other reasonable decision procedure is generally more justified)

and

- to decide whether majority rule or some other procedure is justified, citizens have to deliberate about the substantive value of alternative procedures.

A natural way to spell out (2) is to say that if, after having deliberated with each other, citizens *agree* that majority rule is a justified procedure, it is indeed a justified procedure. So one way of making sense of their acceptance of both (1) and (2) would be to suppose that Gutman and Thompson assume that citizens in fact *agree* on this. However, this can hardly be correct. After all, their whole theory of deliberative democracy centers on the acknowledgment of the fact of persistent moral disagreement. Furthermore, it would introduce a pernicious element of actual consent theory into their approach.

A second way to make sense of their acceptance of both (1) and (2) would be to suppose that Gutman and Thompson assume that reasonable citizens *would* agree that majority rule is justified if citizens were to carry out deliberation about the matter to the bitter end. However, this move is not available to those endorsing DSL because part (2) precludes theorists from circumventing the actual deliberation among citizens which is paramount to usurping the "legitimate democratic authority"[75] of citizens. This conundrum only shows once again that DSL cannot be the final word when it comes to the legitimacy of political decision-making. Deliberative democrats, against their own predilections and assertions, so far did not offer arguments which adequately deal with the fact of disagreement and the ensuing question of the procedural legitimacy of decision procedures.

I shall argue in the subsequent section that deliberative democrats are better off conceiving the legitimacy of decision procedures as integral to

---

[74] Gutman and Thompson (1996): p. 32.
[75] See *fn* 110 *supra*.

part (1) of the reasonable-acceptability version of DSL, the claim that a law L or a set of institutions I has legitimate authority over those to whom they apply if and only if they can be justified in terms of reasons all could reasonably accept/not reasonably reject. Hence, insofar as they make claims about decision-making procedures, they ought to eschew the deliberation-dependence that comes with part (2) of DSL, that is, with the claim that there is no deliberation-independent criterion for determining reasonable acceptability.

This, I will argue, will get them further down the road toward a comprehensive conception of democracy including both parts of the story of democracy, deliberation, and decision-making. Doing so, I will leave the exclusive focus on the normative dimension of deliberative democracy behind and, returning to its epistemic dimension, elucidate what can carry us further. What I will show is that epistemic considerations help us to limit the set of reasonably acceptable decision procedures to procedures which are *sensitive to reasons* formed in deliberation and citizens' post-deliberative judgments grounded on them. However, even if a modest epistemic investment of this kind brings us closer to a selection of decision procedures, it is not enough to single out one of a number of reasonably acceptable decision procedures. Eventually, I will argue that there lies promise in pushing epistemic considerations further still. We might be able to single out a specific decision procedure if we have reason to believe that it tracks not only reasonably acceptable outcomes but the most reasonable options. A discussion of attempts of doing so, and where they fail, will show what such an argument would have to look like in order for it to be a candidate for a public justification of a decision procedure of this type. The argument itself, finally, will have to wait until we leave this chapter behind. It will gradually emerge out of Chaps. 3–5 of this book.

The Epistemic Dimension of Deliberative Democracy

After having discussed at length the normative dimension of conceptions of deliberative democracy, I now turn to an aspect that I have heretofore neglected. This is the fact that deliberative democrats not only view public deliberation from a normative angle as a context of justification which ensures the legitimacy of the exercise of political power. Deliberation also has an epistemic role to play in democracy. Most importantly, it enhances the quality of decisions and does so because in an ongoing process of public deliberation, information is more widely dispersed among citizens. This can include, among other things, moral arguments and factual considerations bearing on the issue at stake. On the other hand, it fosters the moral competence of citizens. For instance, it forces them to adopt the perspectives of others and evaluate the impact decisions would have on them from these perspectives. This role-taking practice is a key moral competence. If we thus take on board certain idealizations deliberative democrats usually accept regarding the overall competence and sincerity of reasoners engaged in deliberative processes and the overall quality of these processes, it does not seem unreasonable to suppose that deliberation increases the chances that options surviving the process meet the criterion of reasonable acceptability posited by DSL. Public Deliberation is "a kind of filtering device, taking out the egregious forms of ignorance regarding interests and justice."[76] It does not have to resolve all disagreement between citizens. Deliberation only has to display a tendency to weed out options which fail in light of the reasonable acceptability conception of DSL. The minority might still disagree with the decision because they do not believe it to be the *best* option among all reasonably acceptable options. However, they might not disagree with the claim that it constitutes a reasonably acceptable option in the first place. The question is how the other side of democracy, post-deliberative decision-making, links up with this epistemic dimension of deliberative democracy.

In light of disagreement about what constitutes the best among a set of legitimate options, deliberative democrats have resorted to procedural values. They argue that in light of the fact that DSL limits the available set of options to a set of reasonably acceptable options but does not single out any specific option, we ought to retreat to procedurally legitimate decision procedures, such as majority rule, which are not reasonably rejectable. It is this underlying ideal of political equality which confers procedural legitimacy to procedures that produce decisions which are, or

---

[76] Christiano (1997): p. 248.

have a tendency to be, also substantively legitimate. This tandem of procedural and substantive legitimacy endows decisions with what we might call *full legitimacy*. It is important to keep in mind, though, that both dimensions of legitimacy are grounded in the same normative standard. Notice that, in this view, the decision procedure tracks reasonably acceptable outcomes. It does not track the most reasonable outcomes. It might single out any decision in the set of eligible options and what ultimately justifies the procedure is this tracking claim, the strength of which is still to be assessed, and its fairness, not any epistemic virtues on top of these properties.

In what follows, I will make three points. First, I will show that there is some, albeit very limited, epistemic import in the conception of legitimate decision procedures deliberative democrats advocate. This epistemic import blocks, in David Estlund's apt phrase, a wholehearted "retreat to fairness."[77] This, deliberative democrats can readily admit as this deviation from fairness is a requirement internal to DSL. However, and this is the second point, while the deliberative democrats' weak epistemic proceduralism identifies a range of reasonably acceptable decision procedures, it does not single out a specific decision procedure.[78] Deliberative democrats might simply bite this bullet. Yet this would leave their theories incomplete as a comprehensive theory of democracy, encompassing both public deliberation and democratic decision-making. I believe, however, that we plainly ought to expect more of a theory of democracy. This leads to the third point I shall make. Can we inject more epistemic considerations into a justification of democracy which is nevertheless in tune with the deliberative standard of legitimacy? In particular, is there a procedure which can track the most reasonable of the set of reasonably acceptable options? If there is, the claim that it is a bestness-tracking procedure itself has to be justified in terms of reasons which are reasonably acceptable in order for deliberative democrats and others accepting part (1) of DSL to endorse it. Otherwise, it will fail a crucial criterion of legitimacy. What, then, could be such a justification? Recall that as a way of respecting

---

[77] Cf. Estlund (2008).
[78] I adopt Estlund's labeling here. Epistemic proceduralism is any view which combines a commitment to fairness with a claim to epistemic virtues of certain fair procedures. Cf. Estlund (2008): p. 98 ff.

the moral judgments of others which figure in reasonable disagreement about justice, deliberative democrats who adhere to the reasonable-acceptability conception of DSL eschew claims about what reasonably acceptable option might be the most reasonable. Consequently, it seems quite puzzling how a justification which respects reasonable agreement and nevertheless relies on bestness-tracking properties can get off the ground. We shall see that it is not an easy undertaking indeed, and I demonstrate below how some attempts to draw on epistemic considerations in order to identify particular decision procedures fail this hurdle. Laying the groundwork for arguments to come in the subsequent chapters, I then introduce a distinction between second-order reasons for accepting the bestness-tracking claim which do not stand in a pernicious kind of conflict with first-order reasons for accepting or rejecting any particular option as the best option available. This might sound opaque at this point. I will explain the distinction in more detail below.

Procedural Fairness and Deliberation David Estlund argues convincingly that the proceduralism which deliberative democrats endorse is not compatible with a wholehearted "retreat to fairness." He invites us to consider the epitome of fairness, a coin flip. Furthermore, to incorporate nothing but fairness, the coin flip would have to be completely insensitive to any features of persons. In other words, it would select between options without any reference to whether anyone actually endorsed the options (and without giving weight to the fact of how many people endorsed which) or any other feature of the persons for whom the decision is made. Any such consideration pulls away from the criterion of full anonymity which Estlund sees at the heart of the idea of fair proceduralism which the coin flip exemplifies. He defines it thus:

> A procedure is fully anonymous if and only if it is blind to personal features: its results would not be different if any features of the relevant people were changed.[79]

---

[79] Estlund (2008): p. 80.

Fairness alone, in other words, does not need to accord any positive decisiveness to individuals. It is compatible with the idea of equal influence that *no one has any influence* in the decision-making at all, that is, equal *negative* influence. Democrats in general, however, do not want this kind of fairness. Instead they want fairness *cum* responsiveness to the preferences of citizens. These might be personal preferences understood as interests as they figure in certain public choice approaches. Or they might be preferences understood as judgments as they figure in theories of deliberative democracy. Deliberative democrats, Estlund now argues, thus do not simply endorse a proceduralism which reduces to fairness. Instead, they mix fairness with other principles which explain why the procedure is not only fair but also accords citizens equal *positive* influence over outcomes. For one, they want the procedure to be sensitive to personal features. These are not just any features, of course. The procedure should not be sensitive to race, for instance. What deliberative democrats want is sensitivity to preferences understood as judgments. In this way, the decision procedure is sensitive to reasons (based on which citizens make their judgments) and connected to the deliberation, an exchange of reasons, preceding the decision-making. As Estlund remarks, "[i]nsofar as procedural fairness is really the point, the deliberation is superfluous. Insofar as the deliberation is important to the theory, the view shifts away from procedural values and toward epistemic ones."[80] Furthermore, Estlund argues that deliberative democrats cannot be pure proceduralists. They cannot hold that the legitimacy of decisions is an exclusive product of properties of the procedure. They cannot endorse both a procedure-independent standard of legitimacy such as part (1) of DSL and such a thoroughgoing investment in procedural legitimacy.[81] This, it seems, is correct, for deliberative democrats care about something else than fairness and procedures. As is evident from part (1) of DSL, the reasonable-acceptability requirement, they care about substantive legitimacy as well. And as is evident from part (2) of DSL, they care about the judgments of citizens as outcomes of the deliberative process about the reasonable acceptability of what is at stake in decision-making.

---

[80] Estlund (2008): p. 96.
[81] See also Forst (2012): p. 186 *fn* 105.

Deliberation and Sensitivity to Preferences Hence, deliberative democrats have every reason to endorse decision procedures that are sensitive to preferences (understood as judgments). For them, the ultimate aim of the entire process of decision-making is to arrive at decisions which can be justified in terms of reasons that fit part (1) of DSL, that is, decisions which are reasonably acceptable/not reasonably rejectable (or could be the result of an ideal process of deliberation).[82] These reasons are uncovered and "constructed" in deliberation. Surely, there will be disagreement about which are the *best* of the set of reasonably acceptable reasons. However, all agree that the reasons others endorse do not violate the criterion of reasonable acceptability. They provide a public justification for the preferred course of action.

Estlund is right to assert that to the extent that deliberative democrats have ever suggested such a thoroughgoing endorsement of procedural fairness as just expounded, they are mistaken. Instead, deliberative democrats should endorse a decision procedure that is (1) fair because this is a reasonably acceptable way of reaching decisions because it concurs with the ideal of political equality, and that (2) selects from among reasonably acceptable options. The way to sort out reasonably acceptable options is, according to deliberative democrats, a process of deliberation which precedes the decision-making and ensures that citizens come to accept and propose options for which they are given reasonably acceptable justifications (and give them in turn). Hence, both deliberation and sensitivity of the decision procedure to such "deliberative" preferences are integral to DSL. However, it is deliberation and not the decision procedure which ensures the generation of adequate preferences.

Spoiled for Choice? Now we come to the second point I have mentioned in the introductory remarks, the specification of decision procedures. Here, deliberative democrats are in a situation which could be described as quite comfortable or as the opposite, quite inconvenient. Which way one's feelings lean depends on one's opinion of the reasonable aims of a theory of democracy. The problem, if it is one, is that deliberative democrats now face a choice situation at the procedural level which is analogous to the

---

[82] This is not to say that the decision process is only of instrumental value to them.

choice situation we face at the substantive level. The question is which of a number of reasonably acceptable social choice procedures we ought to adopt. Among them, we presumably find any procedure which features the kind of sensitivity to judgments deliberative democrats care about and which accords with a procedural conception of political equality. The requirement of procedural equality, we might reasonably assume, excludes dictatorships and like approaches even if they were to select reasonably acceptable options. The answer to the question as to which citizens get their way has to be reasonably acceptable. Hence, there is a presumption of equality of influence. Thus narrowing down the field of decision procedures is actually one of the principle advantages that approaches which mix a normative with an epistemic dimension, such as deliberative democracy, have over purely epistemic theories. The latter struggle to explain what equality of influence adds to the epistemic benefits of public debate and certain institutional feedback mechanisms.[83]

Including equality of influence as an implication of the criterion of reasonable acceptability does not exclude, however, the random and thus fair selection of any citizen with the power to make the decision according to their view of the best, that is, most reasonable decision. This proposal, also known as "Queen for a Day," gives each citizen an equal chance to be decisive. Because it selects among citizens and not among all possible options (whatever they might be), it is obviously sensitive to judgments. Once this is recognized, "[o]ne begins to see how much like voting Queen for a Day is, or could be. [...] It is fair, and it can take place after individual views are shaped by public deliberation."[84] The same holds for decision-making through a lottery randomly selecting among all options citizens endorse after deliberation. And the same also holds for majority rule. Consequently, all three proposals, "Queen for a Day," the lottery, and majority rule, meet the criteria of reasonable acceptability laid down by DSL.[85] Crucially then, DSL does not single out any decision procedure. As I said above, whether deliberative democrats feel comfortable with this

---

[83] See, for example, Tallisse (2009) and Anderson (2006).
[84] Estlund (1997): p. 193.
[85] There might be more such procedures. It suffices to make my point, however, that there is more than one.

situation depends on their attitude toward the reasonable reach of a theory of democracy. Personally, I believe that a conception of democracy which has to stop here is an impoverished one. Decision-making is simply one and, for some people, even the defining aspect of democracy. Hence, we could, and I believe we should, expect more from democratic theory. Some proponents of deliberative democracy seem to concur with this estimate. Clearly, they are not comfortable with leaving the decision-making side of democracy alone. In fact, as I demonstrated in the first part, the default position among them seems to be that we ought to endorse majority rule as the adequate decision procedure.

Bestness and Majority Rule We have seen, however, that contrary to what some deliberative democrats have claimed, there is no intrinsic connection between DSL and majority rule. There is no requirement that the procedure picks out the option of which *a majority* believes it is the best among all reasonably acceptable options. There are two reasons for this. First, bestness in this sense is simply not an integral part of DSL. It goes beyond the reasonable acceptability which is the moral lodestar of many deliberative democrats. Second, majority rule is not the only decision procedure compatible with the ideal of political equality. There are others, of which "Queen for a Day" and the lottery are examples, which are not versions of majoritarian decision-making but nevertheless accord equal positive influence over outcomes to citizens and thus ought to count as reasonably acceptable. Notice, however, that the consensus conception of DSL does not seem to rule out appeals to bestness. We can reasonably suppose that what reasonable and competent citizens would agree on in an ideal discourse is indeed the *best* solution to the issue at stake. This might be why theorists endorsing this version of DSL more actively produced arguments to support the connection between majority rule and bestness. I will presently discuss such an argument.

It seems to me that the only way, then, in which sensitivity to bestness as conceived by a majority could enter a justification of majority rule is if the judgments of the majority would be the most reliable guide to what is objectively the best among all legitimate options. In other words, deliberative democrats could claim majority rule to be the only reasonably acceptable decision procedure *if and only if* the presumption is justified that majority rule has a tendency to track bestness in this sense.

This brings us close to the third point I have foreshadowed in the introduction, an increase of the epistemic component in the justification of decision procedures. Hence, I turn next to the supposed tendency of majority rule to track bestness and argue that the (epistemic) justifications deliberative democrats have offered for the bestness-tracking claim of majority rule do not constitute *public* justifications in the sense of being reasonably acceptable to all citizens. Later on, I argue that a public justification based on the epistemic merits of a decision procedure has to provide second-order reasons that trump the first-order reasons based on which citizens consider the rejection of outcomes as the best outcomes among all reasonable acceptable alternatives (see Dependent versus Independent Reasons). It is still too early to spell out this idea more fully, however.

The Argument from the Presumption of Rationality Invoking a "presumption of rationality" attributed to the outcomes of majoritarian decision-making some deliberative democrats also advance epistemic arguments for majority rule. They claim that the background condition of ongoing deliberation ensures that the judgment of the majority can be justifiably regarded as the rational course of action. This, they say, is because it registers the state of the deliberation at the time of the vote. Thus Jürgen Habermas states:

> Majority rule retains an internal relation to the search for truth inasmuch as the decision reached by the majority only represents a caesura in an ongoing discussion; the decision records, so to speak, the interim result of a discursive opinion-forming process. To be sure, in that case the majority decision must be premised on a competent discussion of the disputed issues, that is, a discussion conducted according to the communicative presuppositions of a corresponding discourse. Only then can its content be viewed as the rationally motivated yet fallible result of a process of argumentation that has been interrupted in view of institutional pressures to decide, but is in principle resumable. [...] To be sure, majority decisions on questions that have been treated discursively certainly do not draw their

legitimating force from the changeability of majority proportions per se. The latter is necessary, though, if majority rule is not to undermine the legitimating force of an argumentation process meant to ground *the reasonable presumption that fallible decisions are right*.[86]

It is clear from this statement that in Habermas's view, the fact that it is a majority that voted for a legislative proposal is not itself the decisive factor in the legitimacy of the thus enacted law. Somehow the fact that the majority formed the *belief* that the legislative proposal enhances the justice of political arrangements and did so in a properly deliberative setting is what matters. Hence, an epistemic relation holds between the fact that it is a majority and the fact that it formed a belief in the relevant way. Assuming that the majority formed its belief in the relevant way, we can regard it as a justified belief. The majority followed a rational procedure of belief-formation. Assuming that other relevant conditions are also met, for example, they are competent reasoners, they can thus regard their belief as a justified, rational belief (which might be regarded as the same; enlisting both attributes helps me to bring out the point I want to make). Consequently, if their judgment prevails in the collective decision-making, they ought to regard the outcome as a justified, rational course of action.

As it stands, however, the minority formed their judgment in the same deliberative process as did the majority. Hence, they participated in the same reliable procedure of belief-formation; and assuming that other relevant conditions are also met, they can thus also regard their belief as a justified, rational belief. If this is right, they are justified in rejecting the majority's judgment *as the correct judgment* and indeed only act rationally when they do so. The epistemic relation that Habermas posits between the fact that the other side is in a majority and the fact that they formed their belief in the relevant way is not obvious to them.[87] Both sides are in an epistemically symmetrical situation and thus have equal support for their respective judgments. This, of course, only holds if we abstain from judging

---

[86] Habermas (1996): p. 179f.; my emphasis.
[87] See also Gaus (2008) for an interesting argument that simple majority rule does not track ideal discourses.

76 Conciliatory Democracy

the merit of their beliefs based on their content. In the next chapter, I will argue that this (formal) epistemic symmetry has important consequences.

Seyla Benhabib provides another example for the role the presumption of rationality sometimes plays in an epistemic justification of decision procedures. Interestingly, her own justification of majority rule along these lines straightforwardly runs into contradictions. She proposes the following:

> [N]ormative justification of majority rule as a decision procedure following from this model [of deliberative democracy]: in many instances the majority rule is a fair and rational decision procedure, *not because legitimacy resides in numbers* but because if a majority of people are convinced at one point on the basis of reasons formulated as closely as possible as a result of a process of discursive deliberation that conclusion A is the right thing to do, then this conclusion can remain valid until challenged by good reasons by some other group. It is not the sheer numbers that support the rationality of the conclusion, but *the presumption that if a large number of people see certain matters a certain way as a result of following certain kinds of rational procedures of deliberation and decision-making, then such a conclusion has a presumptive claim to being rational until shown to be otherwise.*[88]

So far, this is the straightforward argument from a presumption of rationality. According to Benhabib, processes of deliberation enhance the practical rationality of decisions principally for two reasons: (1) in order to convince others of their proposals, participants to deliberation are forced to present their views from an impartial standpoint thus making it accessible to others in the sense that they can see its justice and see that it is mutually advantageous; and (2) the process of deliberation imparts information on participants which they did not possess before. This includes knowledge of other participants' various perspectives through which they view the issue at stake and of the manifold ways in which a decision could affect them.[89]

Surprisingly and confusingly, however, Benhabib immediately goes on to claim that

---

[88] Benhabib (1996): p. 72; my emphasis.
[89] Cf. Benhabib (1996): p. 71f.

2 Deliberative Democracy and the Normative Authority... 77

[t]he simple practice of having a ruling and an opposition party in democracies in fact incorporates this principle: we accept the will of the majority at the end of an electoral process that has been fairly and correctly carried out, *but even when we accept the legitimacy of the process we may have grave doubts about the rationality of the outcome.*[90]

This, it strikes me, is absolutely correct. While the rationality of the result is often in doubt, we might still regard the will of the majority as the legitimate decisive factor in the process. However, this last statement straightforwardly negates what she claimed in the very sentence preceding it.

It is worthwhile to take a step back and look at the situation from where we started: because actual discourses are bound to generate disagreement, we employ a decision procedure. The fact of disagreement, however, *simply means* that the outcomes of the procedure are contested. After all, we enlisted the procedure to arrive at a solution to disagreement. Hence, whatever the outcome might be, it will prefer one position in the disagreement over another. Those on the losing side, of course, will describe their opposing judgments as supported by reasons which they perceive as good—and indeed better—reasons. Otherwise, it would hardly make sense for them to disagree in the first place. It is dubious, then, why they should share the presumption that the result of the majoritarian decision procedure tracks bestness. Recall Benhabib's remark that "this conclusion can remain valid *until challenged by good reasons by some other group.*"[91] Obviously, the minority will claim exactly that: that they challenge the conclusion with good reasons. They have done so *before* the vote has been taken, and they continue to do so after the vote has been taken. In their eyes, the vote did not change the epistemic status of the opposing side in any way.

An important point to note in this is that Habermas and Benhabib fail to provide an epistemic justification that meets publicity as accessibility. Their proposed link between the rationality of the judgment of the majority and the overall rationality of the outcome of majoritarian decision procedures is not accessible to the minority to which it is (also)

---

[90] Benhabib (1996): p. 72; my emphasis.
[91] See *fn* 136 *supra*.

addressed. To them, the reason why the outcome should count as the rational one remains opaque.

As I have indicated, a bestness-tracking claim might be more naturally proffered from those accepting the consensus conception of DSL. Hence, it should not surprise us that the argument from a presumption of rationality appears in Habermas's and Benhabib's writings. Another way to read "rationality" in Benhabib's remarks, however, is to equate it with reasonable acceptability. The claim would then be that the result of majoritarian decision-making has the presumptive claim to being reasonably acceptable. Habermas seems to endorse this argument at one point, stating that

> [b]ecause of its internal connection with a deliberative practice, majority rule justifies the presumption that the fallible majority opinion may be considered a reasonable basis for a common practice until further notice, namely, until the minority convinces the majority that their (the minority's) views are correct.[92]

This, however, leads us back to where we started. The presumption that the outcome of a post-deliberative decision procedure is reasonably acceptable is wholly owed to the presumption that deliberation produces reasonably acceptable judgments and the fact that the decision procedure is sensitive to post-deliberative judgments. There is nothing in the fact that a *majority* endorses a certain judgment that grounds the presumption about outcomes. The point still holds then, that *any* reasonably acceptable procedure that is compatible with the ideal of political equality that is itself reasonably acceptable, ought to count as legitimate. There still is no argument from a presumption of rationality of outcomes to majority rule. The argument we just rehearsed fails to publicly justify its epistemic components.

Dependent versus Independent Reasons I believe that the above discussion not only shows the insufficiency of a particular epistemic argument for majority rule. It also helps to draw an important, more general conclusion regarding the bearing of the requirement of publicity as

---

[92] Habermas (1996): p. 306.

accessibility on epistemic justifications for decision procedures. It illustrates the more general point that an epistemic justification of a decision procedure invoking bestness-tracking propensities can meet the requirement of reasonable acceptability if and only if it severs the reasons for accepting a decision or objecting to it from the (epistemic) reasons for accepting the procedure. This is because these epistemic merits of the decision procedure are only accessible to the majority *and* the minority if their justification does not draw (exclusively) on the reasons the majority has for accepting the outcome in its substance.

To convey this point more clearly, it is helpful to make use of some conceptual tools. I shall distinguish between two types of reasons. The first type I call "dependent reasons." They are reasons for accepting or rejecting a decision which figure in the reasoning of citizens about what the best decision would be. I shall call the second type "independent reasons."[93] These are reasons for accepting or rejecting the claim that a decision procedure tracks bestness which do not figure in the reasoning of citizens about what the best decision would be. Now we can state that a demand of moral deference, in order to be reasonably acceptable, has to be justified in terms of independent reasons. If we assume that disagreement is reasonable and that both parties are justified in holding their preferred alternative to be the most reasonable, it is plainly not enough to cite the dependent reasons endorsed by the majority as a justification for the demand. The minority has their own *dependent* reasons which they justifiably regard as superior. To put the matter differently, to the minority the majority's endorsement of dependent reasons does not constitute evidence that they made a mistake.

Before further developing this distinction for the epistemic dimension of democracy, I want to point to a case with which most readers will already be familiar. The distinction between dependent and independent reasons has a parallel along the normative dimension of democracy. A reasonable conception of justice *J* could thus specify reasons determining the justice of a law *L*. Hence, *J* could give you reasons for accepting or

---

[93] We could also call them impartial or neutral reasons. However, this invites confusion with the impartiality or neutrality of justifying reasons as, for example, political liberalism demands it. See, for example, Rawls (1996).

rejecting L which *depend on* (your acceptance of) J. On the other hand, a conception of democratic legitimacy DL distinct from J could specify reasons which are independent from (your acceptance of) J and which determine the legitimacy of the decision procedure through which L is enacted. Hence, DL could provide independent reasons for accepting or rejecting L, that is, independent of your reasons derived from J. These independent reasons would presumably not, or not in the first instance, refer to the substance of L but to its provenance, that is, whether it was enacted in procedurally appropriate ways. What we end up with is the familiar situation that we might have reasons for accepting a law on procedural grounds even though we reject it on substantive grounds.[94] In this case, in the terminology I adopt here, our independent reasons for accepting L trump our dependent reasons (dependent on J) for rejecting it.[95] Provided L stays within the bounds of the reasonable, the legitimate enactment of L gives you a peremptory reason not to take your reasoning based on J as a guide to the question of whether or not you should accept the outcome as authoritative.

The situation is analogous along the epistemic dimension. A public justification of a bestness-tracking claim in regard to a given decision procedure cannot simply rely on a reasonable, yet also reasonably contested, conception of justice. That a decision procedure tracks the conception of justice which one deems the most reasonable is not a reason in support of a bestness-tracking claim that other reasonable citizens who think that *their* conception of justice is the most reasonable could reasonably accept. They might accept that the procedure possesses some epistemic virtues, such as a tendency to select one among a number of reasonable conceptions of justice. However, they might still believe that theirs is the *most* reasonable. Their reasons for accepting outcomes as reasonable could also be a partial overlap of reasons the majority cites in support of their position and the reasons the minority relies on in justifying their position. However, the reasonable acceptance of these epistemic merits

---

[94] This is where Wollheim (1962) locates his famous paradox of democracy.
[95] Another normative analogue are reasons to compromise. They are independent of what you might want to do when you do not see a need to compromise. The need to compromise, however, gives you a reason not to act on your dependent reasons (see also Chap. 5; Conciliatory Democracy and the Politics of Compromise).

does not entail a reasonable acceptability of a demand of moral deference. Hence, whatever reasons we might offer for a bestness-tracking claim to reasonable citizens holding reasonable conceptions of justice would have to be independent reasons, that is, reasons which do not figure in the reasoning of either party to the disagreement.

Just as in the normative case, spelled out above, the independent reasons to accept a procedure as a better guide to the truth trump the dependent reasons citizens might have to reject this claim. The challenge then is to identify independent reasons of this kind. We can analyze this trumping relation in two ways. Recall the distinction between rebutting and undercutting defeaters, which I introduced in the last chapter (see Chap. 1; Procedure-Independent and Procedure-Dependent Access to the General Will): Assume you hold the belief B based on evidence E. You then acquire countervailing evidence E' defeating your justification for B on the basis of E. E' could defeat their justification for B on the basis of E in two ways. It could be a *rebutting defeater*, that is, it could be better evidence for *non-B* than E is for B. Alternatively, it could be an *undercutting defeater*, that is, evidence undermining the evidential connection between E and B. You might be justified in holding B on the basis of a testimony you have received, for instance. However, you might learn later that the person who gave the testimony is a pathological liar, was drugged, or for some other reason untrustworthy. This new information now undermines your justification for B based on the testimony. Evidence which is an undercutting defeater, then, is *higher-order evidence*, evidence about your evidence.

The point I have been trying to make with reference to dependent and independent reasons is that if we allow for reasonable disagreement in the first place, we cannot cite the dependent reasons of the majority as a defeater of either kind of the justification the minority offers for their belief. They cannot be rebutting defeaters because each side to the disagreement is justified in believing their judgment to be *the most* reasonable. And for the same reason, they cannot be undercutting defeaters either. Hence, we must turn to independent reasons to justify a bestness-tracking claim. These could well be rebutting defeaters. For instance, the minority could become aware of powerful reasons that lead them to agree with the majority which have not yet been introduced in the debate between the two sides.

Again, this parallels the legitimacy/justice distinction along the normative dimension. In the normative case, these independent reasons in one way or another refer to an ideal of equality in political decision-making which (ordinarily) trumps reasons derived from conceptions of justice. In the normative case, they serve as undercutting defeaters for the rejection of the outcome based on dependent reasons.[96]

In the epistemic case, on the other hand, there might also be independent reasons which are undercutting defeaters for a rejection of outcomes based on dependent reasons. Without giving away too much, I might already now impart on the reader that the conciliatory conception of democracy I develop in the chapters to come tells a story in this vein. Political disagreement as such, I shall argue, constitutes higher-order evidence which undermines the evidential connection between your first-order evidence (your dependent reasons) and your belief about what the most reasonable outcome would be. I draw on the epistemic significance of disagreement between equal epistemic authorities and the rationality of seeking epistemic conciliation of their judgments. Together with the tendency of a complex array of democratic decision-making institutions, these considerations constitute the independent reasons which support and publicly justify the bestness-tracking claim with regard to democratic decision procedures.

Notice a further parallel between the normative authority of legitimate decision-making and the epistemic authority of decision procedures tracking bestness. Just as we have a normative reason to *comply* with normatively authoritative outcomes, we have reason to *defer* to the outcomes of epistemically authoritative decision procedures. How the conciliatory conception addresses this issue will become evident in the last chapter (see Chap. 7; The Ambitiousness of Conciliatory Democracy and Weak Deference).

---

[96] The legitimate enactment of *L* gives you a *peremptory reason* for action if the reason excludes other reasons from deliberation about what ought to be done. H.L.A. Hart (1982) introduced the term in the essay "Commands and Authoritative Legal Reasons." In an effort to shift the emphasis from the level of deliberation to the level of action, Joseph Raz uses the term "pre-emptive reasons" (1986, 38 ff.).

References

Ackerman, B. (1980). *Social Justice in the Liberal State*. New Haven, CT: Yale University Press.
Ackerman, B. (1994). Political Liberalisms. *The Journal of Philosophy, 91*(7), 364–386.
Anderson, E. (2006). The Epistemology of Democracy. *Episteme. A Journal of Social Epistemology, 3*, 8–22.
Benhabib, S. (1996). Toward a Deliberative Model of Legitimacy. In S. Benhabib (Ed.), *Democracy and Difference. Contesting the Boundaries of the Political*. Princeton, NJ: Princeton University Press.
Bohman, J. (1998). Survey Article: The Coming of Age of Deliberative Democracy. *The Journal of Philosophy, 6*(3), 400–425.
Bohman, J., & Rehg, W. (1997). Introduction. In J. Bohman & W. Rehg (Eds.), *Deliberative Democracy. Essays on Reason and Politics* (pp. ix–xxx). Cambridge, MA: MIT Press.
Bohman, J., & Richardson, H. S. (2009). Liberalism, Deliberative Democracy, and "Reasons that All Can Accept". *The Journal of Political Philosophy, 17*(3), 253–274.
Christiano, T. (1997). The Significance of Public Deliberation. In J. Bohman & W. Rehg (Eds.), *Deliberative Democracy Essays on Reason and Politics* (pp. 243–279). Cambridge, MA: MIT Press.
Christiano, T. (2009). Waldron on Law and Disagreement. *Law and Philosophy, 19 (4)*, 513–543.
Cohen, J. (1989). Deliberation and Democratic Legitimacy. In A. Hamlin & P. Pettit (Eds.), *The Good Polity: Normative Analysis of the State* (pp. 17–34). Oxford: Blackwell. Page numbers cited in the text refer to the version available on the author's website.
Cohen, J. (1998). Democracy and Liberty. In J. Elster (Ed.), *Deliberative Democracy* (pp. 185–231). Cambridge: Cambridge University Press.
Cohen, J. (2009). Reflections on Deliberative Democracy. In J. Christman & T. Christiano (Eds.), *Debates in Political Philosophy* (pp. 247–265). Cambridge: Blackwell.
Edgar, A. (2006). *Habermas: The Key Concepts*. London: Routledge.
Estlund, D. M. (1997). Beyond Fairness and Deliberation: The Epistemic Dimension of Democratic Authority. In J. Bohman & W. Rehg (Eds.), *Deliberative Democracy. Essays on Reason and Politics* (pp. 173–205). Cambridge, MA: MIT Press.

Estlund, D. M. (2008). *Democratic Authority: A Philosophical Framework*. Princeton, NJ: Princeton University Press.

Forst, R. (2002). *Contexts of Justice. Political Philosophy beyond Liberalism and Communitarianism* (J. M. M. Farrell, Trans.). Berkeley, CA: University of California Press. This work originally appeared in German under the title *Kontexte der Gerechtigkeit. Politische Philosophie jenseits von Liberalismus und Kommunitarismus*, Suhrkamp Verlag, Frankfurt a.M., Germany, 1994.

Forst, R. (2012). *The Right to Justification. Elements of a Constructivist Theory of Justice* (J. Flynn, Trans.). New York: Columbia University Press. This work originally appeared in German under the title *Das Recht auf Rechtfertigung. Elemente einer konstruktivistischen Theorie der Gerechtigkeit*, Suhrkamp Verlag, Frankfurt a.M., Germany, 2007.

Gaus, G. F. (2003). Liberal Neutrality: A Compelling and Radical Principle. In G. Klosko & S. Wall (Eds.), *Perfectionism and Neutrality* (pp. 137–165). Lanham, MD: Rowman & Littlefield.

Gaus, G. F. (2008). The (Severe) Limits of Deliberative Democracy as the Basis for Political Choice. *Theoria: A Journal of Social and Political Theory, 117*, 26–53.

Gutman, A., & Thompson, D. (1996). *Democracy and Disagreement*. Cambridge, MA: Harvard University Press.

Gutman, A., & Thompson, D. (2004). *Why Deliberative Democracy?* Princeton, NJ: Princeton University Press.

Habermas, J. (1984). *A Theory of Communicative Action* (Vol. I–II, T. McCarthy, Trans.). Boston, MA: Beacon Press. This work originally appeared in German under the title *Theorie des Kommunikativen Handelns, Bd. I-II*, Suhrkamp Verlag, Frankfurt a.M., Germany, 1981.

Habermas, J. (1992a). *Moral Consciousness and Communicative Action* (C. Lenhardt & S. W. Nicholson, Trans.). Cambridge: Polity Press. This work originally appeared in German under the title *Moralbewusstsein und kommunikatives Handeln*, Suhrkamp Verlag, Frankfurt a.M., Germany, 1983.

Habermas, J. (1992b). *Postmetaphysical Thinking. Philosophical Essays* (W. M. Hohengarten, Trans.). Cambridge, MA: MIT Press. This work originally appeared in German under the title *Nachmetaphysisches Denken. Philosophische Aufsätze*, Suhrkamp Verlag, Frankfurt am Main, Germany, 1988.

Habermas, J. (1995). Reconciliation Through the Public use of Reason: Remarks on John Rawls's Political Liberalism. *The Journal of Philosophy, 92*(3), 109–131.

Habermas, J. (1996). *Between Facts and Norms: Contributions to a Discourse Theory of Law and Democracy* (W. Rehg, Trans.). Cambridge, MA: MIT Press. This work originally appeared in German under the title *Faktizität und Geltung. Beiträge zur Diskurstheorie des Rechts und des demokratischen Rechtsstaats*, Suhrkamp Verlag, Frankfurt am Main, Germany, 1992.

Habermas, J. (1998). In C. Cronin & P. De Greiff (Eds.), *The Inclusion of the Other: Studies in Political Theory*. Cambridge, MA: The MIT Press. This work originally appeared in German under the title *Die Einbeziehung des anderen. Studien zur politischen Theorie*. Frankfurt am Main, Germany: Suhrkamp Verlag, 1996.

Hart, H. L. A. (1982). Commands and Authoritative Legal Reasons. In H. L. A. Hart (Ed.), *Essays on Bentham* (pp. 243–269). Oxford: Oxford University Press.

Larmore, C. (1987). *Patterns of Moral Complexity*. Cambridge: Cambridge University Press.

Larmore, C. (1999). The Moral Basis of Political Liberalism. *The Journal of Philosophy, 96*(12), 599–625.

Manin, B. (1987). On Legitimacy and Deliberation (E. Stein & J. Mansbridge, Trans.). *Political Theory, 15*, 338–368.

Michelman, F. I. (1997). How Can the People Ever Make the Laws? A Critique of Deliberative Democracy. In J. Bohman & W. Rehg (Eds.), *Deliberative Democracy Essays on Reason and Politics* (pp. 145–173). Cambridge, MA: MIT Press.

Rehg, W., Bohman, J. (1996). Discourse and democracy: The formal and informal bases of legitimacy in Habermas' Faktizität und Geltung. *Journal of Political Philosophy, 4*(1), 79–99.

Rawls, J. (1996). *Political Liberalism* (2nd ed.). New York: Columbia University Press.

Rawls, J. (1997). The Idea of Public Reason Revisited. *The University of Chicago Law Review, 64*(3), 765–807.

Scanlon, T. M. (1998). *What We Owe to Each Other*. Cambridge, MA: Harvard University Press.

Sen, A. (2009). *The Idea of Justice*. Cambridge, MA: Harvard University Press.

Tallisse, R. B. (2009). *Democracy and Moral Conflict*. Cambridge: Cambridge University Press.

Weber, M. (1978). In G. Roth & K. Wittich (Ed.), *Economy and Society*. Berkeley, CA: University of California Press.

Wollheim, R. (1962). A Paradox in the Theory of Democracy. In (Eds.) Laslett, P. & Runciman, W.G., *Philosophy, Politics and Society* (pp. 71–87), Cambridge: Basil Blackwell.

Wittgenstein, L. (1998). On Certainty. In G. E. M. Anscombe & G. H. von Wright (Eds.), *The Collected Works of Ludwig Wittgenstein* (D. Paul & G. E. M. Anscombe, Trans.). Oxford: Blackwell.

3

The Epistemic Authority of Citizens

Thus far, political disagreement has appeared as a source of dismay for political philosophy. It has appeared in this light principally in three ways. Rousseau explicitly stated that widespread political disagreement is a symptom of a state in decline. Deliberative democrats, on the other hand, struggle to cope with "the problem of political disagreement" as it threatens to undermine attempts to develop the deliberative standard of legitimacy into a full-fledged theory of democracy. In particular, political disagreement has torpedoed various bestness-tracking arguments in favor of certain democratic decision procedures.

In the remainder of the book and beginning with this chapter, I hope to show that the focus on political disagreement as a *problem* which political philosophy has to solve in one way or another ought to be replaced by an approach that uses disagreement as a *resource* for an adequate conception of democracy. This shift of perspective offers new and important insights into the role of political disagreement in a justification of democracy.

A Rousseauian Starting Point My argument for what I shall later introduce as the conciliatory conception of democracy starts with two commitments which are present in Rousseau's democratic theory (see Chap. 1;

Sovereignty as the Normative and Epistemic Authority of the People). The first commitment is the commitment of reasonable citizens to treating each other as *equal normative authorities*, that is, as persons with an equal right to take the results of their deliberations as prima facie reasons for action. In the political realm, this commitment translates into granting others the right to participate as equals in the collective decision-making. The second commitment is the commitment to regard them as *equal epistemic authorities*, that is, as prima facie equally reliable judges of the rightness of political decisions. Rousseau took the second commitment to be fundamental. I phrase this point in terms of two dimensions of the significance of political disagreement. They are intertwined because often the epistemic dimension underlies the normative dimension or adds a layer to the significance of political disagreement. Crucially, then, disagreement carries not only normative weight, or, put differently, political disagreement is not only a moral problem. It often confronts us as an epistemic problem as well. And it appears as a normative problem at least partly because of its epistemic import.

According to my interpretation of Rousseau, he took the commitments to the equal epistemic and normative authority of citizens to justify their exclusive right to the (democratic) exercise of political power over themselves, that is, their political sovereignty (see Chap. 1; Sovereignty as the Normative and Epistemic Authority of the People). Importantly, the epistemic component in his justification of democratic decision procedure through which citizens exercise their sovereignty led him to specify supermajoritarian decision-making as the only legitimate decision procedure. In the next chapter, I will return to Rousseau and his analysis of the epistemic significance of political disagreement (see Chap. 4; Rousseau's Version of the Equal Weight View). I will argue that he was correct in attributing epistemic significance to the judgments of reasonable citizens of a well-ordered society in general, yet misguided in adopting a dismissive attitude toward the epistemic significance of widespread political disagreement. He saw the latter as evidence that citizens lack the commitment to give motivational primacy to the common good and/or vote insincerely. A claim I will make in this chapter is that widespread disagreement does not necessarily have these implications. Instead it is the outcome to be expected in decentered deliberation about sufficiently complex issues even when citizens are reasonable and rational.

This also undermines the idea that supermajoritarian decision-making is a feasible way of reaching political decisions (see also Chap. 1; The Simplicity Assumption).

Enter Deliberative Democracy The next building block in my argument for conciliatory democracy introduces the ideal of deliberative democracy and the normative criterion of reasonable acceptability. The normative criterion of reasonable acceptability describes the requirement that the justification of the exercise of political power has to be *accessible* from the diverse perspectives of reasonable citizens. The justification has to be *public* in that sense. Deliberative democrats argue that because of this, post-Enlightenment political philosophy ought to conceive legitimacy as tied in essential ways to the public deliberation of reasonable citizens (see Chap. 2; From Justifiability to Deliberation). According to Rousseau, reasonable citizens are those who meet the sincerity requirement and the requirement to give motivational primacy to the common good in the exercise of political power. The ideal of deliberative democracy introduces the further requirement that they seek to justify the exercise of political power vis-à-vis other reasonable citizens in terms of reasons they could reasonably accept as treating them as equals in relevant respects (see Chap. 2; The Reasonable-Acceptability Conception of DSL).[1]

While endorsing many of the aims and sharing many of the ideas which motivate deliberative democracy, I have also argued that we should not conceive legitimacy as presupposing justification in actual deliberation all the way down (see Chap. 2; Provisionality and Majority Rule). At the very least, when it comes to the legitimacy of decision procedures, political philosophers have to adopt the role of a Rousseauian lawgiver. The principle reason for this is that we need decision procedures precisely because public deliberation ordinarily produces disagreement. This, however, need not discourage us. We can safely let go of this thoroughly deliberative conception of legitimacy and nevertheless accord an important role to public deliberation and, in addition, tie our

---

[1] I shall introduce an expanded conception of reasonableness suitable to the conciliatory conception of democracy (see Chap. 4; The Idea of a Well-Ordered Society and an Expanded Conception of Reasonableness).

justification of democratic decision procedures in a direct way to the ideal of public deliberation (see also Chap. 7; The Normative and the Epistemic Dimension of Conciliatory Democracy). If we want to give room to the ideal of deliberative democracy, post-deliberative decision procedures ought to be judgment-sensitive because the aim is to select from reasonably acceptable options which have survived the deliberative process. This argument got us quite far in a public justification of democratic decision procedures. It narrowed the range of available decision procedures to those which treat citizens as political equals. As we have also seen, however, the argument does not recommend any specific decision procedure over others which accord equal weight to the judgments of citizens (see Chap. 2; Spoiled for Choice?).

A promising way out of this predicament is to insert a stronger epistemic component into the justification of democracy in the form of a bestness-tracking claim. There might be an argument that certain procedures are better than others at tracking the best understood as the most reasonable of a number of reasonable options which survived the deliberative process (see Chap. 2; Bestness and Majority Rule). Importantly, however, according to the normative criterion of reasonable acceptability, this bestness-tracking claim itself has to be a claim which all reasonable citizens could reasonably accept. We have seen that this is very difficult to achieve (See Chap. 2; The Argument from the Presumption of Rationality). We have also seen that a structural feature of an argument in support of a bestness-tracking claim is that it has to invoke independent reasons, that is, reasons which are independent from and trump the (dependent) reasons citizens have for rejecting the outcomes of the procedure (see Chap. 2; Dependent versus Independent Reasons).

From Deliberation to Conciliation Starting with this chapter, I prepare the reasonably acceptable argument for a stronger epistemic component in a normative justification of democracy. Ultimately, the claim is that citizens regarding each other as equally reliable judges of the rightness of political decisions ought to pursue the epistemic conciliation of their conflicting judgments. Because the complex set of democratic decision procedures I describe in Chaps. 5 and 6 is the only decision-making mechanism with an inbuilt tendency to produce outcomes corresponding to the outcomes of epistemic conciliation, we ought to endorse them. In a sufficiently deliberative democracy, our best bet of getting it right is to conciliate our judgments with those of other reasonable citizens. And our best lead to what such conciliation would amount to are the outcomes of this set of decision procedures. The argument is reasonably acceptable and thus qualifies as a component of a public justification of democracy because it relies on *independent reasons* to explain the bestness-tracking claim inherent in the argument. These independent reasons function as *undercutting defeaters* with respect to the dependent reasons of citizens and the epistemic support they offer for their judgments which figure in political disagreements (see Chap. 2; Dependent versus Independent Reasons).

A first step toward this conclusion, which I take in this chapter, is to defend the claim that the reasonable citizens of deliberative democracies ought to regard each other as equal epistemic authorities with respect to their epistemic role in decision procedures. A defense of this claim requires that we reject moral elitism, the thesis that political expertise is unevenly distributed across the population. I provide four arguments why moral elitism is false.

In the course of the discussion of these arguments, I take a moment to consider how these arguments and his own assumptions undermine John Stuart Mill's political philosophy, often cited as the paragon of moral elitism. Furthermore, I diffuse some worries about the standing of experts in light of a commitment to regard other reasonable citizens as equal epistemic authorities. Finally, I introduce a further argument, the debate room argument, which builds on the conclusions of the first three arguments against moral elitism mentioned above. I take it to show that political disagreement is the outcome to be expected in decentered deliberation about sufficiently complex issues even under ideal circumstances. Furthermore, such disagreement need not be irrational, that is, the result of cognitive error, or unreasonable, that is, the result of insincerity on part of the participants. I close this chapter with a question: *how ought reasonable citizens to react to such rational and reasonable disagreement with other reasonable citizens whom they regard as equal epistemic and equal normative authorities?*

The Equal Epistemic Authority of Citizens

The Challenge of Moral Elitism A powerful objection for treating others as equal epistemic authorities is the argument from complexity. The regulation of modern societies is a complex task which requires a political expertise. Such expertise is unevenly distributed across society. Hence, we should not treat citizens as equal epistemic authorities in the political domain. Call this view *moral elitism*. Moral elitism can quickly turn into an *epistemic political elitism* when we add to it the claim that some, namely the political experts, have a greater claim to rule than others.

It is noteworthy that these views are fully compatible and in fact sometimes rest explicitly on a moral egalitarianism. The claim is simply that some are more capable than others in bringing about a society in compliance with an egalitarian morality. Hence, moral egalitarianism can be combined with epistemic political elitism. This poses a challenge to those philosophers who draw a straightforward line from the criterion of reasonable acceptability to political egalitarianism. If epistemic considerations can be brought to bear on the right to participate in decision-making, we need to have more to say on what blocks this move. David Estlund, who finds it "is very difficult to deny"[2] that "some (relatively few) people know those normative standards [by which political decisions ought to be judged] better than others,"[3] offered the normative argument that an identification of political experts is not reasonably acceptable, thus blocking the move from moral elitism to epistemic political elitism.

The argument for conciliatory democracy does not follow Estlund and others in countering the threat posed by the moral elitist on moral grounds. Instead, I develop a battery of arguments supporting the claim that given the background conditions of deliberative democracy with multiparty competition, citizens ought to regard each other as equal epistemic authorities in a very specific sense, namely concerning their epistemic role in the decision procedures of modern democracy. Furthermore, taking what is by many considered the prime example of moral elitism,

---

[2] Estlund (2008): p. 31.
[3] Estlund (2008): p. 30.

I engage with J.S. Mill's theory of democracy. My discussion of his ideas shows that contrary to the popular and, I would argue, superficial reading of his work, it is replete with presuppositions of a relatively high level of moral competence of the general public. This makes Mill an unreliable witness in the case for a strong moral elitism. At the same time, it shows that moral elitism is an idea which is more difficult than we might think to transform into an epistemic political elitism.

The arguments I develop in support of regarding the reasonable citizens of a well-ordered society as equal epistemic authorities are the following:

(1) The Argument from Multidimensional Complexity
(2) The Local Knowledge Argument
(3) The Practice-Based Argument
(4) The Argument from Institutional Expertise

Arguments (1) and (2)—the argument from multidimensional complexity and the local knowledge argument—establish the claim that for any reasoner, it is irrational to have high initial credence in their judgments even if they take themselves to be generally competent in judging the matter at stake. Thus, we should expect differences in expected reliability between reasoners to be limited from the outset. Arguments (3) and (4)—the practice-based argument and the argument from institutional expertise—establish the claim that the gap in expected reliability that might nevertheless exist between citizens concerning their epistemic role in the decision procedures of modern democracy can be closed by practices of deliberation and the epistemic benefits provided by certain democratic institutions. Taken together, these arguments make plausible the assumption that in a sufficiently deliberative democracy, a sufficiently large number of citizens are *in fact* equal epistemic authorities with respect to this role.

In the section about the (un)reasonableness of political disagreement, I eventually present a fifth argument, *the debate room argument*. It draws on arguments (1)–(3) and serves as an explanation for the persistence of disagreement even under ideal conditions. It shows, *pace* Rousseau, that disagreement need not be unreasonable, that is, the outcome of insincere reasoning, or irrational, that is, based on erroneous reasoning. This leads to the question addressed in Chaps. 4 and 5: how ought reasonable citizens to react to such rational and reasonable disagreement with other reasonable citizens whom they regard as equal epistemic and as equal normative authorities?

The Small Differences As already stated, the first set of arguments aims to demonstrate that any differences that might exist in the expected reliability of competent reasoners about justice are bound to be limited. The idea is roughly this: if we take into account the precariousness of our status as competent reasoners about the social conditions of perfect justice and the complexity of the subject matter, we ought to acknowledge that nobody can reasonably claim to be highly reliable in their judgments about justice. Instead, from the outset, all we are entitled to is a relatively low credence in our beliefs about justice. The comparison of our cognitive abilities starts at the bottom, so to speak, rather than at the top of a scale rating the competence of moral reasoners.

The arguments offer two considerations why we should be skeptical of our own ability to arrive at correct judgments about justice as an ideal regulating social institution. The first consideration takes into account the enormous complexity of the subject matter. Justice as an ideal regulating social institution is bewilderingly complex, a fact often understated by philosophers. To order the numerous normative demands that arise from the various aspects of justice in a consistent set under the guidance of basic principles and to bring the relevant empirical knowledge to bear on our decisions is a task that takes us to—and often past—the limits of our cognitive abilities. The second consideration takes into account our inability to oversee decentered practices of collective reasoning. Because of this limitation, we do not, at any point in public deliberation, have at our disposal the entirety of the cognitive resources of collective reasoning. The assumption must then be that in cases of disagreement, reasoners have not accessed all information available at the collective level. In other words, participants base their beliefs on *incomplete* evidence, a fact which recommends that participants adopt an attitude of intellectual humility toward their own judgments.

The Argument from Multidimensional Complexity[4] As noted above, the argument from complexity in support of moral elitism states that the regulation of modern societies is so complex that we are forced to admit the existence of moral experts who know better how to give shape to a just world. It might come as a surprise, then, that I cite an argument from multidimensional complexity in support of an epistemic political egalitarianism. In short, the argument is roughly this: the task of promoting justice in the modern world is *so* complex that individuals can no longer make a plausible claim to superior political expertise. If the task significantly overextends everyone's individual cognitive resources, the case for anyone's expertise to be discernibly superior to that of others is weakened.

On the one hand, complexity arises along the normative dimension. Looked at from a certain angle, the idea that we could order our perceived normative demands in a consistent set with the help of a few basic principles arrived at in reflective equilibrium or through some other method seems preposterous. What is more likely is that no matter how much we try, we end up juggling various demands and, if we are lucky, arrive at a theory that leaves many questions, including the relative ordering of many of these demands, unanswered. It actually seems that the more we reflect on justice, the more difficult it becomes to arrive at a clean-cut picture of what justice requires of us (see The Entropy of Reason below).

To illustrate the complexity, suppose that we, as philosophers, would face the task of arriving at an answer to the following question: "*What is it that justice demands of us in our circumstances?*"

Before answering this question, it is worthwhile noting what philosophers nowadays discuss under the heading of justice. Topics include, to name just a few, political justice, social justice, gender justice, rights of minorities, historical justice, global justice, environmental justice, and justice toward future generations. As if this incomplete list were not enough, we can further subdivide these categories. Under the heading of social justice, for instance, we find surmised a whole range of issues such as the justice of health care, the economic order, the tax system, and so on. Global justice, on the other hand, covers issues ranging from the global distribution of resources to freedom of movement, the legiti-

---

[4] This argument from multidimensional expertise expands on arguments offered in Ebeling (2016).

macy of borders, the justice of global political institutions, and many more. In short, each subdivision raises a wide array of issues on its own. Furthermore, all of these aspects of justice and the issues arising within them are intertwined, which only adds to the complexity of our task. The justice of migration policy, for instance, is intertwined with the legitimacy of national legislation (does the nationally constituted polis have the right to determine its migration policy unilaterally? Does it have the right to close its markets to products produced abroad?), social justice at the national level (if society is a system of cooperation why would outsiders have a right to enjoy the benefits of cooperation?), the global redistribution of resources (e.g., a duty to compensate for inequalities), historical justice (e.g., colonialism), environmental justice (e.g., a duty to compensate for the effects of climate change), the justice of global political and economic institutions (including the lack thereof), and so on. This is but one example but I trust that it suffices to get the point across.[5]

In addition, the empirical world is very complex. We have to assess the right means to our ends, and means–ends relations in the social world are notoriously difficult to gauge. Governing modern societies requires expert knowledge across many different fields of empirical research. Questions of public health, energy supply, transport, IT infrastructure, administrative reforms, macroeconomics, and public finance are but few examples. Furthermore, at least some of the questions we face are made more complicated by our limited ability to predict future developments and how they shape the world humans will inhabit.[6] Suppose a hundred years from now the technology will exist to allow future generations to reverse the effects of global warming. Or suppose that genetically modified grain will grow in areas not arable given current conditions or will be according to current projections. How should these possibilities affect our current

---

[5] Another aspect of the complexity of justice is conceptual. Conceptions of justice can be described as embedded in political theories, which themselves can be seen as interpretations of a complex conceptual web including a host of other concepts and conceptions thereof that inform each other. Political theorizing can be helpfully analyzed as attempts in producing a coherent cluster of conceptions of such concepts as liberty, equality, authority, legitimacy, power, and so on. Justifying a contested conception of justice, one thus quickly enters a terrain of interrelated conceptions, appeal to which only reveals more disagreement and complexity; cf. Gaus (2000): pp. 26–46.

[6] To give the idea an intuitive plausibility, consider if our specimen alive a century ago could have predicted the scientific and social developments that occurred.

course of action? How should we assess the risks associated with our current course of action? Should we assign comparatively limited resources to research institutions dedicated to the problem instead of using a relatively vast amount of resources to fight climate change?

In light of this multidimensional complexity of governing the modern world, if asked "*What is it that justice demands of us in our circumstances?*" it seems the most reasonable answer a contemporary philosopher could give is this: "*That's pretty complex.*"

I say "contemporary" because the task has not always *seemed* so complex. Philosophy, scientific progress, and emancipatory social movements have all contributed to a greatly enlarged notion of justice and the common good. We have broadened the reach of our reflections about the demands of justice to include the interest of those who have been neglected locally as well as of those who have been neglected globally, and the interests of future generations. Even philosophers who do not subscribe to a version of cosmopolitanism nowadays have to develop views which takes these considerations into account if only to refute them eventually. If there is progress in political philosophy, a big part of it is the insight that justice is an ideal which pertains to many more issues than previous generations have thought and that we developed a much deeper understanding of our moral commitments and what they entail. While these developments should be hailed as progress, they surely do not make it easier to conceive a just world. We now see ourselves confronted with a plethora of moral demands and duties, some of which we already acknowledge, and some that are made by others or on their behalf and which, at the very least, we take to deserve very careful scrutiny.[7] An increased awareness of this complexity is partly what motivated the idea of deliberative democrats that adequate justifications for the exercise of political power have to be the product of a collective effort of reasoning about justice.

The increased complexity of our modern-day morality imposes severe cognitive burdens on us. Thus, even if it might be hard to admit, especially for philosophers who spend their whole life working out and

---

[7] Consider, for instance, the animal rights and liberation movement.

refining their favorite conception of justice and its real-world implications, it nevertheless is a basic truth of modern life that most of our moral judgments are made under circumstances of significant uncertainty.[8] In light of this, the idea seems preposterous that we could easily arrive at a coherent framework which integrates the various moral demands we face—even taking into account only those we already acknowledge—and implement it with the empirical expertise necessary for the task. The crucial point is that while we need to at least try to develop such a coherent framework in order to have any reasoned basis for our judgments, it is clearly unreasonable to advocate our conclusions about what ought to be done with great confidence. The epistemic attitude demanded in such circumstances is one of severe intellectual humility. In other words, to the extent that we regard ourselves as competent reasoners about justice, we ought to ascribe a low level of reliability to our judgments about the just course of collective action.

The Local Knowledge Argument[9] The second argument draws on the idea that political deliberation in complex societies engenders a decentered deliberative setting. In such a setting, participants cannot gain knowledge of the global validity status of arguments in relation to the overall process of deliberation.[10] All they can resort to is their knowledge of the local validity status of arguments within their restricted deliberative sphere. Imagine the following setting:

---

[8] See Landemore (2014) for an argument that cites our ignorance about future developments in support for an epistemic political egalitarianism.

[9] This argument draws on Hayek's criticism of centralized economies based on their insufficient ability to gain and process information about the dispersed preferences of the members of large and complex societies. Cf. Hayek (1991). My version of the argument was inspired by my reading of Gaus (2008).

[10] I use the validity status of an argument to refer to its current status in an ongoing process of deliberation. The argument counts as valid as long as no defeating argument has been offered.

Debate Room 1. A group of people is randomly assigned seats at different tables in the same room. They then proceed to discuss the justice of a proposed policy for a limited amount of time. After the discussion is interrupted, people seated at different tables disagree about the justice of the proposed policy.

This example aims to mirror the decentered deliberation under ideal conditions that the inhabitants of the public sphere engage in in a deliberative democracy as Habermas and others envision it.[11] More specifically, each table represents one of many deliberative spheres, which together constitute the public sphere in its entirety. The room represents the public sphere and the decentered deliberative process as a whole. The random assignment of seats at the different tables is due to the assumption that citizens of a deliberative democracy are maximally open toward differing perspectives and arguments made by others. Taken together, they represent the full spectrum of pluralistic perspectives present in modern societies.

While everybody follows and participates in the deliberation at their table, they do not have access to the deliberation carried out at the other tables. Hence, while they can judge the current validity status of a given argument at their table, they cannot do the same for the other tables. It is easily possible, of course, that arguments currently counted as valid at their table have been defeated at other tables or vice versa. The fact that disagreement remains after the deliberation has been carried out at each table indicates that not everyone has taken the same arguments into account.[12] Crucially, participants do not know how the arguments they regard as valid have fared or would fare at a table different from their own (nor if they were to change their mind, would they come to know

---

[11] Cf. Habermas (1996): p. 299 and Benhabib (1996): p. 69f.

[12] This is so presuming that all reasoners are sufficiently competent so that it would be unreasonable to blame the disagreement on the incompetence of others alone. The fact that disagreement remains after participants have engaged in deliberation is partly explained by the incompleteness of evidence due to the complexity of the subject matter. See the argument from multidimensional complexity above.

the arguments regarded as valid at different tables). Hence, while participants try to discuss the justice of a proposed policy with as many people, try to consider as many arguments, and try to include as many different perspectives as they can, they are never able to obtain knowledge of the deliberative process as a whole and the global validity status of arguments. This is exactly what it means to engage in "decentered" deliberation. Rather than observing the *centered* deliberation of a small number of representatives who all, to stay with the debate room metaphor, sit around one big table, they engage in a *decentered* deliberation, sit around different tables without knowing and having access to what is going on at the other tables. While a decentered deliberative setting has epistemic benefits as more arguments can be voiced and more perspectives made visible, the setting significantly increases our cognitive burdens in that it makes it impossible to all available information relevant to the formation of our judgment of the issue at stake. Within a decentered public, this god's eye view on the deliberative process is not available to anyone. Given that the outcome of the deliberation is disagreement, participants should be conscious of the fact that defeating arguments might still be "out there." The fact of disagreement makes this consideration especially pertinent. For this reason, they should exercise caution in their adoption of a belief regarding the global validity status of an argument on which they base their support of or opposition to the proposed policy. In other words, participants confronted with persistent disagreement in a decentered deliberative setting should assign a low level of credence to their beliefs.

Both of the above arguments recommend an attitude of intellectual humility.

Closing the Gap The second set of arguments starts where the first has left off. It shows how ongoing public deliberation and the existence of democratic institutions can close the gap in the political competence of citizens with respect to their epistemic role in the decision procedures of modern democracy. I cite two considerations to accomplish this. One is the educational effect of the practice of deliberation which shapes the choices we face in politics. Another is the fact that democratic institutions generate epistemic benefits which every citizen can reap to an equal extent when they vote for the political party closest to their preferred choice. Both support the claim that citizens can justifiably regard each other as equal epistemic authorities with respect to their epistemic role in the democratic decision procedures.[13]

The Practice-Based Argument The first argument in this set is practice-based. Participants to the deliberative practices of a democratic society increase their competence in moral reasoning and their factual knowledge base and develop and further a shared sense of justice. It is the practice of deliberation itself which levels competence in moral reasoning. Furthermore, citizens collectively shape the choices they face as a community in ongoing processes of public deliberation.

The idea is a simple one. Recall the example used in the preceding argument. The example can easily be expanded to convey the idea that political participation increases and levels the relevant competences over time. This is not a particularly novel argument, and I do not believe it is in need of much elaboration. It has been made time and again and the idea is present in every contemporary theory of deliberative democracy.[14]

Debate Room 2. In the imagined setting, a group of people is randomly assigned seats at different tables in the same room. They then proceed to discuss the justice of a proposed policy for a limited amount of time. We now expand this setting and suppose that the session does not stop after one round of debate. Instead, the whole procedure is repeated numerous times with the debates covering a wide array of issues.

As the number of rounds increases, so does the participants' exposure to various normative and instrumental considerations pertaining to the

---

[13] Yet another consideration, which I do not elaborate here, invokes a moral reason to treat others as equal epistemic authorities based on the claim that we owe opacity respect to others once they pass a certain threshold of moral competence; cf. Carter (2011). My arguments to establish the small differences in expected reliability can be seen as laying the epistemic foundation for such an argument.

[14] This does not imply that the educational effects of participation are what ultimately justify participatory procedures. For this position see, for example, Pateman (1970); for the critique of similar approaches as self-defeating, see Elster (1985). The educative function is an important side effect of participation, however.

various matters at stake. They become acquainted with more perspectives on all issues at stake, they learn about more arguments for and against a given option, and they gain knowledge about a greater number of instrumental considerations bearing on the issues at stake. Importantly, they also become increasingly aware of the interconnectedness of the various issues under discussion and the considerations voiced in the many rounds of debate. We can thus assume that over time, they develop a more and more coherent and integrated moral outlook from which to approach questions of political morality. Furthermore, they extend their moral competence in other ways than just absorbing and processing information. The confrontation during debate with other reasonable citizens who do not share the same perspective on life and might come from different cultural and social backgrounds fosters their moral competence of mutual perspective-taking. As the relevant information is now widely dispersed among participants and key moral competences strengthened, existing gaps in the expected reliability of judgments between participants are narrowed, and differences in expected reliability between reasoners should be expected to shrink over time. Sustained participation closes the moral competence gap.

An Interlude on J.S. Mill's Epistemic Political Elitism Instead of elaborating on what I take to be an uncontroversial point, I focus on how this dynamic unfolds in and ultimately threatens to undermine the theory of representative democracy advocated by J.S. Mill, one of the forerunners of the deliberative democracy school and, at the same time, the paragon of moral elitism. A particularly interesting illustration of this dynamic can be found in J.S. Mill's arguments in his *Thoughts on Parliamentary Reform*[15] and his *Considerations on Representative Government*[16]. At the same time, a close analysis of his theory of democracy shows that it might be more difficult to translate moral elitism into a coherent political theory than its adherents suspect.

---

[15] Cf. Mill ([1859] 1977); henceforth *T*.
[16] Cf. Mill ([1861] 1977); henceforth *C*.

Mill famously argues that while the suffrage ought to be extended to (almost) everyone, not everyone ought to be given an equal vote. Instead, those with a higher degree of knowledge and moral sophistication—including both moral competence and moral motivation—ought to be given more votes than the less educated.[17] This is to be to the benefit of the intellectually inferior classes and Mill assumes that they would ultimately agree to his voting scheme given the transparency of the beneficial effects the outcomes of the thus instituted political process would have for them and for society as a whole.

Mill points out that one central benefit of democratic participation and by extension of democratic political regimes is the education of the citizenry. To deprive citizens of their opportunities for participation deprives them of one of the central means to further their intellect and moral competence. In criticizing the idea of a benevolent despot, he makes the point negatively stating that if a despot were to rule—benevolent as they may be—

> the public at large [would] remain without information and without interest on all the greater matters of practice; or, if they have any knowledge of them, it is but a *dilettante* knowledge, like that which people have of the mechanical arts who have never handled a tool. Nor is it only in their intelligence that they suffer. Their moral capacities are equally stunted. Wherever the sphere of action of human beings is artificially circumscribed, their sentiments are narrowed and dwarfed in the same proportion.[18]

A little further into his argument for democracy, he states the same idea positively arguing that

> [s]till more salutary is the moral part of the instruction afforded by the participation of the private citizen, if even rarely, in public functions. He is called upon, while so engaged, to weigh interests not his own; to be guided, in case of conflicting claims, by another rule than his private partialities; to

---

[17] The details of the voting scheme need not interest us here. Mill conveniently assumed that the attainment of a higher level of education correlates positively with a higher level of moral sophistication.

[18] T, p. 400f.

apply to every turn, principles and maxims which have for their reason of existence the common good: and he usually finds associated with him in the same work minds more familiarized than his own with these ideas and operations, whose study it will be to supply reasons to his understanding, and simulation to his feeling for the general interest. He is made to feel himself one of the public, and whatever is for their benefit to be for his benefit. Where this school of public spirit does not exist, scarcely any sense is entertained that private persons, in no eminent social situation, owe any duties to society, except to obey the laws and submit to the government.[19]

Citizens as Subjects and Agents of Justification One could read Mill as exclusively speaking of participation of the individual citizen in their capacity as voter. In this capacity, general participation in representative democracies is indeed rare. However, the public function of citizens and their participatory actions are not exhausted by casting a vote. Instead, the public role of *citizens as voters* casts them into a complex net of justificatory practices including rights to justification and duties to justify their own actions undertaken in that capacity. First, citizens *qua* voters are "answerable to the public"[20] and have a duty to justify their actions to those whom they disagree with. In this respect voting for political representatives differs from voting in private associations because in the former case, voting "is strictly a matter of duty; he [the voter] is bound to give it according to his best and most conscientious opinion of the public good."[21] The duty to justify ones vote derives partly from the instrumental value of publicity for the common good orientation of citizens' voting behavior.[22]

Second, *representatives* have to justify their actions to their constituency (and to everyone else). While due to their superior intellect their justifications might not need to be couched in terms of reasons which their electorate could easily understand, they have to at least make their deliberations transparent to the electorate.[23] Mill avoids the charge of circularity by arguing that the citizens' ability to effectively criticize those

---

[19] T, p. 412.
[20] C, p. 493.
[21] Ibid.
[22] Mill makes all of these points in his argument for the public mode of voting. See C, Chap. X, pp. 488ff.
[23] Cf. C, p. 501.

who hold higher function does not qualify all citizens for the exercise of those higher functions. Nevertheless, the representatives' duty of justification only makes sense in light of the presupposition that citizens can at least evaluate whether the representatives' decision was based on grounds that appropriately take their interests into account and fulfill the criterion of common good orientation.

Third, the way the role of *citizens as voters* is conceived, including the unequal distribution of votes, has to be justified to them. This latter arrangement has to be justified to the intellectually inferiors in terms of moral reasons. Not only does this have to be done in terms of moral reasons, but in terms of *reasons they can in fact accept* as establishing the moral worth of the arrangement. Mill states that "[i]t is [...] necessary that this superior influence [of the intellectual superior] should be assigned *on grounds which he [the intellectual inferior] can comprehend*, and *of which he is able to perceive the justice.*"[24] Mill of course thinks that his own theory establishes the moral grounds of the arrangement, which implies that the intellectual inferiors have to at least be capable of understanding the aspects of the theory that do so.[25] The Millian voting scheme with its unequal distribution of votes has to meet this publicity condition based on a form of moral respect owed to all persons. Notice that this publicity condition is much stronger than the formulation of reasons reasonable citizens *could* accept. According to Mill, "[e]very one has a right to feel insulted by being made a nobody, and stamped as of no account at all."[26] I venture that for Mill, this holds just as much for the right, though not the equal right, to have a say in decision-making as for the need to justify the way political power is distributed in terms of reasons all members of society can accept. Not to be the subject of political justification is to be made a nobody, and "stamped as of no account at all."

Hence, contrary to the popular reading of Mill as a radical proponent of moral elitism, his conception of democracy includes a strong

---

[24] C, p. 474; my emphasis throughout.
[25] Mill thinks that the intuitive idea that the opinion of one's intellectual superiors should count more even in governing one's own life suffices to show that it is prudent to defer to their opinion. However, this rationale does not establish the *justice* of the arrangement.
[26] C, p. 474.

justificatory dimension, which in turn presupposes a significant level of moral competence on part of the intellectually inferior.

Mill and Equal Epistemic Authority Indeed, if the idea of equal epistemic authority over the common good were put on trial, one could find an unexpected witness for the defense in Mill. The picture of political participation that emerges from the aspects of the public function of citizens and voters to whom justification is owed and from whom it can be demanded is much more complex than citizens simply casting a vote for a candidate. The rights and responsibilities coming with the public status as citizen and voter already by themselves presuppose a high degree of moral competence. Up to a point, Mill conceives voters to be equal epistemic authorities *in the negative sense* that they, as subjects of justification, are able to comprehend the justifications offered to them and acknowledge them as establishing the moral worth of the political institutions they are subject to and of the actions of their representatives. To the degree that they are conceived as capable of justifying their own actions to others, that is, as agents of justification, their moral competence exceeds the passive competence of this negative conception of equal epistemic authority. Hence, political participation even by ordinary citizens presupposes a relatively high level of moral competence in their active participation in the political affairs of the society of which they are a part.

Furthermore, Mill held that political participation drastically enhances the moral competence of citizens. Mill in fact recognized that increased participation brings groups closer toward epistemic peerhood in practical reasoning because it ingrains in them a sense of justice and an orientation toward the common good and transmits knowledge about means–end relations between the members of the groups.

Consider the following quotes:

> It is by political discussion that the manual labourer, whose employment is a routine, and whose way of life brings him in contact with no variety of impressions, circumstances, or ideas, is taught that remote causes, and events which take place far off, have a most sensible effect even on his personal interests; and it is from political discussion, and collective political action, that one whose daily occupations concentrate his interests in a

small circle round himself, learns to feel for and with his fellow-citizens, and becomes consciously a member of a great community.[27]

In this passage, Mill argues that political participation can greatly expand the intellectual faculties even of those intellectually most disadvantaged.[28] He even goes so far as to explicitly state that, on certain questions, the socially and intellectually near-to-lowest classes can approach the status of equal epistemic authorities:

> When a subject arises in which the labourers as such have an interest, is it regarded from any point of view but that of the employers of labour? I do not say that the working men's view of these questions is in general nearer to truth than the other: but *it is sometimes quite as near*.[29]

However, since he thought that a plural voting scheme would have to be of a permanent nature, he cannot have thought that the gap between intellectual capabilities would disappear completely over time. Presumably then, he either thought that the benefits of political participation for workers hit a ceiling beyond which no further benefits are incurred or that opportunities for participation have a natural limit in modern society, hence limiting the opportunities to develop one's competences. His argument for *representative* democracy provides evidence for the latter thesis. This is apparent in his summary of the argument, where he remarks that

> the participation should everywhere be as great as the general degree of improvement of the community will allow [...] but since [in large republics] all cannot [...] participate personally in any but some very minor

---

[27] C, p. 469.
[28] Further testimony to this emphasis is Mill's remark that even the rare occasion of jury duty or to serve in parish offices has an effect on members of the lower classes which "must make them [...] *very different beings*, in range of ideas and development of faculties, from those who have done nothing in their lives but drive a quill, or sell goods over a counter" (T, p. 411). Admittedly, this statement is also testimony to his low regard of the general intellectual capacities and moral competence of the lower classes.
[29] C, p. 405; my emphasis.

portions of the public business, it follows that the ideal type of a perfect government must be representative.[30]

Keeping in line with Mill's thinking, one might conjecture that workers actually have a much steeper learning curve and that the transmission of knowledge is asymmetrical since they would learn much more from their intellectual superiors than the other way around. On the other hand, in Mill's scheme the intellectual superiors have much greater opportunities for political participation and hence many more opportunities to develop their sense of justice and incur factual knowledge about means–end relations.[31] Furthermore, it is worth noting that the intellectual superiors would equally face limits grounded in the limit of their intellect and potential participation with only the representatives left as those fully dedicated to political decision-making.

In any case, it is crucial to note that even for Mill the near-to-lowest classes count at least as equal epistemic authorities *in the negative sense* in that they are able to understand and reliably evaluate the merits of political justifications addressed to them. To the extent that they are thought capable of justifying their actions to others, their competence presupposed by and enhanced through political participation exceeds the negative conception of equal epistemic authority and presupposes a sufficient level of competence to actively participate in these justificatory practices. Furthermore, he took them to approach the status of equal epistemic authorities in the full sense on at least some issues.

The Problem of Disagreement among Representatives There is another problem with Mill's moral elitism. According to it, the constituents ought to defer to the opinion of the representative in many instances. This is because they can discern their representative's intellectual superiority without it necessarily being the case that they agree with them on many issues. However, they presumably can also discern the intellectual superiority of the representatives of other constituencies or at least trust

---

[30] C, p. 412.
[31] In this context, it is interesting to consider that participation could be broadened to include, for example, workplace democracy and other decentralized participatory designs.

that the electoral process reliably selects the intellectually superior to be the representatives of other constituencies. A parliament thus elected will include some representatives who disagree with their own representative and more closely mirror their own political judgments. Why, then, should they defer to *their* representative and not feel encouraged to hold on to their opinion in light of the fact that representatives of other constituencies, themselves intellectually superior to them and often at least equal to their own representative, agree with them? This is another point where Mill's conception of democracy runs into problems. Even if we grant intellectual asymmetries, the fact of disagreement among representatives and the baseline of considerable presupposed moral competences of the electorate can justify that those who make up the latter hold on to their opinions. Furthermore, such intra-level disagreement between representatives can erode the relations of epistemic trust between the electorate and representatives as a group and the epistemic trust which citizens place in the outcomes produced by such an elitist decision procedure supposedly geared toward bringing political competence to bear on decisions.

In addition to this, the disagreement between representatives gives rise to another question. If the electoral system ensures that the intellectually superior are elected into office, the elected representatives, before they learn of their disagreement, have reason to believe that the other representatives are rather similar in their moral competence and their judgments about justice similarly reliable. Disagreement between representatives, then, is a case of disagreement between persons who have reason to regard each other as similarly reliable epistemic agents. The question then is: how should *they*—the representatives—react to disagreement among themselves? Off-hand, it seems implausible that they ought to defer to the judgments of others. After all, they were elected because of their special qualifications to make these kinds of judgments. We thus face the question of what, if it is not deference, is the rational reaction to political disagreement between people who regard each other as similarly reliable in judging the content of the common good? I shall return to this question in the next chapter.

The Argument from Institutional Expertise The argument from institutional expertise cites another crucial consideration in favor of equal epistemic authority. Importantly, modern democracies are representative democracies. Though to different degrees in different countries, most matters are decided by elected representatives. This means that citizens need not decide many of the complex issues that arise when trying to govern the world according to their preferred conception of justice. They can rely instead on their representative to translate a more general value judgment into the specifics of public policy-making.

In modern societies, however, even the representative's competence faces severe limits. Normally, they cannot develop in-depth knowledge about more than a few fields of public policy. Like the ordinary citizen, they therefore rely heavily on their political party to guide them through the policy space. In our times, political competence has become less an attribute of politicians than an attribute of the impersonal functionality of bureaucratic entities such as political parties. Political parties and representative institutions help us to come to terms with the "evident epistemic holism of political knowledge."[32] For, "[a] great deal of policy appears to be holistic in exactly this way: that is, one cannot successfully evaluate policy within one particular subdomain without some substantial regard for the effects of such policy in a wide range of other subdomains."[33] The party machinery with its working groups, specialized committees, and incorporation of expert knowledge can effectively gather information and integrate the more abstract value judgments of citizens into a *sufficiently coherent* and *sufficiently specific* conception of justice. They are the political experts in modern politics:

> Within the process of an increase of complexity in politics, "competence" seems to emigrate from the individual and their ability, skill, and charisma and to take on the character of impersonal, efficient task fulfillment, protection of interests, and provision of services according to the functionality of a huge organizational, administrative, and structuring apparatus. The fact that leading politicians are nowadays as a matter of course identified in

---

[32] Fuerstein (2008): p. 81.
[33] Ibid.

public as the representatives and "spokesmen" of their respective parties mirrors the relation of dependence.[34]

I provide a detailed discussion of the role of party ideology and party programs below (see also Chap. 6, Party Ideology and Programs).

Importantly, the epistemic benefits of multiparty systems and the institution of representative democracy are provided to the citizenry at an equal degree as the party position and the representative's judgment are available to, and voted on, by all. Voters can cast their vote for the party whose position corresponds most with their value judgments at a fairly abstract level and rely on the party to translate the values endorsed into a consistent set of policies which take into account a wide array of instrumental considerations and empirical knowledge not available to each voter or each representative individually. As a consequence, these institutional arrangements further level the epistemic status of citizens.

As Rousseau pointed out, "the evidence [about the common good] can be in the natural and political laws *only when they are considered in abstraction*. In any particular government, which is a composite of so many diverse elements, *this evidence necessarily disappears*" (LtoM, 1; my emphasis throughout). Individuals on their own lack a good deal of information on the specifics of public policy-making, which undermines the idea that they have independent access to how the common good "considered in abstraction" bears on public policy. Hence, we need procedures and political institutions which pool dispersed knowledge relevant to effectively translating abstract judgment about justice into effective public policy (see Chap. 1; Legitimacy without Procedures?). Implicit in this idea is that political knowledge can be compartmentalized in this way. We can, for instance, distinguish the knowledge of (or judgments about) general principles of justice from the "[k]nowledge of the nuts and bolts [of] administrative facets of governance (drafting legislation, running committees, etc.).""[35]

---

[34] Cf. Richter (2011): p. 172 (my translation).
[35] Fuerstein (2008): p. 76.

The argument of institutional expertise thus explains why *citizens ought to regard the judgments informing their votes as equally reliable given the relevant threshold of comparison defined by their epistemic role in the decision procedures of modern democracies*. It is in this sense that the reasonable citizens of a well-ordered society ought to count as equal epistemic authorities.

In the conciliatory conception of democracy, political parties play two roles. The first is the one just presented, namely the leveling of the epistemic status of citizens. The second is to aid in the epistemic conciliation of conceptions of justice. What I mean by this and how it is done, I will explain in Chap. 5.

The (Un)Reasonableness of Political Disagreement

There are two noteworthy consequences of the above arguments. Of particular interest here are the argument from multidimensional complexity, the local knowledge argument, and the practice-based argument. All three are part of a justification of the commitment of reasonable citizens of deliberative democracies to regard other reasonable citizens they disagree with as equal epistemic authorities, that is, as prima facie equally reliable judges of the rightness of political decisions according to a procedure-independent criterion of rightness (reliable in an epistemic sense). The argument from multidimensional complexity and the local knowledge argument, however, serve not only as arguments to establish the claim that differences in the expected reliability between reasoners are limited. They also explain why *disagreement is the outcome to be expected* of any decentered reasoned debate with a sufficient level of complexity *even under ideal circumstances*. By extension, this also holds for public deliberation, which is simply a special case of a debate with these characteristics.

Importantly, the conditions under which public deliberation proceeds are such that (1) participants are exposed to *non-identical* evidence, and (2) the assumption is justified that this evidence is *comparable*, that is, epistemically on par with the evidence all other participants obtain throughout the process. Hence, *the disagreement in question need not be irrational*, that is, the product of cognitive error, *or unreasonable*, that is, the product of insincere reasoning on part of the participants. Rather, it is *disagreement between persons who obtain non-identical but epistemically symmetrical evidence*.

The Debate Room Argument The following example will help to bear out these conclusions.

> **Debate Room 3.** In the imagined setting, the members of a relatively large group comprised of persons of various backgrounds roughly mirroring the pluralism of modern-day societies are randomly assigned seats at different tables in the same room. They then proceed to discuss the justice of a proposed public policy for a limited amount of time.[36] After some time, these groups are dissolved and each person is again randomly assigned seats at different tables in the same room. Hence, the make-up of the groups is bound to be very different from the first round of debate. Each group now proceeds to discuss the justice of the proposed public policy for a limited amount of time with these different persons who they find at their respective table. This process is repeated several times.

It is a feature of public deliberation about sufficiently complex issues that while the deliberators are maximally open to others and the deliberation itself is maximally open to input by all members of society, there are natural constraints on how much input can be absorbed synchronously in any deliberative sphere and by each participant. The separation of the tables is meant to mirror these constraints. The first constraint is the complexity of justice (see The Argument from Multidimensional Complexity). The set of arguments bearing on the question is too extensive for the participants at any one table to consider the complete set. Taken individually, participants face cognitive limits in their capacity to take all pertinent considerations into account in their reasoning. The second constraint is the structure of modern society. The pluralism of modern societies is too deep for its full spectrum to be present at any one table.

---

[36] It is assumed that the issue at stake is sufficiently complex in the rough sense that the deliberation cannot produce a consensus between participants in the time available to them. Actual, observed disagreement on political questions is an indicator that public deliberation on political issues is sufficiently complex in this sense.

The idea is that no deliberative sphere is so encompassing as to include members of all social groups. Due to these constraints, the relevant information available at each table differs and is necessarily incomplete. It is thus assumed that participants do not learn of all arguments and cannot familiarize themselves with all perspectives even after many rounds of debate. Furthermore, they do not gain knowledge of the global validity status of arguments currently under discussion (see The Local Knowledge Argument). The continuous participation in this form of decentered public deliberation, however, levels the gap in competence between participants (see The Practice-Based Argument).

Local Consensus and Global Disagreement Assume—however unlikely this might strike you as—that a Habermasian consensus (an agreement for the same reasons) emerges at each table. Since at each table, participants are exposed to different arguments bearing on the issue and to perspectives reflecting only a limited spectrum of the pluralism of modern societies, however, the participants at different tables are bound to arrive at judgments that differ from those made at other tables. Hence, any consensus formed under these conditions would be restricted to each table and thus hold only locally. In other words, in the debate room, any consensus arrived at would be a local consensus. This readily follows from the assumption that, in the first round of debate, the different information available to different groups makes it rational to arrive at conflicting judgments.

Of course, access to the various deliberative spheres is not restricted to those currently participating in them. And it is certainly not assumed to be in the ideal theory of deliberative democracy. Instead, it conceives participants as maximally open to new input, and all perspectives and arguments potentially receiving uptake by each participant. Hence, we can imagine new deliberative spheres forming as participants tap into deliberative processes they have not previously been a part of.

Debate Room 3 Cont'd. After some time, these groups are dissolved and each person is again randomly assigned a seat at a table in the same room. Hence, the make-up of the groups is now bound to be very different from the first round of debate. Each group now proceeds to discuss the justice of the proposed public policy for a limited amount of time. This process is repeated several times.

After thus being introduced to a new deliberative sphere, participants learn about different arguments and perspectives bearing on the issue. These arguments might attack assumptions underlying their previously formed opinion on the issue under discussion or include independent considerations. Importantly, participants can gain a deeper understanding of the complexity of a question also by understanding the interconnectedness with other issues. This transmission of information, of course, is not a one-way affair. The newly introduced participants communicate information they have obtained in the previous round of debate which was not present within the deliberative sphere they now find themselves in. Hence, being the ideally open-minded deliberators that they are, some or all participants are likely to adjust their views upon the new information they obtain. The same process of information exchange simultaneously takes place at all other tables in the room. Thus, the alteration of judgments is a comprehensive phenomenon in the debate room. As in the first round of debate, we can in principle imagine a local consensus forming at the various tables. Again, however, these will differ in correspondence to the information available, which is assumed to differ and be incomplete in each sphere.

Hence, even if the mix-up of participants makes new information available to the participants within each newly constituted deliberative sphere, the judgments based on the total information now available in each deliberative sphere still differ from those made from within other spheres. While the consensus might have shifted, it still remains confined to a deliberative sphere and local in nature.

Global Consensus and the Entropy of Reason By itself, the process described above does not guarantee the persistence of disagreement over time, however. One could argue that after a sufficient number of rounds of debate all participants at all tables would be familiar with all or nearly all arguments made as, after a certain number of rounds of debate, all could have at least indirectly learned of the arguments made by all others. In such a state of full information, the argument provides no reason why a *global* consensus between all participants could not, in principle, be possible.

This objection, however, is ill-advised for two reasons. First, it neglects the role of the argument from multidimensional complexity, which established that given the enormous complexity of the issues at stake, no reasoner is in a state of total information even after a large number of rounds of debate. Second, the objection assumes that the information exchanged in the totality of the deliberative process is *static* when it really is *dynamic*. If the information we are confronted with were static, our situation would be one where each reasoner starts out with a subset of the total information I concerning an issue. For the sake of the example, let the total information in the debate room reasoners are confronted with at point t_1 of the deliberative process comprise the subsets I_{a-z}. In an ongoing process of deliberation, each reasoner could then obtain the information available to all the other participants, starting from $I_a + I_b + I_c \ldots$ until eventually arriving at point t_2 of the deliberative process at which the total information I_{a-z} is available to them. A consensus could form if all participants evaluated the complete set of information in the same way.

Reasoned debate with a sufficient level of complexity, however, is inherently dynamic in the sense that reasoners are likely to construct (or discover) new arguments and reasons which they have not previously been aware of. Hence the new information they obtain and process collectively leads to an expanded total information I', which is *not* identical to I_{a-z} but includes new information I_α they were not previously aware of. Thus, the total information processed in public deliberation at t_2 is comprised of the subsets $I_{a-z+\alpha}$. One might say at this point that everything that is entailed by the original complete set of information I_{a-z} is part of the original set, which is why the distinction between this set and another set including I_α is illusory. However, it is hard to see how an entailment I am not aware of can be said to be part of the information I am *confronted* with when deliberating. The example thus helps us to gain an understanding of the dynamic growth of the total information processed in reasoned debate. Due to this dynamic growth, the information participants are confronted with does not display a tendency to form a unified complete set, which is itself static and comprised of static subsets that have been collectivized at the global level. Instead, reasoned debate about sufficiently complex issues simply produces *additional* information. After each round of deliberation in the debate room, then, participants will have altered and *expanded* subsets of the total information on which to base their judgments.

Thus again, in the standard case, after each round of debate, participants base their judgments on different, only locally available sets of information and, accordingly, ought to arrive at different judgments about the issue at stake. Due to the entropy of reason, that is, the dynamic growth of information, the information available in each deliberative sphere is bound to be incomplete after any number of rounds of debate.

The debate room argument thus helps to illustrate why disagreement is to be the expected outcome of deliberation in a decentered public *even under ideal circumstances* without the constraint of the limited time available in real-world deliberations.

Consensus as the Motivational Requirement and the Telos of Deliberation Yet, if disagreement is the expected outcome of deliberation even under ideal circumstances, why engage in deliberation at all? Is the motivating force to do so not the hope to convince others of the truth of my opinion and thus reach agreement? If, due to the complexity of contested issues and the dynamics of decentered deliberation, I cannot reasonably hope to convince others of my opinion, why make the effort at all?

A first point to note here is that we do not need any special insights into expected outcomes of deliberation under ideal circumstances in order to recognize this question as pertinent. Under the very real circumstances of actual deliberation, we regularly encounter persistent disagreement with other competent reasoners. However, we also see that deliberation remains a stable practice over time in spite of this fact. Thus, the expectation to convince others cannot be our sole motivation to engage in deliberative practices. Furthermore, if consensus is not to be expected, we cannot expect that the public use of reason will lead us to converge on a truth that will be recognized as such by all. Hence, our desire to gain a level of certainty in a belief based on the fact that the public use of reason leads to such a shared belief cannot be the only motivation at work either. Even worse, persistent disagreement between competent reasoners is often seen as putting into question the truth-aptness of an issue altogether.

However, the lack of agreement need not cast doubt the epistemic benefits of public deliberation. As John Stuart Mill points out,

> [t]he beliefs which we have most warrant for, have no safeguard to rest on, but a standing invitation to the whole world to prove them unfounded.[37]

To expose our beliefs to criticism has epistemic benefits even when it does not lead to agreement. *In a first step* in the dialectic of disagreement, the fact that, from *our* perspective, our own beliefs survive the criticism voiced by others is a reason to believe that we are warranted to hold them.[38] Another view deserves a hearing because it

> may possibly be true. Those who desire to suppress it, of course deny its truth; but they are not infallible. [...] To refuse a hearing to an opinion, because they are sure that it is false, is to assume that their certainty is the same thing as absolute certainty.[39]

To engage in deliberation is not only an attempt to convince others of one's own beliefs but also, and crucially, to expose these beliefs to criticism and give other opinions the hearing they deserve in an attempt to arrive at the most justified beliefs judged *from our perspective*. From this perspective, deliberation is a cognitive resource for us in arriving at beliefs with a rich informational basis which includes the perspectives of others. This self-interest in arriving at justified beliefs in the face of doxastic opposition provides a plausible motivational basis for our continued engagement in deliberative practices. Given our cognitive imperfections and the structural limits of our acquisition of information, it is an adequate expression of intellectual humility and respect for the opinions of others.

---

[37] Mill (1991): Chap. 2, para. 7.
[38] However, persistent disagreement gives us all the more reason to acknowledge our own fallibility.
[39] Mill (1991): Chap. 2, para. 3.

Furthermore, our effort to treat others justly is itself bound with our effort to arrive at well-justified beliefs about what is just. If we were not to make a sincere effort to arrive at well-justified beliefs about what justice requires of us, we could not be said to make a sincere effort to treat others justly. If part of making a sincere effort to arrive at justified beliefs about what justice requires of us is to expose our view to public criticism, to engage in deliberation is part and parcel of a duty to justice (see also Chap. 7; The Normative and the Epistemic Dimension of Conciliatory Democracy).

Rational and Reasonable Disagreement and Symmetrical Evidence As we have seen, we ought to regard disagreement as the standard result of decentered reasoned debate even under ideal circumstances. I said earlier, however, that the argument also explains why *the disagreement* in question *need not be irrational*, for example, the product of cognitive error, *or unreasonable*, for example, insincere reasoning on part of the participants. Instead, we can explain the disagreement in terms of the different sets of information participants in deliberation are confronted with. It should by now be easy to see that this second claim follows from the explanation of the persistence of disagreement over time, and I want to refrain from repeating myself. However, up until now, I have said nothing in support of the further claim, made at the beginning of this section, that persistent disagreement is not only a rational and reasonable outcome of decentered debates on complex issues, but, at least in the case of public political deliberation, can be regarded as *disagreement between persons* who obtain *non-identical but epistemically symmetrical evidence*.

What supports this last claim is that the conditions under which public deliberation proceeds are such that (1) participants are exposed to nonidentical evidence, and (2) the assumption is justified that this evidence is *comparable*, that is, on par with the evidence all other participants obtain throughout the process. I have argued for the first point extensively. The second assumption follows from the way the debate room example is set up. The public sphere is inhabited by persons who regard each other as equal epistemic authorities and who are in persistent reasonable and rational disagreement with each other. Crucially, however, they do not know the grounds for the disagreement with persons who are not members of their deliberative sphere. This follows from the fact that they have, at any point t in the deliberative process, only local knowledge of the information available to them in their respective deliberative sphere. In this setting, participants are not warranted to assume that their evidence is epistemically superior to that available in other deliberative spheres.

Below, I will discuss an epistemological principle dubbed "Independence". The principle states that downgrading the epistemic status of your opponent is permissible only if your reason to do so is independent of your and their reasoning that lets you two make your respective judgments. The purpose of this principle is to preclude the arbitrariness of downgrading the epistemic status of the judgment of a presumed equal epistemic authority on the matter simply on the basis that you disagree with them. The impermissibility of downgrading their judgment based on an arbitrary presumption that, because you disagree, their evidence must be inferior is simply an extension of the Independence principle. Given the fact that you justifiably regard other participants as equal epistemic authorities and the fact that evidence is widely distributed among participants, the presumption in regard to the evidence available to your epistemic peers ought to be that their evidence is on a par with yours. Interestingly, then, we can describe disagreement which is the outcome of decentered reasoned debate with a sufficient level of complexity as a case of disagreement which need not be the result of insincere or erroneous reasoning or cognitive error on part of the participants. Furthermore, the persistent fact of disagreement between competent reasoners in any actual decentered deliberation with a sufficient level of complexity should put in doubt the notion that the information locally available to each participant is sufficient to judge the issue at stake with a high level of confidence. *Actual* disagreement between competent reasoners points to cognitive error on part of some participants or the availability of comparable, that is, epistemically symmetrical, evidence available to different participants supporting different conclusions. This leaves the second part of the disjunction. Actual disagreement points to the availability of comparable, that is, epistemically symmetrical, evidence available to different participants supporting different conclusions. In more general terms, the argument shows that the persistent, actual disagreement which reasonable citizens encounter in decentered public deliberation about sufficiently complex issues is an epistemically worrisome feature, which ought to affect the credence that participants assign to their beliefs.

This is an extremely interesting result in its own right, and it leads to a question to which I now turn: *how ought reasonable citizens to react to such rational and reasonable disagreement with other reasonable citizens whom they regard as equal epistemic authorities and as equal normative authorities?*

References

Benhabib, S. (1996). Toward a Deliberative Model of Legitimacy. In S. Benhabib (Ed.), *Democracy and Difference. Contesting the Boundaries of the Political*. Princeton, NJ: Princeton University Press.

Carter, I. (2011). Respect and the Basis of Equality. *Ethics, 121*(3), 538–571.

Ebeling, M. (2016). Epistemic Political Egalitarianism, the Role of Political Parties, and Conciliatory Conception of Democracy. *Political Theory, 44*(5), 629–656.

Elster, J. (1985). *Sour Grapes. Studies in the Subversion of Rationality*. Cambridge: Cambridge University Press.

Estlund, D. M. (2008). *Democratic Authority: A Philosophical Framework*. Princeton, NJ: Princeton University Press.

Fuerstein, M. (2008). Epistemic Democracy and the Social Character of Knowledge. *Episteme: A Journal of Social Epistemology, 5*(1), 74–93.

Gaus, G. F. (2000). *Political Concepts and Political Theory*. Boulder, CO: Westview Press.

Gaus, G. F. (2008). The (Severe) Limits of Deliberative Democracy as the Basis for Political Choice. *Theoria: A Journal of Social and Political Theory, 117*, 26–53.

Habermas, J. (1996). *Between Facts and Norms: Contributions to a Discourse Theory of Law and Democracy* (W. Rehg, Trans.). Cambridge, MA: MIT Press. This work originally appeared in German under the title *Faktizität und Geltung. Beiträge zur Diskurstheorie des Rechts und des demokratischen Rechtsstaats*, Suhrkamp Verlag, Frankfurt am Main, Germany, 1992.

Hayek, F. A. (1991). The Use of Knowledge in Society. In R. M. Ebeling (Ed.), *Austrian Economics*. Hillsdale, MI: Hillsdale College Press.

Landemore, H. (2014). Democracy as Heuristic: The Ecological Rationality of Political Equality. *The Good Society, 23*(2), 160–178.

Mill, J. S. ([1859] 1977). Thoughts on Parliamentary Reform. In J. S. Robson (Ed.), *The Collected Works of John Stuart Mill, Volume XIX: Essays on Politics and Society*. Toronto, ON: University of Toronto Press.

Mill, J. S. ([1861] 1977). Considerations on Representative Government. In J. S. Robson (Ed.), *The Collected Works of John Stuart Mill, Volume XIX: Essays on Politics and Society*. Toronto, ON: University of Toronto Press.

Mill, J. S. (1991). On Liberty. In J. Gray (Ed.), *On Liberty and Other Essays*. Oxford: Oxford University Press.

Pateman, C. (1970). *Participation and Democratic Theory*. Cambridge: Cambridge University Press.

Richter, E. (2011). *Was ist politische Kompetenz? Politiker und engagierte Bürger in der Demokratie*. Frankfurt a.M.: Campus.

4

The Epistemology of Political Disagreement

The lengthy discussion in the previous chapter about the reasons for reasonable citizens of deliberative democracies to treat other reasonable citizens as equal normative authorities[1] and to regard them as equal epistemic authorities[2] leads us to the following question:

> How ought reasonable citizens to react to their rational and reasonable disagreement with other reasonable citizens whom they regard as equal epistemic authorities and as equal normative authorities?

In this chapter, I set out to answer part of this question. More specifically, I try to lay the foundations for an answer to how reasonable citizens ought to react *rationally* to disagreement with other reasonable citizens

---

[1] Recall the definition of equal normative authorities as persons to whom they grant the right to take the results of their deliberations as prima facie reasons for action. In the political realm, this commitment translates into granting others the right to participate as equals in the collective decision-making.

[2] Recall the definition of equal epistemic authorities as prima facie equally reliable judges of the rightness of political decisions according to a procedure-independent criterion of rightness (reliable in an epistemic sense).

© The Author(s) 2017
M. Ebeling, *Conciliatory Democracy*,
DOI 10.1057/978-1-137-57743-6_4

whom they regard as equal epistemic authorities. The question as to what a rational reaction to political disagreement between reasonable citizens in a deliberative democracy looks like and why the answer to that question eventually leads us to endorse the conciliatory conception of democracy will take time to answer. The epistemic dimension of the significance of disagreement will be the focus of this chapter. In Chap. 5, we shall see how the conciliatory conception of democracy reconciles the epistemic with the normative dimension. In line with the discussion in Chap. 2, I will show that the answer to the epistemic significance to the political disagreement provides us with an epistemic component of a public justification of democracy which can help us to specify decision procedures that are among the set of reasonably acceptable answers to the normative significance of political disagreement (see Chap. 2, esp. Spoiled for Choice?).

Taking a step back, we can see how we got thus far. In the first chapter, I discussed in detail how Rousseau approached the problem of political disagreement. The reason for this detailed discussion was twofold. First, Rousseau was one of the few thinkers in the history of political philosophy who recognized that the political judgments of citizens as such carry epistemic significance. Furthermore, given his analysis of the epistemic significance of agreement as higher-order evidence which can undermine the first-order evidence supporting the diverging judgments of other citizens, he was able to recommend specific democratic decision procedures. This recommendation he based on a bestness-tracking claim in their favor which is a component of a normative justification of democracy. Supermajoritarian decision-making, he told us, is the only method which can give us a level of confidence approaching certainty that our exercise of political power is an expression of the general will and is thus legitimate. We have also seen that Rousseau was dismissive of widespread disagreement in the sense that it does not, according to him, constitute higher-order evidence pointing in either way. The reason for this dismissive attitude lies in his belief that in a well-ordered society whose citizens are sincere and give motivational primacy to the common good, (near) unanimity is the result to be expected. If citizens do not reach nearly unanimous verdicts for or against a legislative proposal, this is evidence that the state is in decline and the citizenry corrupted (see Chap. 1; Deference, (Near) Unanimity, and Levels of Confidence). This reasoning would, if correct, constitute a public justification of supermajoritarian democratic rule. Alas, Rousseau is mistaken, or, at the very least, his theory is not applicable to contemporary societies (see Chap. 1; The Simplicity Assumption).

As I have argued in Chap. 3 (see The Debate Room Argument), disagreement is the outcome we ought to expect of decentered deliberation in pluralistic societies about issues with a sufficient level of complexity. Because this is the case, we cannot simply dismiss widespread disagreement as epistemically (or morally) insignificant. Instead, we ought to take it seriously. A second consequence from the reasonable expectation of disagreement is that it is very unlikely to obtain second-order evidence (near unanimity of judgments in Rousseau's case) that could make us virtually certain that the exercise of political power tracks justice or the general will. All we can do is to take our best shot under conditions of severe uncertainty. I believe, however, that this conclusion should not discourage us from making a publicly justifiable bestness-tracking claim in favor of certain decision procedures. My argument for the conciliatory conception of democracy is, in a nutshell, that endorsing the outcomes of democratic decision procedures is our best shot at getting it right.

The epistemology of disagreement between equal epistemic authorities is the reason why scrutinizing the epistemic dimension of political disagreement eventually leads us to endorse the conciliatory conception of democracy. In the course of this chapter, I will offer different views of how to analyze disagreement of the kind that concerns us. I will reject some views along the way and eventually a variant of a view called *Equal Weight View* will come up on top. It is this view that recommends *epistemic conciliation* as the appropriate reaction to the cases of disagreement under consideration.

Because the conciliatory conception of democracy, as you might have guessed, follows the Equal Weight View in this aspect, this chapter lays important stepping stones for the arguments in the following chapter. Hence, the current chapter is an important building block of my overall argument for the conciliatory conception of democracy I present in Chap. 5.

This chapter introduces the notion of *peer disagreement*, which stands at the center of the epistemological debate I will presently engage in. As will become clear in the following paragraphs, the notion of epistemic peerhood is an obvious analogue to the notion of equal epistemic authority. For now, I shall adopt the jargon of the peer disagreement debate and use the term "epistemic peers" rather than sticking to "equal epistemic authorities." One reason for doing so is that the epistemological debate I now turn to is primarily concerned with theoretical reasoning and the idea of equal epistemic authority introduced in the last chapter pertains to practical reasoning. At the center of my discussion of the debate stands the aforementioned Equal Weight View and an epistemological principle named "Independence", which those accepting the view typically endorse. According to the Equal Weight View, it is rational to alter the credence in one's belief in cases of peer disagreement when there is no independent reason not to do so.[3] In some cases, this results in an increase in credence. In others, it prescribes epistemic conciliation of the credence levels of epistemic peers.

The attentive reader will know by now that my ultimate aim in this section is to defend this conciliatory attitude. I do so by showing that other views on the subject of peer disagreement are either implausible or inconsistent. Furthermore, I defend Independence against a number of challenges raised against it. It thus proves to be a more resilient principle than often supposed. However, its resilience comes at too high a price. Eventually, I will present an objection to the Equal Weight View that is itself based on a strong reading of Independence. In order to rescue the Equal Weight view from what had looked like the jaws of defeat, I offer a weaker reading of Independence that limits its significance to the permissibility of the local downgrading of the epistemic status of one's peer. This presupposes a distinction between two types of downgrading, local and global, which I introduce and explain below. I then supplement the Equal Weight View—now equipped with a weak reading of Independence—with a dynamic model of epistemic peerhood, which bases the permissibility of global downgrading in the absence of independent reasons on an evolving history of high-confidence dis/agreements.

---

[3] What counts as an independent reason will become clear in the course of the discussion.

This is the point at which I return to the political disagreements of reasonable citizens. I apply the dynamic model of epistemic peerhood to this class of disagreements and expand it into a conception of public reason, that is, the shared reason of the reasonable citizens of a well-ordered society. I call this conception of public reason "Democratic Public Reason". It is the epistemic frame of the political disagreements which arise between reasonable citizens. These disagreements are largely low-confidence disagreements about the just exercise of political power. And as the dynamic model of epistemic peerhood suggests, it is at this level that citizens ought to seek to conciliate their judgments with those of citizens with whom they disagree. This is the point of entry for the conciliatory conception of democracy which I turn to in the subsequent chapter.

Epistemic Peerhood and Views on Offer

I now return to the question that shall keep us occupied throughout this chapter: how ought we to rationally react to political disagreement as a case of disagreement among equal epistemic authorities?

To answer this question, one has to familiarize oneself with the epistemology of peer disagreement. To clarify: with regard to a given question, two persons are epistemic peers if they regard each other as equally reliable in answering the question correctly. For example, they regard each other as

- equally familiar with the evidence and the arguments bearing on the question;
- equals with respect to general epistemic virtues such as intelligence, freedom from bias, alertness, and so on.[4]

In general terms, then, the question under discussion is how we ought to rationally respond to the fact that people whom we regard as equally competent reasoners disagree with us on many issues. In the terminology

---

[4] See Elga (2007) for a definition along these lines. The two points narrowing down the notion are mentioned in Kelly (2005): p. 10. It is crucial that the definition given here spells out epistemic peerhood in terms of an ascription of epistemic status by others, not in terms of an objective possession of that status!

adopted here, then, the question at stake is: what is the rational response to disagreement with one's epistemic peer?

First-Order and Second-Order Evidence I have introduced the distinction between higher-order and first-order evidence along with the distinction between rebutting and undercutting defeaters in Chap. 1 (see Procedure-Independent versus Procedure-Dependent Access to the General Will). I shall recap them briefly. Assume that your first-order evidence E for a given belief B is a testimony by a person P whom you trust (and assume for the time being that this trust is justified in light of everything you know about the person). Given this assumption, you are justified in believing B. At a later point, you receive additional information to the effect that P is a pathological liar, was drugged when they gave their testimony, or were untrustworthy for whatever other reason you might fancy to imagine. This new information constitutes new evidence that your original evidence (the testimony) did not in fact justify believing B. It defeats your justification for believing B on the basis of E. Furthermore, it is an *undercutting defeater*. It does not rebut your justification by way of giving you better evidence which supports *non-B* as a *rebutting defeater* would do. Instead, it defeats your justification by way of undermining the evidential connection between E and B.[5]

One point at issue in this debate is whether actual disagreement with an epistemic peer provides additional, second-order evidence about the significance of the original, first-order evidence on which the peers initially based their beliefs.[6] And if it does, to what extent does this new evidence require a revision of the original credence in your belief based on the first-order evidence? The answers given to this question open up a broad spectrum of possible views which at its extremes takes the form of the following radically opposed views.[7]

---

[5] See Chap. 1; Procedure-Independent versus Procedure-Dependent Access to the General Will for more on the undercutting/rebutting defeater distinction.

[6] On this point, see Feldman (2006, 2009) in particular.

[7] The debate is sometimes framed in terms of an all-or-nothing model of belief (cf. Feldman 2006: p. 235), but mostly operates with various degrees of credence invested in one's beliefs (Cf. Christensen 2007: p. 189 and Elga 2007). I will proceed on the assumption that the degree-of-belief model is

4 The Epistemology of Political Disagreement

On one extreme, we find the *Right Reasons View*.[8] This view asserts that all that matters in the assessment of the rationality of the parties is their reaction to their first-order evidence. The fact that an epistemic peer disagrees with them should *not* figure in their reasoning in a decisive manner. If anything, double-checking one's own reasoning after learning about the disagreement should make one *more* confident of one's own judgment. The conclusion adherents of the Right Reasons View draw is "epistemic egoism without apology."[9]

On the other extreme, we find the *Equal Weight View*.[10] Characteristic of this position is an attitude of according a lot of significance to one's disagreement with an epistemic peer. Supporters of this position argue that if we take the notion of epistemic peerhood seriously, it entails that in many instances of disagreement, it is rational for epistemic peers to adjust their credence in their own judgment toward the credence the disagreeing peer has in their judgment until they meet half way. What we ought to do in such cases is to split the difference between us. In other words, the claim is that rationality demands that we take into account the judgment of our epistemic peer as new evidence bearing on the assessment of the issue at stake. It then demands that we lower our confidence in our own judgment until we reach full epistemic conciliation.

An example of a view that attempts to avoid both extremes is the *Total Evidence View*. This view acknowledges that disagreement can be evidence that one has misjudged one's original evidence. Thus, disagreement

---

applicable to peer disagreement. This opens the possibility of being rationally required to revise one's credence in a belief while nevertheless maintaining it. The standard Bayesian convention has it that the credence one invests in a given belief is assigned a numerical value between 0 and 1 inclusive; 1 represents maximal confidence that the proposition is true, 0 represents maximal confidence that the proposition is false. A state of perfect agnosticism is represented by 0.5.

[8] It is also sometimes called *Steadfast View*.

[9] Kelly (2005): 31.

[10] The Equal Weight View is sometimes labeled "conciliationism," which emphasizes the fact that it advocates "splitting the difference" in credence in cases of peer disagreements. In these cases, according to the view under consideration, peers ought to conciliate. This label, however, is misleading given the fact that the view also prescribes an *increase* in credence in cases of peer agreement. If two peers have a credence of say 0.95 and 0.9 in a shared belief, they should, after becoming aware of this fact, arrive at a credence higher than their original credence. Popular defenses of the Equal Weight View were undertaken by, for example, Elga (2007), Christensen (2007, 2009), and Feldman (2006, 2009).

can provide a reason to lower the credence in one's original belief formed in response to one's original or first-order evidence. Interestingly, Kelly sees this view as an improvement over the Right Reasons View, in whose formulation he played a significant part. He now argues that there is no abstract epistemic principle which determines how to react to peer disagreement. Whether revision of your original credence is in order depends on the relative strength of the first-order and second-order evidence rather than on formal features of the situation. The view allows for a flexibility which makes it indistinguishable from the Equal Weight View in the analysis of certain paradigmatic cases and from the Right Reasons View in the analysis of others.

In what follows, I lay out the main motivations behind these different views and point to their characteristic features and (sometimes ulterior) assumptions. This quite naturally unfolds the dialectic of the debate and lays bare the contested issues.

The Right Reasons View There are a number of intuitions motivating the Right Reasons View. One is that we face widespread and persistent disagreement on a whole range of issues. To argue that we would have to remain agnostic about all or most of them can strike one as an absurd consequence of any epistemological position. Another intuition, and maybe the more important one, is that when we face disagreement about these issues, we usually believe that we have the best reasons on our side. Even if we cannot convince our counterpart, and given that they cannot convince us, we attribute the mistake to them. Our confidence in our beliefs on the issue survives the disagreement unscathed. In any case, even if we are wrong, the rationality of our beliefs must relate back to why we are wrong. Having the right reasons on our side simply must matter. If in such cases agnosticism were the rational attitude, one of us would get rationality for free so to speak. The fact that one of us did not respond to the first-order evidence correctly would drop out of the picture completely.

In contrast, the Right Reasons View holds that what ultimately matters in the justification of one's belief that p is that the first-order evidence in fact supports p. Actual disagreement can have some epistemic significance regarding our belief that p in that it can point us to blind spots or performance mistakes in our reasoning. The fact that someone disagrees with us does not, however, have any ultimate significance concerning the rationality of our belief. What matters is whether we got it right or not and whether we got it right for the right reasons. If we did, disagreement drops out of the picture. Ultimately, then, the epistemic significance of actual disagreement is no different from hypothetical disagreement. Both are only of significance if we are wrong.

To illustrate: on the present view the case for or against the Ptolemaic system, for instance, does not depend on the contingent fact that no one defends it anymore. If we do not have a reason to believe it now, as we assume is the fact, we would not have had a reason to believe it before the seventeenth century even though most people did. Copernicus, Galileo, and Kepler were just as justified then to believe that the Ptolemaic system is wrong as they would be today. This example gives color to an intuitively convincing point the Right Reasons View rides on, namely that "the case for a given view itself is no stronger in virtue of the fact that that view has actual defenders."[11]

The moral of the story: What matters in the evaluation of the rationality of your belief is that it is the correct response to the relevant first-order evidence. It is thus wrong to hold that rationality requires you to abandon your justified belief when learning that an epistemic peer disagrees with you. To think otherwise would mean that having the right reasons on your side does not matter. The second-order evidence provided by the disagreement would swamp the first-order evidence.

The Equal Weight View Interestingly, the adherents of the Equal Weight View challenge the Right Reasons View in the exact opposite way. Their argument is that under the latter view, it is the second-order evidence which implausibly drops out of the picture completely. Not only does it drop out of the picture, but it does so for arbitrary reasons. This, they submit, follows directly from the fact that you regard your opponent as your epistemic peer prior to the disagreement. Take the following examples:

---

[11] Kelly (2005), p. 31.

Horse Race. You and your friend watch a horse race. It ends with a close finish. When the race is over, however, you are quite confident that Horse A has won. You then come to learn that your friend, whom up until now you have regarded as equally competent in accurately determining the winning horse, is equally confident that Horse B has won.[12]

Restaurant. "Suppose that five of us go out to dinner. It's time to pay the check, so the question we're interested in is how much we each owe. We can all see the bill total clearly, we all agree to give a 20% tip, and we further agree to split the whole cost evenly, not worrying over who asked for imported water, or skipped desert, or drank more of the wine. I do the math in my head and become highly confident that our shares are $43 each. Meanwhile, my friend does the math in her head and becomes highly confident that our shares are $45 each. How should I react, upon learning of her belief?"[13]

The Right Reasons View suggests that in both cases the rationality of your response to the disagreement is wholly determined by who is right. If you are right, you should stick to your guns. If your friend is right, you should switch sides. End of story.

This is absurd. If you think that, prior to the disagreement, your friend is indeed your epistemic peer, you should by definition take her to be equally likely to have arrived at the correct answer. If you assign less or no weight to your friend's belief *only after* learning about the disagreement, however, you treat the fact that you disagree as new evidence that you are the better judge. This is obviously a mistake. Quite simply, you are betraying your commitment to regard your friend as an epistemic peer. Moreover, you are doing so arbitrarily as the downgrading of their epistemic status is not based on any new evidence justifying a belief in your epistemic superiority. The point is that all other things being equal, the mere fact that you disagree with someone should not count as evidence that the other person is wrong.[14] What we ought to do then in Horse

---

[12] Elga originally introduced the example to the debate. Cf. Elga (2007): p. 486.
[13] Christensen 2007: p. 8f.
[14] This is Elga's (No) Bootstrapping Argument. Cf. Elga (2007), pp. 486ff.

Race and Restaurant, the Equal Weight View has it, is to suspend judgment on the question of who won the race and on whether our share of the bill is $43 or $45 respectively. Importantly, this holds independently from whose belief is *in fact* correct.

Notice, however, the conclusion the Right Reasons View advocates is only absurd if we adopt a first-person perspective to evaluate the rationality of your doxastic reaction to peer disagreement. Since we are concerned with the significance of our respect for actual political disagreement, this is the perspective we indeed ought to adopt. Doing otherwise would amount to the stubborn assertion that we are right and therefore rational in sticking to our previous belief. This, however, is exactly what it is *not* to respect disagreement.[15] The God's eye perspective is not available to us in the epistemically precarious context of public deliberation. Consequently, I base my answer on how to react rationally to political disagreement to a large extent on the Equal Weight View. This is an important point as it will prove paramount to clearly distinguish the perspectives underlying our intuitions when we evaluate the merits of the different answers on offer.

The Total Evidence View An example of a hybrid view is the Total Evidence View, which Thomas Kelly also proposed.[16] Interestingly, this is a revision of the Right Reasons View he defended at an earlier point.[17] To better understand the motivations behind this view, it will be fruitful to understand what provoked him to change his mind about his original take on the significance of peer disagreement.

The main reason why he did so was his desire to accommodate a very strong intuition most people, himself included, share. The intuition is the following: if I count a large group of people as my peers and, after assessing the evidence, learn that all of them disagree with me on a given question, it would be extremely implausible not to let that fact affect my

---

[15] Furthermore, we eventually want this analysis to usher in an action-guiding theory of democracy.
[16] Cf. Kelly (2010).
[17] Cf. Kelly (2005).

judgment *even though* I had been justified in confidently holding my belief prior to learning about the disagreement.[18] Call this "the many peers objection."

Notice first that the Right Reasons View cannot accommodate this intuition. Whether or not you are justified in holding your belief depends on whether your evidence supports that belief. Ultimately, his desire to develop a response to the objection led Kelly to reject a god's eye perspective on rationality. Accordingly, he rejected the Right Reasons View in favor of a view which adequately takes into account our fallibility in assessing the evidence and supports the idea that *actual* peer disagreement can indeed provide evidence that we are in circumstances where taking into account that fallibility is particularly pertinent. Consider Kelly's own example:

> **Conjecture.** Suppose you are a mathematician who thinks long and hard about a mathematical conjecture well known in the mathematical community. For a long time you do not have an opinion either way regarding the truth or falsity of the conjecture in this sense being perfectly in tune with the rest of community. Then a little further down the road to your own surprise you succeed in proving the conjecture. After this Eureka moment you become skeptical of your own success and double-check your proof. The result is confirmed and you are subsequently extremely confident that the conjecture is true. Suppose further that this confidence is fully justified. The conjecture is in fact true and your proof is valid. Then the unexpected happens. You show your proof to your colleagues, one colleague at a time. The first one rejects your proof, so does the second, and the next until eventually a large number of your colleagues have expressed their dismissal of your proof. Suppose further that meanwhile your proof has been circulated in the mathematical community at large and the *entire* community rejects it.

---

[18] This of course also holds the other way around. If all your peers agree with you, you are justified in increasing the credence in your belief. Furthermore, this need not be anonymous agreement. Presumably it is enough to have a large majority on your side to justifiably increase your credence. Assuming for a moment that you would have to remain agnostic if the epistemic community was divided at exactly 50:50, even a simple majority might have a buffering effect on your duty to lower your credence and consequences for the permissibility of maintaining your belief. This also bears on Rousseau's attitude toward the epistemic significance of political disagreement (see Chap. 1; The Epistemic Significance of Political Disagreement).

"In the face of this consensus," Kelly now holds, "it would be unreasonable for you to remain practically certain that The Conjecture is true."[19] He now feels the need to accommodate the intuition behind the many peers objection, thus buying into the objection, and consequently reconsiders his originally held Right Reasons View. He furthermore, and this is the important part, concludes that "if you are rationally required to be less confident after *all* of your peers have disagreed with you, then it would seem that you are also required to be at least somewhat less confident after even *one* of your peers disagrees with you."[20]

The Independent Reasoning Condition A note on the Many Peers Objection is in order here. The number of peers is not by itself as decisive a factor as one might suppose. The objection is subject to the condition that the disagreeing peers arrived at their beliefs independently.

An example:

Oxford versus Harvard on the Analytic/Synthetic Distinction. G.A. Cohen states that philosophers of his generation who received their training in Oxford almost universally believe that the distinction is philosophically important. In contrast, "people of my generation who studied philosophy at Harvard rather than at Oxford for the most part *reject* the analytic/synthetic distinction. And I can't believe that this is an accident. That is, I can't believe that Harvard just *happened* to be a place where both its leading thinker rejected that distinction and its graduate students, for independent reasons—merely, for example, in the independent light of reason itself—also came to reject it. And vice versa, of course, for Oxford. I believe, rather, that in each case students were especially impressed by the reasons respectively for and against believing in the distinction, because in each case the reasons came with all the added persuasiveness of personal presentation, personal relationship, and so forth."[21]

---

[19] Kelly (2010): p. 27.
[20] Ibid.
[21] Quoted in Kelly (2010): p. 38. The emphasis is Cohen's.

The relevance of Cohen's point for the Many Peers Objection is that in this case, numbers do not matter. Even if, say, Oxford had trained a much greater number of philosophers during the same time than Harvard, that fact alone would not give the objection any grip. What matters is that they arrived at their belief "in the independent light of reason itself," not based on "personal relationship, and so forth."

Notice that a defender of the Right Reasons View need not buy into the many peers objection at all. Kelly, for instance, could simply remain adamant in his claim that *what really matters* is the correct response to the first-order evidence. If all my peers disagree with me, so what? Let them be wrong. The fact that our shared first-order evidence justifies my belief and not theirs fatally undermines the force of their objections and strips the fact that they disagree with me of all epistemic significance. If this rebuttal of the Many Peers Objection is in principle available to Kelly, there must be a further reason that explains why he nevertheless abandoned the Right Reasons View and sought to accommodate the intuition behind the objection. As I have already hinted at, the reason is to be found at a deeper level. He gave up the perspective that supported the view and on which the potential rebuttal of the objection thrives. Instead of assessing the rationality of our doxastic responses to evidence from a third-person standpoint exclusively, he now aims to take into account the first-person perspective with all its epistemic imperfections and ensuing fallibility. From this perspective, the fact that all our peers disagree with us on a certain question is deeply unsettling and should dramatically lower the confidence we have in the result of our deliberations. He concludes thus:

> One should give some weight to one's peer's opinion even when from the God's eye point of view one has evaluated the evidence correctly and he has not. But why? Exactly because one does not occupy the God's eye point of view with respect to the question of who has evaluated the evidence correctly and who has not.[22]

---

[22] Kelly (2010): p. 28.

He nevertheless maintains that only in extreme cases does the second-order evidence provided by disagreement completely override the first-order evidence at hand, thus asserting that his new view, the Total Evidence View, can accommodate the intuition behind the Many Peers Objection without suffering from the shortcomings of the Equal Weight View. He consequently maintains that "[w]hat *is* quite implausible [about the consequences of the Equal Weight View in cases of peer disagreement among a small number of peers], I think, is the suggestion that you and I are rationally required to make *equally* extensive revisions in our original opinions, given that your original opinion was, while mine was not, a reasonable response to our original evidence (Kelly 2010: 13)." Hence his original objection against the Equal Weight View still stands: in most cases, the first-order evidence should play an important role in determining the rational response to one's *overall* or *total* evidence.

Independence and Downgrading Under Scrutiny

The discussion of the different views so far raises three important questions: (1) *Rationality*. If the adoption of a stance of agnosticism by both parties is equally rational, does rationality come at the cheap? What role does the first-order evidence still play in an assessment of the rationality of their beliefs? (2) *Independence*. Is it a formal feature of peer disagreement that one always needs an independent reason, that is, independent from the reasoning that gave rise to the disagreement, in order to discard or assign lower reliability to the belief of one's epistemic peer? Or can the reason for doing so arise from the substance of the disagreement itself? (3) *Downgrading*. When if ever is one allowed to downgrade (or upgrade) the epistemic status of a person one takes (not) to be one's epistemic peer? If you at some point regard another person as your peer, are you required to *always* do so, no matter how often and on what issues you disagree? Is there no way out of epistemic peerhood?

There is an easy answer to the first question. The adherent of the Equal Weight View can maintain that the overall rationality of a belief derives from two sources: first, the correct response to the first-order evidence; and second, the correct response to the second-order evidence, that is, to peer disagreement. Equally weighing the judgments of peers is the rational response to second-order evidence and the view does not make a statement about the full rationality of the disagreeing peers. Even though both parties might ultimately end up with the same credence in a belief, this can still be more or less rational depending on how they responded to the first-order evidence at hand.[23] The other two questions, however, are of a much more intricate nature and will stay with us throughout the remainder of this chapter.

Local and Global Downgrading and Independence As a matter of clarification, I want to introduce a distinction between two types of downgrading the epistemic status of a peer or a judgment which are often confused in the literature.[24] They raise different questions, however.

Call the first type "local downgrading": it is to downgrade a particular judgment, that is, the epistemic status of the opponent restricted to a particular instance of disagreement.

This differs from the second type. Call it "global downgrading": it is to downgrade the general epistemic status of the opponent in regard to a certain domain unrestricted to particular instances of agreement and disagreement.

Motivated by the desire to avoid arbitrary downgrading of the epistemic merits of a peer's judgment, Equal Weighers have endorsed a principle they term *Independence*. As Christensen puts it,

> [i]t attempts to capture what would be wrong with a P-believer saying, e.g., "Well, so-and-so disagrees with me about P. But since P is true, she's wrong about P. So however reliable she may generally be, I needn't take her disagreement about P as any reason at all to question my belief."[25]

---

[23] Christensen (2009): p. 9.
[24] For reasons of brevity, I will subsequently refer to downgrading the epistemic status of X simply as downgrading of X.
[25] Christensen (2011): p. 2.

Roughly, Independence states that locally downgrading your opponent is permissible only if your reason to do so is independent of your and their reasoning that led you to make your respective judgments.[26] Such reasons are plentiful. Take the following slightly altered examples:

> **Horse Race on LSD.** Imagine the same setting as in Horse Race only that you now come to learn a few facts about your friend that you have not been aware of earlier. Suppose that horse races bore your friend to death. In order to make the event more enjoyable for him, he has consumed a large quantity of LSD prior to his arrival. You have not realized this at an earlier point because you, unlike your friend, find horse races most exhilarating and were captivated by the event. Now, a third person enters the picture and tells you about your friend's altered state of mind.

Not implausibly, you would conclude that his perception might be affected by the drug and subsequently downgrade the reliability of his perceptual judgment. You are allowed to do so because the fact that your friend is tripping on LSD gives you an independent reason to downgrade the reliability of his perception. The reason is independent of your or his actual perception of the horse race. It is thus independent of your respective evaluation of the first-order evidence at stake. This point can be generalized to the effect that whenever you have reason to believe that, in a given situation, your peer lacks the relevant epistemic credentials (e.g., intelligence, freedom from bias, alertness) to be on par with you, you ought to downgrade the expected reliability of his judgment in that situation.

However, the principle is taken to have a much wider application. Even if you have no immediate independent reason to locally downgrade your peer, there might still be an independent reason available for doing so. A further example helps to illustrate the point:

> **Extreme Restaurant.** In this case, all the relevant background conditions are equal to those in Restaurant. The only difference is that while the result of your calculation is still $43, your friend is now equally confident that

---

[26] Kelly notes some difficulties with Christensen's formulation of the principle and offers a revised version. See Kelly (manuscript): pp. 8–12.

the correct result is $450. As it happens, this result for your individual share of the total bill is higher than the overall sum stated on your bill.

Is the Equal Weight View committed to the extremely counterintuitive conclusion that in this case, too, you are forced to assign equal weight to your friend's judgment and hence adopt a stance of agnosticism? Not surprisingly, adherents of the view answer in the negative. Presumably then, there must be an independent reason which allows us to discount our peer's judgment. In the case at hand, Christensen invokes a common sense check on the reasoning of your peer. The check consists in the simple and highly reliable operation of determining whether the total is higher than your share. If it is not, the result your friend arrived at must be wrong. Furthermore, you have reason to believe that she did not perform this common sense check on her own reasoning, which would have led her to become aware of the result's wrongness. Importantly, thus checking your results is an operation of reasoning that is independent of either your or your friend's calculation. In addition, its reliability is much higher than either your or your friend's reliability in mental arithmetic. For these reasons, common sense checking gives you an independent reason to remain confident that the correct result is $43.

The Case against Independence A number of additional arguments have been brought forward against Independence, all to the effect that disagreement often allows us to downgrade the epistemic status of persons in permissible ways. The participants to the discussion are not always clear, however, on whether their main concern is local or global downgrading or both, and how their view bears on either.

Endorsing the Total Evidence View is one such way to attribute to the substance of the disagreement the justifying power to locally downgrade an opponent. To recapitulate, the view suggests that there is no principled way of arbitrating between first-order and second-order evidence. What is reasonable to do is a function of the relative strength of either kind of evidence. Thus, one can conceive situations in which it is permissible to stick to one's guns when facing disagreement and others in which equally weighing judgments is the rational thing to do.

Kelly seems to conceive the strength of the second-order evidence of peer disagreement as determined mainly by the number of peers disagreeing with you given they have reasoned independently. He thus states that "[a]s the number of peers increases, peer opinion counts for progressively more in determining what it is reasonable for the peers to believe, and first-order considerations count for less and less."[27]

The Strength of the First-Order Evidence As Conjecture suggests, your first-order evidence could be particularly strong when you recognize a mathematical proof as such. In such a case in which the first-order evidence is very robust, the substance of the disagreement or what is at stake in the disagreement can justify *locally* downgrading your opponent. You might still be required to lower your confidence slightly. But, as Kelly now maintains, since you can be quite sure that you got it right in this particular instance, your own confidence is not significantly questioned. Things change if you are dealing with a large number of peers who nearly unanimously disagree with you. Kelly also believes that the Total Evidence View can invoke the same considerations to explain the permissibility of *global* downgrading when disagreement is persistent or spans across many issues or instances. It is not clear to me, however, how the same consideration, that is, the relative strength of evidence, explains the permissibility of both types of downgrading. His Total Evidence View is a thesis about the rationality of belief revision in cases of peer disagreement which has implications for the permissibility of local downgrading. It is plainly not a thesis about and does not have obvious implications for the rationality of the revision of the general epistemic status of a party to the disagreement, that is, for the permissibility of global downgrading. Hence, the question of the permissibility of global downgrading still needs to be addressed.

The Total Evidence View has another problem. Kelly oscillates between an omniscient third-person perspective and a first-person perspective with an inbuilt reflective awareness of its fallibility. His desire to accommodate the different intuitions bearing on the analysis of the epistemic

---

[27] Kelly (2010): p. 34.

significance of peer disagreement leads him to state the matter on the one hand thus:

> One should give some weight to one's peer's opinion even when from the God's eye point of view one has evaluated the evidence correctly and he has not. But why? Exactly because one does not occupy the God's eye point of view with respect to the question of who has evaluated the evidence correctly and who has not.[28]

On the other hand, he maintains:

> If God is rewarding people in proportion to how well their beliefs reflect their evidence with respect to this particular hypothesis [a hypothesis that is or is not supported by the evidence], He would have no basis for rewarding them more handsomely than He rewards us, since all four of us are doing maximally well. Again, that conclusion seems difficult to endorse.[29]

Because Kelly does not decide which of these perspectives is to be given priority in an account of the epistemology of peer disagreement, his view now appears as an unstable hybrid of elements of both the Equal Weight View and the Right Reasons View.

This point against the Total Evidence View can be generalized. Indeed, it seems that much of the confusion in the peer disagreement debate stems from the fact that the assessments of the rationality of reactions to peer disagreement are made from inconsistent perspectives. Thinking about these issues, it is incredibly difficult to lay to rest the powerful thought that one person is, in fact, right.

Given the fact that I am concerned with a proposal of how the citizens of a deliberative democracy ought to react to their rational and reasonable disagreement, I leave the Total Evidence View behind at this point. Ultimately, the aim is to arrive at an answer that could be action-guiding for citizens. And to be so, it has to be an answer which is wholeheartedly committed to their first-person perspective. As the discussion has shown, this is something the Total Evidence View is not.

---

[28] Kelly (2010): p. 28, my emphasis.
[29] Kelly (2010): p. 16, my emphasis.

The Substance of the Disagreement But again, there remains the idea that the substance of the disagreement and the initially extremely high confidence in your belief must somehow matter for the permissibility of downgrading our opponents. Ernest Sosa has argued that in a certain type of cases, at least local downgrading does not incur the charge of arbitrariness even though the Independence principle is violated.[30] Consider the following example:

> **Restaurant Double-Checked A.** The situation is the same as in Restaurant. You calculate the amount of the individual share of the bill in your head and arrive at the results of $43 and $45 respectively. This time, however, the story continues. You, being as punctilious as you are, take out pen and paper and do the calculation on paper. Subsequently, you check your on-paper calculation with a calculator and find the result confirmed. It is $43. Having been absorbed by the task, you did not pay further attention to your friend and therefore do not know what he has been up to in the meantime.

Sosa now argues that if your checks on your reasoning justify an increased credence in your belief and you do not also have an independent reason to increase the credence in the belief that you are your friend's peer, it follows that your friend should decrease their credence in the latter belief and debunk you of your symmetrical epistemic status. In other words, you should no longer count your friend's mental math result of $45 as on par with your double-checked result of $43. He takes this to be an argument against Independence and in support of the claim that local downgrading can be permissible based on the substance of disagreement.

Notice, however, that the example as described does not violate Independence. *The increased reliability of the chain of reasoning* that supports the belief that you are right that the individual share of the bill is $43 and not $45 carries the weight here. It is not the contested belief or reasoning itself that makes downgrading permissible. If this is correct, the example simply describes an independent reason to downgrade your peer. This becomes even clearer when one alternates the example further still.

---

[30] Cf. Sosa (2010).

Restaurant Double-Checked B. The situation is the same as in Restaurant Double-Checked A. Only now, after you triumphantly announce the reconfirmed result of your calculation to your friend, he bursts out laughing. After regaining his composure, he apologizes and tells you what triggered his laughing fit. While you were busy doing the calculation on paper and again with your calculator of choice, he has done exactly the same. Yet he, too, found his earlier result confirmed by his double-checking. He is now extremely confident that the individual share is indeed $45.

How are you to react to this new situation? What happened is that while you had reason to increase your credence in your belief after double-checking, you now have received independent evidence that ought to likewise make you believe in an increased reliability of your friend's reasoning. Hence, if you are to treat your friend as a peer again (and so you should) and refrain from arbitrary downgrading, you ought to again revise the credence in your belief and split the doxastic difference with your friend (not the bill, though for pragmatic reasons that might also be advisable at some point). Presumably, Sosa agrees with all this. After all, he talked about a case in which you did *not* have independent evidence to belief that your friend's reliability had increased. Yet what the revised example bears out is that the rational responses to the disagreement alternate in each scenario but this is independent from the *substance* of the disagreement. Hence, the explanation for the difference in rational responses (your expected reliability) must be independent from the issue at stake. Independence is not violated.[31]

The Argument from Personal Information But do we really have to split the difference between us even in Restaurant Double-Checked? A seductive argument why one might not appeals to the availability of personal information. In the case of disagreement between us, the argument goes, I am in a better position to rule out some conditions which might distort

---

[31] Notice that the example bears some similarity to Extreme Restaurant. In that example you have independent reasons to locally downgrade your friend which consist in the reliability of the common-sense check on *his* reasoning. It is independent because the common-sense check is *a different kind of reasoning* than the mental math operation itself. In Restaurant Double-Checked A the calculations on paper and with a calculator are equally independent checks on *your* original reasoning, that is, your mental math operation.

our judgment for myself than for you. Through introspection, I can, for example, be confident that I am not experiencing an episode of mental derangement, that I am not drugged, that I am not simply not alert or unfocused, or that I am not lying or joking. While I can be confident that this is true in my own case, I can only assume that it is also true in yours. Given that *someone* must have made a mistake and *something* weird must be going on and that I have reason to be slightly more confident in the appropriateness of my reasoning than in yours, I am justified in attributing the mistake to you.[32]

While seductive, the appeal to personal information of this kind is of little help in the really interesting cases of peer disagreement. It is a distraction rather than a genuine contribution to the analysis of such cases. Why should I be more confident that I am more likely not to be in a state of aberration than you? Sure, I have personal information that I am not - but so do you! And this fact is easily communicable. After such communication has taken place, why should I think that you are more likely to have made a mistake? One possibility would be that you could be in such a state of aberration that you cannot tell anymore that you are - but so could I! Peer disagreement only becomes interesting in hard cases, once we assume that such information has either been communicated or is irrelevant. There remains the possibility of insincerity, which is by all standards very slight, and if the case for even slightly lowering the expected reliability of your judgment depends on this option exclusively, the argument from personal information is weak and ultimately unconvincing. Notice, however, that insincerity can play a significant role in political debate, and if I have evidence of insincerity on your part, I have reason to discard your judgment. This is exactly what caused Rousseau to dismiss widespread disagreement as of epistemic significance, taking it instead, which he took as evidence of insincerity and lack of motivational commitment (see section Rousseau's Version of the Equal Weight View).

---

[32] Personal information is given this role by White and Christensen, who mentions joking as an option. Cf. White (2009): p. 248 and Christensen (2011): p. 9.

The Argument from the Opacity of Evidence Yet another temptation on the road to truth alludes to the opacity of one's evidence supporting one's belief that p. In many cases, our belief in a certain proposition draws support from a variety of sources such as perception, memory, testimony, and inference. It often has a social component, owing to the influence of our intellectual communities over us during our upbringing. These sources all have a subtle and often indiscernible influence on the process of forming our belief. All in all, "[a] belief forms in us over time through the subtle influence of diverse sources."[33] It follows from all this that one's evidence for a given belief on a controversial issue is not always shareable, which makes the assumption that you are my peer dubious given that you are not and cannot be in the position to evaluate the same batch of evidence. Hence, the opacity of evidence, the argument has it, makes it permissible to stick to one's guns in many instances of disagreement. In other words, it allows for reasonable disagreement.

This argument from the opacity of evidence would have a strong appeal if epistemic peerhood presupposed possession of identical evidence. Crucially, however, the evidence need not be identical for the notion of epistemic peerhood to be applicable. It fully suffices if the evidence supporting the other person's belief is *sufficiently similar* in its quality and bearing on the issue at stake. I can very well count you as my peer regarding a given issue if I take you to be equally reliable in responding correctly to a batch of evidence available to you (but not to me) which fulfills these conditions. In short, even opaque evidence does not preclude the possibility of an epistemic symmetry such as expressed in an epistemic peerhood relation (see also Chap. 3; The Debate Room Argument).

Putting these challenges behind us, then, one might still wonder whether Independence in fact overreaches. Granted that it does deliver what Equal Weighers want, namely a principled firewall against arbitrary local downgrading, does it not also restrict downgrading to an implausible degree? If the Equal Weight View has been correct so far in its implications in the examples and in its endorsement of Independence, we are left with some arguably untenable consequences.

---

[33] Sosa (2010): p. 290.

Spinelessness One of them is the problem of spinelessness. Given that in many cases of disagreement about controversial issues we do not have independent reasons for locally downgrading our presumed peers' judgments, we seem to be required to adopt a stance of agnosticism toward many issues subject to persistent and deep disagreement. This problem is only aggravated by the fact that (most of) our judgments concerning these issues involve reasoning that cannot be as neatly delineated from a wider web of beliefs and reasoning as the above examples suggest. Given this fact, reasons which are independent from our reasoning are much harder to come by. Just how many of our background reasons does the disagreement implicate? In these circumstances, Independence is not only much harder to come by; it is not even clear what it amounts too. I return to this problem when I discuss the dynamic model of epistemic peerhood and a conception of democratic public reason in the next chapter.

The Many Disagreements Objection Leaving this problem aside for the time being, I want to raise another worry. Given the strength of Independence, once we determine which epistemic status to ascribe to someone, the *global* downgrading of that person becomes impermissible. This holds at least as long as, which is often the case, no independent reason is available to justify global downgrading. Such a reason would have to invoke the discovery of some permanent lack of epistemic virtue or capability which undermines the general reliability of the other person's judgments, for instance, a permanent impairment of vision, a math deficiency, or a mental condition. Reasons of the kind often do exist and frequently make global downgrading permissible. The continuous disagreements with another person themselves, however, would not suffice to legitimate global downgrading. That particular instances of disagreement cannot translate into permissible global downgrading follows from the fact that local downgrading is subject to the constraints of Independence. The latter implies that each particular judgment that figures in peer disagreements has to be counted as on par with yours if no independent reason makes local downgrading permissible. In other words, in each particular instance, you have to regard your opponent as equally likely to be correct. If each particular judgment is to be counted as on par with yours, even a long chain of disagreements will not suffice to make global downgrading permissible. Hence, the impermissibility of global downgrading based on many disagreements is a direct consequence of the impermissibility of arbitrarily downgrading a peer locally, which is, in turn, a direct consequence of Independence. This, however, is highly implausible. At least to some degree our assessment of another person's general epistemic status is, and ought to be, influenced by the fact that we agree or disagree on many issues or in many instances. The challenge is that once that assessment is made, the general epistemic status should not be locked-in in the sense that it is unalterable by future agreements and disagreements. But this is exactly what Independence requires if global downgrading based on instances of disagreement is not to be subject to the charge or arbitrariness.

What the discussion suggests is that given a commitment to treat your opponent as an epistemic peer, it is more difficult than anticipated to make a convincing case against Independence. We are still stuck with the question of the permissibility of global downgrading based on an evolving history of disagreements. The many disagreements objection still stands. And we still face a downgrading puzzle. Global downgrading based on instances of disagreement violates Independence. Insular peer disagreements taken separately are subject to Independence and, if the above arguments are sound, cannot serve to locally downgrade your opponent. By extension, global downgrading based on an evolving history of disagreements is impermissible given Independence. The inability to refute the many disagreements objection renders the Equal Weight View implausible. It cannot be the end of the story. Any plausible philosophical view on peer disagreement has to allow for some flexibility in the ascription of epistemic status based on an evolving history of dis/agreement. What we need, then, is a dynamic model of epistemic peerhood.

Rousseau's Version of the Equal Weight View As I have already suggested in Chap. 1 (see The Epistemic Significance of Political Disagreement), Rousseau held a version of the Equal Weight View. What speaks against ascribing the view to Rousseau is that he did not take widespread disagreement between equal epistemic authorities to warrant that they lower their (already low) credence in their judgments. The Equal Weight View suggests, however, that they should in fact remain agnostic about the issue at stake if the numbers are equal on each side, and that they should in general alter their credence according to the distribution of votes. Quite simply, if we weigh each judgment equally, the majority's judgment weighs more. Prima facie, the fact that Rousseau does not embrace this position could justify ascribing to him the Total Evidence View which delivers similar results as the Equal Weight View as large number of disagreeing peers boost the weight of the second-order evidence. However, once we get to the bottom of why we should not take into account more widespread disagreement as evidence bearing on the question at stake, we understand that it is not because it is the weaker part of our total evidence. Rousseau thought that it does not qualify as evidence *at all*. And the reason he offered was an independent reason in the sense of Independence introduced above. Rousseau offered the independent reason that widespread disagreement is evidence that the judgments of other citizens are insincere and that the state is in decline. Hence, they do not constitute evidence about the common good.

As I have shown, Rousseau advanced this line of argument based on an assumption that the legal framework of a well-ordered society, is characterized by its simplicity (see Chap. 1; The Simplicity Assumption). Simplicity guarantees that the general will can be fully evident to citizens, which in turn justifies an expectation of nearly unanimous judgments of citizens. Hence, because of these facts about a well-ordered society, insincerity or a lack of commitment to the common good of a significant part of the citizenry is what best explains widespread disagreement. This reasoning is obviously independent in the required sense from the reasoning about the common good which led the remaining sincere citizens to adopt their original judgments.

As I have also noted, neither the Total Evidence View nor the Equal Weight View by themselves can explain why Rousseau thought that there is a limit to the degree of agreement above which it no longer constitutes evidence about the general will. Rousseau states that "[a]t the other end of the cycle, unanimity returns. That is when the citizens, fallen into servitude, no longer have freedom of will" (SC, IV.2.3). The reason, then, why he introduces this limit is that it is indicative of the fact that people do no longer reason independently about the common good. Instead, they have fallen into servitude and do not follow their own independent reasoning. The free exercise of reason, even when the common good is fully evident, Rousseau seems to suggest, makes it reasonable to expect that a modicum of disagreement will always be present even under ideal conditions. Full unanimity indicates that the independent reasoning condition is not met. He thus again offers an independent reason for deviating from what the results of the Equal Weight View (and in this case also of the Total Evidence View) would be absent independent reasons.

It is also noteworthy that the Independent Reasoning Condition finds a parallel in Rousseau's no communication, or, as I have eventually called it, his no faction condition (see Chap. 1; Background Conditions). We learned that Rousseau thought that citizens ought to reason independently about the common good. Reasoning independently, however, did not imply that there is no communication and thus no public debate between citizens, but only that citizens ought not to form factions which unite their will according to the shared particular will of the group (i.e., the will grounded in the particular interests which all members of the group have in common). In that sense, their will has to remain independent and their vote the result of their own, independent reasoning about the common good.

The conciliatory conception of democracy, which I will eventually argue for in this thesis, equally builds on the Equal Weight View, albeit an expanded version thereof, to analyze the significance of political disagreement. However, at least in the case of modern, pluralistic societies, Rousseau's simplicity assumption proves untenable. The legal regulation of such societies is anything but simple; in fact, it is *very* complex. The arguments in Chap. 3 (section The (Un)Reasonableness of Political Disagreement) showed that, *pace* Rousseau, widespread disagreement is the outcome to be expected of decentered deliberation about issues with a sufficient level of complexity even under ideal conditions. Hence, we should not take widespread disagreement itself to prove that a great number of citizens offer insincere judgments. Disagreement is not only compatible with but a sign of healthy deliberative practices. Rousseau's independent reason for discarding widespread disagreement as evidence about the common good thus falls flat. If we remain committed to the Equal Weight View, and absent other independent reasons, we consequently have to endorse its conclusions also for cases of widespread disagreement.

Toward a Dynamic Model of Epistemic Peerhood

Far from offering to solve or *dis*solve the downgrading puzzle, I want to elaborate on what the intuition underlying the many disagreements objection aims at: a dynamic model of epistemic peerhood. I do not offer a wholesale solution to our quandary and my proposal will not usher in an epistemological principle which would settle the permissibility of global downgrading once and for all. Even less so will it provide a principled solution to particular cases. As far as I can see, the permissibility of global downgrading based on disagreement is of a too gradual and coarse-grained nature to be susceptible to a neat philosophical solution in the form an epistemological principle. The following considerations are only a rough sketch that might help to gain a better understanding of the issue.

Intuitively, it seems plausible to put the matter roughly thus: I have reason to count you as my epistemic peer if we agree repeatedly on the same issue or on many related issues within a certain domain. Stating the intuitive point in this way is illuminating for the following reason: it suggests that in order to take greater strides toward a dynamic model of epistemic peerhood, we might be better off shifting the analysis of downgrading away from cases of one-time or one-issue disagreements toward an analysis of a series of disagreements about the same issue over time or disagreements covering multiple issues within the same domain.

Notice, however, that disagreements and agreements are not all that matter here. Whether I should down- or upgrade you globally is also a function of the confidence I have in my judgment on which we agree or disagree. The following simplified table illustrates the possible constellations between high-confidence dis/agreements and low-confidence dis/agreements. We have four possible pairs:

(1) High-confidence agreements and low-confidence agreements	(2) High-confidence disagreements and low-confidence agreements
(3) High-confidence agreements and low-confidence disagreements	(4) High-confidence disagreements and low-confidence disagreements

In a dynamic model of epistemic peerhood, these different constellations yield a different dynamic of up- and downgrading. I will consider them in turn.

(1) High-confidence agreements and low-confidence agreements (in the same domain):
This case is straightforward. We have reason to increase confidence in our beliefs on both levels. The same-level beliefs are mutually reinforcing on each respective level (high- and low-confidence). There exists no high- to low-confidence interference across levels (see below). There exists an upward epistemic push stemming from high-confidence agreements toward ascribing peerhood status to each other. The reason is that the assumption of high reliability in our own judgment carries over to our opponent if they agree with many of our high-confidence judgments.

(2) High-confidence disagreements and low-confidence agreements (in the same domain):
In this case, there exists the potential for (high- to low-confidence) interference across levels. If many high-confidence disagreements arise, we can *either* maintain our high-confidence beliefs and globally downgrade our opponent *or* seek high-level conciliation if we do not. As I indicated above, this is presumably a gradual and coarse-grained matter where *at some point* the balance tilts toward global downgrading. The higher our confidence in our beliefs, the more are we justified to do so at an earlier point. The higher the confidence we have in the reliability of our own judgments, the lower the confidence in the reliability of our opponent ought to be if we repeatedly disagree. If we demote our opponent from peerhood status, or refrain from assigning it, the fact that we disagree with them will not, or only slightly, affect our confidence in our beliefs on both levels. If they continue to be our peer, we ought to increase the confidence of our previously low-confidence beliefs.

(3) High-confidence agreements and low-confidence disagreements (in the same domain):
 In this case, the high-level dynamic is the same as in (1). High-confidence beliefs mutually reinforce each other. The high reliability each of us assigns to our respective judgments is transferred to an assumption of an equally high reliability of the person we agree with, which pushes us toward an ascription of peerhood status. In addition, this now triggers a high-to-low-level dynamic. Granting peerhood status based on high-confidence agreements exerts pressure to be conciliatory in cases of low-confidence disagreements.
(4) High-confidence disagreements and low-confidence disagreements (in the same domain):
 This final case is similar to (2). The high reliability we assign to our own high-confidence judgments can give us reason to withhold peerhood status. If we do, our confidence in our beliefs ought not to (or only slightly) be affected at both levels. If we have previously assigned peerhood status to our opponent, however, we can *either* maintain (or lower only slightly) our confidence at both levels *or* seek conciliation at both levels. Put differently, we can either globally downgrade our opponent or maintain our belief in their equal reliability. Again, this is a gradual and coarse-grained matter where *at some point* the balance tilts toward global downgrading.

The moral of the story: In this rough sketch of a dynamic model of epistemic peerhood and absent independent reasons to globally downgrade the epistemic status of your counterpart, it is primarily high-confidence dis/agreements that unfold the dynamic behind permissible global down- and upgrading of the status of others.

An example might help to illustrate this schematic categorization of possible dis/agreement pairs on different levels and their respective interaction.

Hazy Clearing A. Suppose you and your friend are out to observe the wildlife in a nearby forest. Eager to maximize your chances for sightings, you begin your expedition very early in the morning. After a longer march, you arrive at a clearing equipped with a hideout. You determine that this is one of the better places to observe animals and get in position. Because it is early in morning, however, the clearing is filled with haze and visibility is poor. You and your friend are filled with excitement and do not despair in view of these adverse conditions. And your dedication is rewarded! Well, at least you think this is the case. You take yourself to have seen a deer briefly appearing in sight and quickly disappearing again. But after telling your friend about your sighting he voices disagreement. He didn't see a deer and remains unmoved by your assurances that he must have missed it. He tells you that he was looking at the exact same spot where you think you saw the deer at the exact time you think you saw it.

Given the poor visibility you do not have reason to be confident in your own judgment. In such a situation you are likely to take disagreement seriously *even without* prior evidence of epistemic peerhood. There is strong pressure toward "splitting the difference" and you do in fact remain agnostic. Maybe there was a deer and maybe there wasn't. With your friend disagreeing with you, you cannot justify holding on to your belief. At the same time, however, you did not obtain evidence that your friend's perception is as reliable as yours, that is, that your friend is your epistemic peer. Maybe there really was a dear and he just didn't see it.

Hazy Clearing B. Even though you are disappointed that your first sighting "didn't count" you unrelentingly continue your observation of the clearing. Meanwhile the sun continues its rise and the air around you slowly warms up. The haze begins to lift. The visibility increases and—there!—again you think you see a deer appearing in sight and quickly disappearing again. You turn to your friend exclaiming "You saw that one? This one you must have seen." He looks at you and tells you that no, he has not and that he is quite sure that no deer appeared at the spot you are pointing to.

What are you supposed to do now? Presumably, you grow more skeptical of your friend's reliability. Given your increased credence, you might still be unsettled by the disagreement and might continue to think of your friend as your peer. You might actually have some leeway and reasonably *either* discount your own judgment *or* downgrade your friend. It does not seem to be a clear-cut case one way or the other.

> **Hazy Clearing C.** By now, you are a little annoyed. You want to enjoy the uncompromised experience of a sighting. Grudgingly, you return to business. You and your friend patiently lie still as the sun starts to shine brightly upon the verdant surroundings. The haze, thick and gray when you arrived, dissipates completely. You enjoy perfect visibility and fixate the clearing. Then you (again?) spot a deer appearing and quickly disappearing but this time in full view. You rejoice. Finally, there is an incontestable sighting. You turn around to your friend, your expression giving away your excitement. "What now?" he asks somewhat dumbfounded, "Don't tell me you have seen one *again!*" You are completely perplexed. "But haven't you?"—"Nope," "Right over there!"—"Nope," "Aw, come on, you are kidding"—"No, I don't know what you are talking about. There was no dear. At least, I didn't see it." This happens repeatedly.

Given your assumption of high reliability of your own perception, you now start to seriously doubt the reliability of your friend's perception. Consequently, you downgrade him globally. You do not anymore believe that his perception is equally reliable.

> **Hazy Clearing D.** As the evening nears and dusk sets in, the haze once again covers the clearing. Visibility decreases to poor levels and you are almost ready to go home. Right before you do so, you spot yet another deer. You are again not very confident in your judgment and your friend disagrees.

But unlike with the first sighting early in the morning you now don't much care anymore for your friend's disbelief and as a result do not drastically lower credence in your judgment. Furthermore, your friend's disagreement with you while enjoying perfect visibility retrospectively affects your confidence in your own judgments in the previous cases. You are now again somewhat confident that you in fact also had some sightings in the morning and reverse your earlier agnostic stance toward the first sighting.

So far the example illustrates some of the dynamics described in an abstract manner earlier. We are dealing with a case of high-confidence and low-confidence disagreements as in (4) above. We deem our perception highly reliable and without further evidence to the contrary we withhold peerhood status from our friend or demote him (assuming here that the repeated cases of extremely high-confidence disagreements have tilted the balance in this direction. As a consequence our confidence at both levels is not or only slightly affected by the disagreements at both levels.

To further illustrate the dynamics of global up- and downgrading, consider a slightly altered version of the example.

> **Hazy Clearing C′.** The haze, thick and gray when you arrived, dissipates completely. You enjoy perfect visibility and fixate the clearing. Then you again spot a deer appearing and quickly disappearing but this time in full view. Only now it is your friend who rejoices and exclaims "Have you seen the deer? Right there in front of us!" pointing at the same spot where you think you also saw the deer. This happens repeatedly.

We now have a case analogous to (3) above. You both are highly confident of your belief that you indeed saw a deer. Furthermore, your high confidence is mutually reinforcing. Because both of you know the other person agrees with you in cases of high-confidence judgments, you both judge each other to be equally reliable and subsequently assign to each other the status of a peer. This high-level dynamic causes a high-to-low-level dynamic. Because you and your friend treat each other as peers based on the assumption of shared expected reliability, both of you are under pressure to be conciliatory at the level of low-confidence judgments. In our example, this means that you have reason to remain agnostic about your sightings at dawn and at dusk.

The moral of the story remains the same: In a dynamic model of epistemic peerhood and absent independent reasons to globally downgrade the epistemic status of your counterpart, the dynamic of permissible global up- and downgrading is primarily determined by high-confidence dis/agreements.

Peer Disagreement and Political Disagreement

I shall now bring this rough sketch of a dynamic model of peer disagreement to bear on the epistemic dimension of the significance of political disagreement and correspondingly on the reasonable commitment of reasonable citizens to regard other reasonable citizens as equal epistemic authorities. In pursuing this strategy, I evince how we can apply this dynamic model of peer disagreement in theoretical reasoning to cases of disagreements in practical reasoning among the reasonable citizens of deliberative democracies. This ushers in an epistemologically charged conception of public reason, which I call "Democratic Public Reason". I show that reasonable citizens are in high-confidence agreement and low-confidence disagreement with other reasonable citizens whom they, in part because of their high-confidence agreement, regard as equal epistemic authorities. As the dynamic model of epistemic peerhood suggests, citizens ought to seek epistemic conciliation at the level of low-confidence disagreements. In the next chapter, finally, I will elaborate on the possibility and the nature of epistemic conciliation of judgments about justice. This opens the door to the final argument for the conciliatory conception of democracy which I elaborate in Chap. 5. I argue there that a set of institutions typically present in modern democracies has a tendency to produce outcomes which help us to achieve epistemic conciliation, or something close to it.

Democratic Public Reason I now turn to applying the dynamic model of epistemic peerhood in theoretical reasoning to practical reasoning. This is the point at which the epistemological debate about peer disagreement offers illuminating insights when applied to political disagreements among equal epistemic authorities. I argue that citizens of a well-ordered democracy face strong pressures toward the epistemic conciliation of judgments on many matters of social justice. The disagreement among citizens on these questions occurs within Democratic Public Reason. Furthermore, I claim that it is rationally permissible for citizens of a well-ordered democracy to globally downgrade individuals who, do not share the framework of Democratic Public Reason.

The Idea of a Well-Ordered Society and an Expanded Conception of Reasonableness In the course of the discussion, I again employ the conception of a well-ordered democracy. I call a democracy well-ordered if it is a deliberative democracy whose citizens are reasonable in the four respects introduced earlier: (1) their votes are determined by their sincere judgments about the justice of the public choices confronting them; (2) they give motivational primacy to the common good (see Chap. 1; The Simplicity Assumption); (3) they actively seek to justify their judgments in terms of reasons other reasonable citizens could accept (see Chap. 2; The Points of Departure); and (4) they share a commitment to treat other reasonable citizens as equal epistemic and normative authorities (see Chap. 3). The idea of a Democratic Public Reason adds to this a fifth requirement of reasonableness. It is that (5) citizens are *meta-rational* with respect to the low-confidence disagreements they have with other reasonable citizens who share the framework of Democratic Public Reason, the content of which will become clearer momentarily, when they engage in public deliberation. Being meta-rational in this context means that they understand and accept the implications of the epistemology of peer disagreement and draw the right conclusions with respect to political disagreements among equal epistemic authorities.[34]

Recall the matrix of dis/agreement pairs:

(1) High-confidence agreements and low-confidence agreements	(2) High-confidence disagreements and low-confidence agreements
(3) High-confidence agreements and low-confidence disagreements	(4) High-confidence disagreements and low-confidence disagreements

Of particular interest for a conception of Democratic Public Reason is the dis/agreement pair (3) high-confidence agreements and low-confidence disagreements, as I have stated in the preceding section.

(3) High-confidence agreements and low-confidence disagreements (in the same domain):

---

[34] This use of "meta-rational" is similar though not identical to the use Tyler Cowen and Robin Hanson make of the term; cf. Cowen and Hanson (2001): p. 24.

In this case, the high-level dynamic is the same as in (1). High-confidence beliefs mutually reinforce each other. The high reliability each of us assigns to our respective judgments is transferred to an assumption of an equally high reliability of the person we agree with, which pushes us toward an ascription of peerhood status. In addition, this now triggers a high-to-low-level dynamic. Granting peerhood status based on high-confidence agreements exerts pressure to be conciliatory in cases of low-confidence disagreements.

Democratic Public Reason, I submit, is constituted by high-confidence agreements about some issues which are accompanied by low-confidence disagreements on many other issues. The upshot is that the reasonable citizens of a well-ordered society face strong pressure toward conciliation at the low-confidence level.

Democratic Public Reason as the Epistemic Framework of Disagreement We now face a question regarding the content of high-confidence agreements and low-confidence disagreements in Democratic Public Reason. At this point, it is useful to invoke the method of reflective equilibrium. According to Rawls, reflective equilibrium stands at the end of a process of reflection, of working "back and forth" between particular moral judgments and principles of justice, which allow us to coherently order these judgments. The starting points of this process of reflection are our considered judgments or convictions, that is, those moral judgments we hold with extremely high confidence before actively trying to establish coherence between our beliefs. Many of these judgments are bound to survive the process of reflection, thus molding the conception of justice we are willing to endorse and imposing limits on the acceptability of conceptions of justice. Among these considered judgments are the condemnation of institutions such as "slavery and serfdom, religious persecution, the subjection of the working classes, the oppression of women, and the unlimited accumulation of vast fortunes, together with the hideousness of cruelty and torture, and the evil of the pleasures of exercising domination."[35] However, Rawls acknowledges

---

[35] Rawls (1996): p. 431.

that we hold judgments "at many levels of generality, from the more particular to the most abstract."[36] We have strong beliefs not only in the injustice of particular institutions but equally so in abstract principles such as the equal moral worth of all.

When reflective equilibrium is reached, the high confidence we have in our initial judgments is at least partly transferred to the conception of justice we hold in reflective equilibrium together with our considered judgments. This is because a theory of justice which coherently orders our initial high-confidence judgments gains justificatory support from the fact that it is compatible with many or most of our high-confidence judgments. The fact that many or most of our high-confidence judgments can be coherently ordered by a conception of justice, on the other hand, lends justificatory support to these judgments. Hence, Rawls seems to think that we are justified in having high confidence in both our considered judgments *and* the conception of justice we hold in reflective equilibrium.[37] In that respect, it is interesting to note that *before* reflective equilibrium is reached, Rawls draws a clear distinction between the levels of confidence we have in different kinds of moral judgments. Before we enter into reflective equilibrium, there are some judgments which we take to be those least likely to be made under distorting influences, such as an excessive attention to our own interests. He names our belief in the injustice of religious intolerance and racial discrimination as examples.[38] Remarkably, Rawls explicitly excludes beliefs about the correct distribution of wealth and authority from those judgments we can hold with high confidence.[39]

I have argued above that in a decentered deliberative setting, Rawlsian reflective equilibrium is inherently unstable (see Chap. 3; The (Un)Reasonableness of Political Disagreement).[40] If this is true,

---

[36] Rawls (1996): p. 275.
[37] He describes the judgments in reflective equilibrium as mutually supporting each other; cf. Rawls (1999): p. 19.
[38] Rawls (1999): p. 18.
[39] Ibid.
[40] This also means that the ideal of full reflective equilibrium is unattainable. Cf. Rawls (1996): p. 384, *fn* 16.

the epistemic link between high-confidence beliefs about baselines of just institutions and beliefs about the correct distribution of resources is broken. Furthermore, the argument from complexity, the local knowledge argument, and the fact of disagreement support the assertion that we are not warranted in holding high-confidence beliefs about many matters of justice. What remains is the high confidence we have in some judgments before we enter reflective equilibrium and which are, in Rawls words, "provisional fixed points" in moral reasoning, meaning judgments which "we never expect to withdraw,"[41] hence, which we are extremely unlikely to change in the course of further deliberation (though this is not impossible, of course).

Albeit lacking the epistemic support of reflective equilibrium, the confidence democratic citizens place in these judgments is not arbitrary. First, there is an independent justification for the confidence we have in these judgments. As Rawls says, they are the ones which are least likely to be made under the distorting effects of self-interest. Second, reasonable citizens of a well-ordered democracy do not form their belief in isolation. Citizens do not arrive at high-confidence beliefs without engaging in comprehensive discussions with their fellow citizens. Hence, their high-confidence beliefs are considered in the sense that they have survived extensive public discussion and have shown themselves to be very resilient after citizens have worked "back and forth" between them and the results of public deliberation. This resilience, when put to the test of the opinion of the public, is of epistemic significance. As J.S. Mill claims, "The beliefs which we have most warrant for, have no safeguard to rest on, but a standing invitation to the whole world to prove them unfounded".[42] It justifies the high confidence citizens of a well-ordered democracy have in these stable beliefs. Hence, a division can be maintained between high-confidence beliefs formed and confirmed in deliberation with one's fellow citizens and low-confidence beliefs on which citizens disagree.

They are in *low-confidence* disagreement because they disagree on many issues on which they are not entitled to hold high-confidence

---

[41] Rawls (1999): p. 18; also Rawls (1996): p. 8.
[42] Mill 1991: Chap. 2, para. 7.

beliefs (see the argument from complexity and the local knowledge argument) and because they recognize this fact.

In the dynamic model of epistemic peerhood sketched above and absent independent reasons making downgrading permissible, high-confidence agreement/low-confidence disagreement constellations put reasoners under pressure to seek conciliation at the level of low-confidence beliefs.

The Permissibility of (Globally) Downgrading Anti-Democrats An additional and no less important consequence of the dynamic model of epistemic peerhood and the conception of Democratic Public Reason concerns the permissibility of globally downgrading anti-democrats. In a well-ordered democracy, the shared high-confidence beliefs held by citizens provide the epistemic framework of Democratic Public Reason. These considered judgments allow us to spell out an epistemically informed conception of reasonableness which promises to be more than a dogmatic assertion of egalitarian principles.

Imagine, for instance, an incorrigible Nazi. Such an ardent believer in Nazi ideology rejects a great many beliefs a reasonable citizen of a well-ordered democracy—I shall call this latter person "democrat" for short-hand—holds with great confidence. The Nazi rejects the democrat's firmly held convictions that discrimination on the basis of race and religion is unjust; that cruelty and torture are moral evils without exception; that slavery and serfdom are moral wrongs without exception; that men and women ought to be equal in important respects, and many more. In particular, the Nazi rejects the idea that citizens ought to be reasonable as defined above. Subsequently, they also reject the idea that an egalitarian distribution of political authority is justified on the basis of the normative requirement of public justifiability in terms of reasonably acceptable reasons (see Chap. 2) and that they ought to justify their exercise of political power to others. In addition, they reject an egalitarian distribution of political authority altogether.[43]

The democrat and the Nazi thus enter into a constellation of high-confidence disagreement combined with either low-confidence agreement or low-confidence disagreement:

---

[43] The same presumably holds for the criterion of reciprocity of advantage (see Chap. 2).

4 The Epistemology of Political Disagreement 163

| (1) High-confidence agreements and low-confidence agreements | (2) High-confidence disagreements and low-confidence agreements |
| (3) High-confidence agreements and low-confidence disagreements | (4) High-confidence disagreements and low-confidence disagreements |

As argued in the above section Toward a Dynamic Model of Epistemic Peerhood, the pressure to conciliate at the level of low-confidence beliefs becomes substantially weaker in (4) as does the justification to increase the confidence at this level in cases of agreement in (2). The citizen of a well-ordered society is now permitted to downgrade anti-democrats from peerhood status and exclude the judgments of these groups from the epistemic conciliation they pursue. This move is warranted from the standpoint of rationality. Apart from the unreasonableness of Nazi ideology from the normative perspective of reasonable citizens, it is also this *epistemic* perspective from which the doctrine of the anti-democrat appears as unreasonable.

Above I have argued that in the cases of (2) and (4), if many high-confidence disagreements arise, we can *either* maintain our high-confidence beliefs and globally downgrade our opponent *or* seek high-level conciliation if we do not. Furthermore, I have expressed my conviction that this is presumably a gradual and coarse-grained matter where *at some point* the balance tilts toward global downgrading. Our confrontation with the Nazi is a case in which the balance has clearly tilted toward global downgrading due to the number and the intensity of our high-confidence disagreements with them.

Without looking at the content of the beliefs reasoners hold, but training one's sight solely on the formal features of their epistemic relations, we have two ways of analyzing the situation at hand. The first is to adopt *the third-person standpoint*. From this perspective, we can observe that in public deliberation involving democrats and anti-democrats, many, maybe even all, high-confidence beliefs about political morality are contested. Because we look only at the formal feature of the epistemic circumstances of rational actors and do not analyze the content of their beliefs and the reasons for holding them, we do not pass judgment on the question whether high confidence in some beliefs is justified, and we have consequently no criterion to help determine the epistemic relations between participants, that is, to sort out who is one's epistemic equal, or superior or inferior to whom, apart from high-confidence dis/agreements (which include beliefs about relevant attitudes and motivational commitments). All we say is that the formal features of their epistemic circumstances suggest that democrats and anti-democrats should not regard each other as equal epistemic authorities. Importantly, this applies to both parties to the (high-confidence) disagreements. Without looking at the content of the beliefs reasoners hold, we can assert that even in the most ideal scenario of public deliberation, there comes a point when reason runs out and, speaking with Wittgenstein, the spade is turned.[44] While democratic citizens might offer arguments supporting their high-confidence beliefs, these will refer to premises which anti-democrats do not share. If they are subsequently rejected, and if this is a general phenomenon of the debate, hence, if the disagreement extends to the most fundamental beliefs reasoners hold, it is hard to see how either party could produce arguments that seem convincing to the disagreeing party. This is exactly the situation the democrat and the Nazi find themselves in.[45] In this setting, all we assert from the external perspective is that it is rational to downgrade the person with whom you find yourself in extensive and persistent high-confidence disagreement. This holds symmetrically for both the democrat and the Nazi.

The second way to analyze the situation is to adopt *the first-person standpoint*. Here, matters are slightly different. First, from this perspective, we observe that our high-confidence judgments are embedded in a web of beliefs which includes mutually reinforcing high-confidence beliefs. Hence, reasons *internal* to the first-person standpoint are readily available which justify our dismissal of the other party as inferior judges of questions of political morality. Furthermore, as the dynamic model argues, high-confidence agreement about these questions is a criterion to

---

[44] See Ebeling (2014) for a detailed discussion of the bearing of Wittgenstein's late philosophy on radical disagreement.

[45] One might object that Nazi ideology is based on false beliefs about facts and that even Nazis should be in a position to recognize this. However, I assume that there is an irreducible evaluative component to their ideology.

sort out whom we ought to regard as equal epistemic authorities. From within the first-person perspective of reasonable citizens, then, there are *reasons* why they ought to consider themselves as superior judges compared to anti-democrats.[46]

From the first-person standpoint, the high confidence we place in our judgments is non-arbitrary for an additional reason. Importantly, the reasonable citizens of a well-ordered democracy do not form their belief in isolation. They do not hold high-confidence beliefs without being engaged in comprehensive deliberation with their fellow citizens. Hence, their high-confidence beliefs are "considered" in the sense that they have survived extensive public deliberation and have shown themselves to be very resilient after citizens have worked "back and forth" between them and the results of public deliberation with their epistemic peers. This resilience, when put to the test of the opinion of the public, is of epistemic significance. It justifies the high confidence citizens of a well-ordered democracy have in these stable beliefs. The beliefs are stable among persons who consistently regard each other as equally reliable judges about the issues at stake. Furthermore, this doxastic stability ensures the stability of the evaluation of epistemic relations among reasonable citizens and vice versa. Hence, the situation is, epistemically speaking, self-stabilizing. Thus, a division can be maintained between high-confidence beliefs formed and confirmed in deliberation with one's fellow reasonable citizens whom one regards as equal epistemic authorities and low-confidence beliefs on which these citizens disagree. A second consequence concerns the democratic practice of seeking low-level epistemic conciliation with the judgments of one's epistemic peers. Persistent high-confidence disagreements absolve the democrat from seeking low-level epistemic conciliation with the Nazi. This makes it permissible and even rationally warranted to exclude the Nazi's low-confidence beliefs from the democratic practice altogether as their input would distort the result of epistemic conciliation of judgments democrats ought to seek with their epistemic peers.

---

[46] Ebeling (2014).

It is crucial to note, however, that nothing of the above serves as a justification of the *content* of the beliefs in question. The approach I pursue starts from shared high-confidence beliefs, and although I do engage with the normative foundations of my approach in Chap. 2, I did very little in terms of justifying these beliefs and the epistemological story I told does little to this effect. Instead, I focused on the *formal* features of epistemic relations among reasoners and analyzed these from the first-person perspective. I argue that from this epistemic perspective, the disregard for anti-democratic positions, which might well be justifiable from a substantive normative perspective as well, is rationally permissible. In this sense, Democratic Public Reason and the justification of democracy spelled out in terms of this conception are self-insulating, albeit in a good way.

Why Democracy? After this exposition of an epistemically charged conception of public reason, two questions still remain to be answered. They are (1) how does epistemic conciliation work in disagreements about justice? and (2) why does it lead us to a justification of democratic decision-making? So far, I have said next to nothing on either of these crucial questions.

References

Christensen, D. (2007). Epistemology of Disagreement: the Good News. *The Philosophical Review, 116*(2), 187–217.
Christensen, D. (2009). Disagreement as Evidence: The Epistemology of Controversy. *Philosophy Compass, 4*(1), 1–12.
Christensen, D. (2011). Disagreement, Question-Begging and Epistemic Self-Criticism. *Philosopher's Imprint, 11*(6), 1–22.
Cowen, T., & Hanson, R. (2001). Disagreement as Self-Deception about Meta-Rationality. https://www.researchgate.net/profile/Robin_Hanson2/publication/2372917_Disagreement_as_Self-Deception_About_Meta-Rationality/links/0046351fac48f73a68000000.pdf. Accessed 11/09/2016.
Ebeling, M. (2014). Wenn der Spaten sich zurückbiegt: Mouffes Wittgensteinianische Analyse radikalen Dissenses und darüber hinaus. *Zeitschrift für Politische Theorie, 5*, 234–253.
Elga, A. (2007). Reflection and Disagreement. *Noûs, 41*, 478–502.

Feldman, R. (2006). Epistemological puzzles about disagreement. In S. Hetherington (Ed.), *Epistemology Futures* (pp. 216–236). Oxford: Oxford University Press.

Feldman, R. (2009). Evidentialism, Higher-order Evidence, and Disagreement. *Episteme, 6,* 294–312.

Kelly, T. (2005). The Epistemic Significance of Disagreement. In J. Hawthorne & T. Gendler (Eds.), *Oxford Studies in Epistemology* (Vol. 1). Oxford: Oxford University Press [page numbers refer to the paper available at his website].

Kelly, T. (2010). Peer Disagreement and Higher Order Evidence. In R. Feldman & T. Warfield (Eds.), *Disagreement.* Oxford: Oxford University Press.

Mill, J. S. (1991). On Liberty. In J. Gray (Ed.), *On Liberty and Other Essays.* Oxford: Oxford University Press.

Rawls, J. (1996). *Political Liberalism* (2nd ed.). New York: Columbia University Press.

Rawls, J. (1999). *A Theory of Justice* (Rev. ed.). Cambridge, MA: Harvard University Press.

Sosa, E. (2010). The Epistemology of Disagreement. In A. Haddock, A. Millar, & D. Pritchard (Eds.), *Social Epistemology.* Oxford: Oxford University Press.

White, R. (2009). On Treating Oneself and Others as Thermometers. *Episteme, 6,* 233–250.

5

Conciliatory Democracy

The ideal at the center of the conciliatory conception of democracy is the epistemic conciliation of the conflicting judgments of citizens regarding each other as equal epistemic authorities. The preceding chapters have established the claims that (1) citizens ought to regard each other as equal epistemic authorities with respect to their epistemic role in the decision procedures of modern democracy (Chap. 3) and that (2) epistemic conciliation is the rational reaction to their disagreements about the common good (Chap. 4). In this chapter, we shall see to what the epistemic conciliation of conflicting judgments about justice amounts and what democracy has got to do with it.

Importantly, the ideal of epistemic conciliation does not amount to the claim that if there is disagreement between an equal number of citizens who regard each other as equal, they should remain agnostic and thus suspend their beliefs about the demands of justice altogether. If we understand the issues at stake correctly, we ought to find the point along a scalar dimension of the issue where our judgments can "meet" (see Epistemic Conciliation about Justice). However, not every issue might lend itself to epistemic conciliation. If it lacks a scalar dimension, if the choice we face is strictly

© The Author(s) 2017
M. Ebeling, *Conciliatory Democracy*,
DOI 10.1057/978-1-137-57743-6_5

binary, the idea of epistemic conciliation in this sense does not get off the ground. On first sight, many issues might strike us to be of exactly this nature. However, if we think them through, a scalar dimension might open itself up in spite of appearances. This is the art of compromise. To the extent that this is not the case, and I shall introduce an example in which this is contested, the conciliatory conception of democracy will not gain traction (see Abortion). I do not take this to be a weakness of my argument. If anything, it shows that it is a conception that takes the complexity of the landscape of political choices seriously. Political philosophy, after all, should not start with the assumption that there is a catch-all solution to political conflicts. I nevertheless believe that many important issues in politics do lend themselves to epistemic conciliation in the sense of finding middle ground along a scalar dimesion. The paradigmatic example is disagreements about distributive justice. I do not choose this aspect of social justice for arbitrary reasons. First, it is the most natural field of application of my theory. We can gain a pretty clear idea of what epistemic conciliation consists in cases of disagreement about distributive justice. Second, in spite of all other demands of justice we might conceive, it remains a fundamental question in modern democracy; and it does so in part because it is a component of claims to justice that do not *primarily* aim at the right distribution of resources in society (see The Continued Importance of the Political Struggle for Distributive Justice).

Yet, what does all this have to do with democracy? This question forms the main part of this chapter. What I will show is that modern democracies have a robust tendency to produce outcomes which tend to correspond to conciliatory judgments about the matters at stake. The reason for this tendency lies in the inbuilt dynamic of multiparty competition and committee voting toward median voter preferences. To substantiate this last claim, I draw on the findings of Public Choice theories, in particular Duncan Black's Median Voter Theorem and Anthony Down's spatial model of party competition (see The Rule of the Majority and the Spatial Model of Voting; and Chap. 6; The Spatial Model of Party Competition). The role of political parties, as we shall see, plays an especially important role in the conciliatory conception. Traditionally, however, these approaches to democratic theory have been associated with minimalist and elitist conceptions of democracy according to which the essence of democracy is electoral competition and the driving forces of this process are political elites with little more in mind than to secure a seat in government. This stands in obvious contradiction to the commitments to deliberative forms of decision-making and the civic-mindedness of the conciliatory conception itself. Hence, we will have to bring into a constructive dialogue theories all too often perceived as being in fundamental opposition to each other (see the section The Adaption of the Spatial Model in Chap. 6). I will show that these two strands of political theory can be reconciled and that the conciliatory conception of democracy is the child of this happy marriage in democratic theory.

In Chap. 7, I will address the question which I have outlined at the end of the second chapter. I have argued there that if we make a bestness-tracking claim in support of democratic procedures (or any other decision procedure for that matter), it comes with a correlated demand to defer to the epistemic authority of such procedures in one way or another. When I made this point, I deliberately left it open to what such a claim would have to amount, partly because different epistemic theories of democracy can spell it out in different ways. What I owe the reader, however, is a description of how the conciliatory conception conceives moral deference, and I shall pay this debt (see Chap. 7; The Ambitiousness of Conciliatory Democracy and Weak Deference). As we shall see, the demand of deference as it features in conciliatory democracy is significantly weaker than the one Rousseau formulates in his correctness theory of democracy. This will thus provide a last point of contact with and a last point of departure from Rousseau's political philosophy. What remains is to connect the dots and tell the story of how we arrived from Rousseau to conciliatory democracy.

Epistemic Conciliation about Justice

In an article on peer disagreement, Richard Feldman notes two different attitudes toward disagreement. In political debates, he states that "victory is the measure of success"[1] whereas nowadays the common consensus on religious disagreement is an attitude of toleration. My argument so far

---
[1] Feldman (2006): p. 414.

has been that a third attitude is available in politics. In the conciliatory conception of democracy, reasonable citizens ought to pursue epistemic conciliation on issues subject to low-confidence disagreement between equal epistemic authorities. The aim of this chapter is to show that this is a cogent ideal.

Consider the horse race example in Chap. 4 (see Horse Race). You and your friend watch a horse race. It ends in a close finish. When the race is over, however, you are quite confident that Horse A has won. You then come to learn that your friend, whom up until now you have regarded as equally competent in accurately determining the winning horse, is equally confident that Horse B has won. The two of you come to the conclusion that none of you is justified in holding a belief on which of the two horses won. You thus conciliate your judgments and assign a credence value of .5 to your belief; in other words, you remain agnostic. Alternatively, we could assign differing credence levels to you and your friend with the conciliation again consisting in "splitting the difference." If you believe that Horse A won with a credence of .8 and your friend has a credence of .4 in the same belief, conciliation requires that you lower your credence whereas your friend raises his with the result of both of you arriving at a credence of .6.

Disagreements in practical reasoning are different, however. They are disagreements about what decision to take, what to *do* in a given situation. Suppose you and your friend are hiking and arrive at a fork in the trail which is not indicated on the map. You face a decision about which trail to follow. Your friend chooses the trail on your right while you decide to follow the trail on your left. While you can make different choices, neither one of you is warranted in believing that they have made the right choice. Neither one of you knows which trail is the right one to follow; hence, from a theoretical perspective, you ought to remain agnostic. However, given the fact that *you have to* continue your hike, that *you have to* arrive at a decision about what to do, your agnosticism cannot translate into a direct behavioral analogue.[2] You want to proceed but neither choice is more rational than the other. Since the resources of rationality are exhausted at this point, you could

---

[2] See Feldman (2006): p. 433 for the original version of this example.

decide to simply follow your preferences, which might be to follow the path which seems more beautiful. If your preferences conflict, you might opt for a random procedure which gives equal weight to your preferences. Whatever you do will take further considerations into account. The theoretical stance of agnosticism does not find a direct behavioral correlate.

However, in the cases of practical disagreement we are concerned with, namely practical disagreements about the justice of the social order of our society, are the resources of rationality also exhausted? Does the ideal of epistemic conciliation make politics a game of conflicting preferences and random decision-making in which anything goes?

I venture that this objection is ill-advised in regard to many, and probably most, political disagreements. Whatever place randomness occupies in a conception of democracy, the epistemic dimension of conciliatory democracy does not give us a reason to include it.

Consider the following example:

Tax Rates. Five legislators have to determine the rate of the income tax. We assume that these legislators regard each other as equal epistemic authorities with respect to the justice of income tax rates. They have argued about the issue for a considerable amount of time and tried to justify their position with reasons others could accept. And they generally believe of each other that they are reasonable in all the other respects in which I have defined reasonableness earlier (see Chap. 4; The Idea of a Well-Ordered Society and an Expanded Conception of Reasonableness). After deliberating sincerely about the issue for a considerable time, then, Legislator 1 prefers a tax rate of 40%, Legislator 2 of 50%, Legislator 3 of 60%, Legislator 4 proposes a tax rate of 70%, and Legislator 5 of 80%.

If these legislators do the right thing and conciliate their judgments, what tax rate should they eventually settle on? The answer is clearly not that they ought to remain agnostic and thus not do anything. None of them believes that it would be just not to raise income taxes at all. What they ought to do is to conciliate their judgments along the scale of possible options. Hence, the correct answer is a tax rate of 60%. This is the outcome they ideally ought to reach given everything we learned about the epistemology about peer disagreement in the preceding chapter. Importantly, this refutes the objection voiced above that given peer disagreement in practical reasoning, no path of action is objectionable. Quite to the contrary, we can now see that one answer is uniquely rational.

However, we might object to this example as an example of conciliation about justice. After all, looking at a decision in isolation says very little about the conciliation of judgments about the justice of social and political arrangements more broadly construed. Consider another example:

> **Bob versus Jerry on Social Justice.** Assume that two persons, call them Bob and Jerry, agree that the distribution of resources in their society raises normative concerns. However, they strongly disagree on the question of which mechanism of distribution is justified in terms of considerations of justice. Bob believes that the distribution of resources ought to be regulated by the mechanisms of a free-market economy exclusively—the only mechanism that, according to him, respects the natural rights of persons and their self-ownership. In other words, Bob believes that any redistribution by the state is unjust. Jerry, on the other hand, believes that the distribution of resources ought to conform to the norms of socialist equality—the only way that, according to him, morally arbitrary differences between persons are compensated for and the only one that enables people to live in community with each other. Furthermore, Jerry believes that justice demands that the state undertake a massive effort of redistributing resources which market mechanisms have allocated unevenly to citizens. Assume further that Bob and Jerry regard each other as equal epistemic authorities on the matter.

In this example, Bob and Jerry agree that *any* distribution of resources in a given society raises demands of justice. What they disagree about is *how much* (re)distribution by the state can be justified in terms of considerations of justice. In other words, they disagree about what point on a scale of possible (re)distribution by the state justice specifies. It is this scale that opens the door for epistemic conciliation of the conflicting judgments of epistemic peers on the question of how much (re)distribution is justified. So we might just say that the case is the same as in the above example. Notice, however, that we can easily expand the example. Bob and Jerry could object to this because they could object to the idea that looking at tax rates in isolation is not what the disagreement is ultimately about. They could thus tell us that they are concerned with a set of freedom-protecting or equality-promoting *institutions*, which come in a complete set and that the conciliation on one issue, such as tax rates, does not address the point at stake. What they might say is that averaging tax rates in cases of peer disagreement is not conciliating judgments *about justice* in this broader sense. Interestingly, this mirrors another aspect of modern democracy. While we have seen an example of majoritarian decision-making on a specific issue, as it could indeed have taken place in any legislative assembly, we now face a question that citizens in their input to the decision procedures of modern democracies are more likely to face. *Citizens*, with the exception of referenda, *vote for political parties* and party positions are typically not one-issue agendas but comprise a broad range of issues. The task of parties, as I shall explain in more detail later, is to work out *sufficiently coherent* and *sufficiently specific* conceptions of justice, thus translating the abstract value judgments of citizens into an integrated set of policy proposals and proposals for institutional reform (see Chap. 6; Party Ideology and Programs). However, while it seems relatively clear how majoritarian decision rules can lead to outcomes which track conciliatory judgments, it is far less clear how democracies can achieve conciliation between conceptions of justice at a grander scale. I shall argue, however, that they can (see Chap. 6; Issue-Specific and Comprehensive Epistemic Conciliation).

As for providing a solution to the problem of how to specify which of a number of reasonable democratic procedures compatible with the ideal of political equality to opt for, notice already now that my examples leave behind the narrow focus on decision procedures with regard to the resolution of a single-choice situation such as majority rule, lotteries, or Queen for a Day proposals (see Chap. 2; Spoiled for Choice?). The bestness-tracking claim these arguments lead up to is not a claim about the advantages of an isolated decision rule or procedure. What I take into view is the complex set of institutions and decision procedures of modern democracies. I take this to be a major point in favor of my approach.

When we thus put off the question of epistemic conciliation between conceptions of justice until further notice, we can turn to another problem.

Distributive justice is a paradigm case in which epistemic conciliation is possible and desirable. It is not, however, the only issue at stake when it comes to the just exercise of political power. There are harder cases to which epistemic conciliation might just not be an answer easily available. This is due to the apparent lack of a scalar dimension of these issues.

Abortion One particularly tough nut to crack is the permissibility of abortion. I do not have in mind persons who agree that abortion is, in principle, permissible but disagree on specifics, such as at what point in the life of the fetus it becomes impermissible. In this case, epistemic conciliation along this temporal dimension might be possible. Instead, I am concerned with otherwise reasonable citizens who disagree persistently and radically on the permissibility of abortion itself. The disagreement is radical because it involves high-confidence judgments. The persons I have in mind are adamantly pro-choice and adamantly pro-life respectively.

Two features are noteworthy with respect to this radical disagreement about the permissibility of abortion. On the one hand, as the scenario has it, citizens are in high-confidence disagreement about the issue. On the other hand, however, they are in agreement regarding all other high-confidence judgments of reasonable citizens about political morality. Furthermore, the low-confidence disagreements about other matters of justice remain. Hence, the situation is a mix of the following constellations of dis/agreements:

(1) High-confidence agreements and low-confidence agreements	(2) High-confidence disagreements and low-confidence agreements
(3) High-confidence agreements and low-confidence disagreements	**(4) High-confidence disagreements and low-confidence disagreements**

Spelling out the consequences of the dynamic model of epistemic peerhood above, I have noted that in the case of (4),

> The high reliability we assign to our own high-confidence judgments can give us reason to withhold peerhood status. If we do, our confidence in our beliefs ought not to (or only slightly) be affected at both levels. If we have

5 Conciliatory Democracy 177

previously assigned peerhood status to our opponent, however, we can *either* maintain (or lower only slightly) our confidence at both levels *or, if possible*, seek conciliation at both levels. Put differently, we can either globally downgrade our opponent or maintain our belief in their equal reliability. Again, this is a gradual and coarse-grained matter where *at some point* the balance tilts toward global downgrading.

Given these alternatives, it is crucial to note a further structural feature of the high-confidence disagreement about the permissibility of abortion: its insularity. This is important because, on balance, the constellation of insular high-confidence disagreement and otherwise pervasive high-confidence agreements does not seem to make global downgrading permissible. As I have stated above, I believe that whether to downgrade or not is a messy question in the sense that the answers we can give are gradual and coarse-grained. In the example at hand, however, I believe it reasonable to maintain that we have not yet reached the point at which global downgrading is an option. In other words, even in the face of insular high-confidence disagreement, citizens can regard each other as equal epistemic authorities. The epistemic conception of Democratic Public Reason can accommodate these kinds of disagreements while it can also show that in other clear-cut cases of wider-scope high-confidence disagreements, such as confrontations with Nazi ideologues, the balance has tipped toward global downgrading (see Chap. 4; The Permissibility of (Globally) Downgrading Anti-Democrats).

The second feature of disagreement about abortion is that it seemingly does not allow for epistemic conciliation. Consequently, even though citizens can still regard each other as equal epistemic authorities in spite of their high-confidence disagreement, epistemic conciliation of their judgments is not an available option, or if it is, it would engender agnosticism. This feature is due to the issue at stake. If the issue at stake is the permissibility of abortion per se, the alternative is *either* pro-choice *or* pro-life. The choice is *binary*. It might be that "it is a poor candidate for moral compromise because the most crucial point of contention is a discrete question: either a woman has the right to abort a pregnancy in her first trimester simply because she does not wish to carry it to term, or she does not. This question of right must be decided one way or another;

there is no via media here."[3] Disagreements about distributive justice are different. In case of the latter, citizens might disagree about what point on a scale of possible redistribution by the state justice specifies; and I maintained that it is this scale that opens the door for epistemic conciliation of the conflicting judgments of equal epistemic authorities on the question of how much redistribution is justified.

We are left with two alternatives. Either the disagreement allows for epistemic conciliation along a scalar issue dimension, in which case there is a uniquely rational answer, or anything goes, in which case we might opt for a random procedure and permit disagreeing peers to stick to their guns. The problem with the second option is that while the parties to the disagreement can maintain their judgments about the issue, their credence nevertheless should be dramatically lowered. This conclusion, however, does not sit well with the phenomenology of radical disagreement about abortion. As the example assumes, and as is usually the case, advocates on both sides ordinarily have very high credence in their beliefs regarding this issue. The analysis thus far suggests that there remain only three possible ways of dealing with this phenomenon. All of them strike me as problematic.

The first possibility is that radical disagreement about abortion, contrary to what I presumed, involves many more high-confidence disagreements about, for example, the sanctity of human life, conceptions of dignity, and the right of women over their body. If this is the case, one might think that the balance has tilted toward the permissible global downgrading of the epistemic status of one's opponents in the debate. Given the remaining high-confidence agreements on a great many issues of political morality, this seems questionable, however. It also seems very undesirable of an account of public reason that it should not be able to accommodate disagreements of this nature. Yet, desirability is not a convincing argument. It is even a point in favor of the idea of Democratic Public Reason introduced in Chap. 4 that it appreciates the fact that radical disagreement has the potential to undo the epistemic framework of public deliberation and dissolve the fundamental commitment of citizens to regard others as equal epistemic authorities. It accounts for the phenomenon of polarization. By

---

[3] Cabuela May (2005): p. 347.

this I mean an increasingly wider scope of high-confidence disagreement with the corresponding increase in *intellectual arrogance*, an attitude of dismissing other citizens as generally less reliable judges of the moral issues at stake in political decision-making.

The second possibility is to bite the bullet and endorse the conclusion that advocates on both sides ought to significantly lower their credence in their respective beliefs. As I have already stated, this ill suits the phenomenology of radical disagreement. However, this might not be an observation to which we ought to give much weight. On a general note and in special regard to the intensity with which the abortion debate is fought out, it is important that we should not allow the *intensity* of our disagreements to spoil our ability to step back from our emotional engagement in political debate. The intensity we sense when we argue in the heat of the moment should not make it impossible for us to adopt a reflective stance characterized by an attitude of intellectual humility. Emotions, of course, do have their place in politics and the emotional engagement of citizens in political debate and action is a sign of a healthy political community and something to be cherished. Ultimately, however, we cannot allow our emotions to carry us away and to stop more seasoned political judgments to enter the discursive arena of politics.

The third possibility, finally, is to argue that, despite appearances, there is room for epistemic conciliation on the matter that does not entail agnosticism. The problem with the preceding analysis of the issue is that it treats the options in the disagreement as binary. But why should we do so? Pro-choice advocates often disagree about *until what point* in the life of a fetus abortions ought to be legal. Pro-lifers, on the other hand, seldom think that abortion is morally impermissible no matter the circumstances. Many accept that exceptions should be made if the pregnancy is the result of a rape, when it poses a risk to the life of the mother, or when it is known that the child-to-be would be born with severe health defects or develop a serious illness in the course of their life. On a more abstract level, we can ask: how permissive should the state be with respect to abortion? In this light, their disagreement does invoke scales along which conciliation seems possible. Conciliation, after all, is also realizable along a scalar dimension if it is between the judgment of a person who rejects all redistribution and the level of redistribution advocated by someone who deems redistribution permissible. Hence, what prima facie might be described as a binary choice really does allow for epistemic conciliation along a scalar dimension specifying a uniquely rational position. Why, then, should pro-life advocates not be required to pursue conciliation along that scale? Their input into the search for epistemic conciliation along this temporal dimension would steer the result toward an earlier stage in the pregnancy. Maybe the solution endorsed in many democratic legal systems, to legalize abortions within the first trimester of pregnancy, can be regarded as just that, an instance of epistemic conciliation. On the other hand, we can rephrase the conflict thus: should the state subsidize abortions or not? In spite of its "either/or" character, the issue thus stated clearly has a scalar dimension. We might likewise ask, *to what extent* should the state subsidize abortions?[4] George Sher argues that the state should be neutral with respect to the question as to whether abortion is worthy of support.[5] But this question—should the state be *either* neutral *or* partial?—also allows for a reformulation introducing a scalar dimension. We can ask, *how* neutral does the state have to remain? There are many ways in which neutrality with respect to religion is implemented in degrees in modern states, for instance. We might thus compare the laical French model with the secular German state, which collects a church tax. Should the state offer support in terms of free professional advice on related health issues or should it subsidize the procedure itself, for instance? All these questions allow for positions which are on different points on a scale and thus for epistemic conciliation and/or political compromise (see Conciliatory Democracy and the Politics of Compromise below).

I am uneasy with all three ways to solve the abortion puzzle. On the one hand, the first option neglects the respect many people engaging in the discussion have, and should have, for the opinions of their counterparts on a wide range of other moral issues. The second and the third options, on the other hand, do not seem to take the opinions involved very

---

[4] Possible answers include, of course, "not at all" and "all the way." More nuanced positions are available, however. Gutman and Thompson, for instance, argue that only pro-choice advocates should pay a tax used to subsidize abortions; cf. Gutman and Thompson (1996): p. 88ff.

[5] From which he considers that it follows that the state should not subsidize abortion; cf. Sher (1981).

seriously. They do not reflect the intensity with which people engaging in the controversy hold their beliefs. In a different light, however, they *do* treat these beliefs and the persons holding them with respect. In fact, they respect both equally. It is precisely this equal respect that supports the relativistic attitude in the second, and the conciliatory attitude in the third reply.

Epistemic Conciliation and Religious Dogmatism Related to this topic, there are two questions with respect to the conciliatory stance toward political disagreements and religious beliefs.

One concerns the point that religious beliefs might inform beliefs about the justice of issues at stake in political decision-making. I have argued that the confidence in beliefs about the justice of these issues ought to reflect our precarious status of competent reasoners. As Rousseau says, reasonable citizens ought to be "wary of their own reason" (see Chap. 1; Self-Regarding Interests and the Virtue of Intellectual Humility). However, this assumption does not sit well with the phenomenology and the often dogmatic nature of religious convictions. One might thus wonder if and how the conciliatory stance of reasonable citizens toward their political disagreements affects their religious convictions and vice versa.

The other problem is of a more general nature. It concerns the question if and how the widespread disagreement about religion and the spiritual life ought to affect the confidence of reasonable citizens in their beliefs about these matters. Reasonable citizens ought to take a conciliatory stance toward their disagreements about justice, but should they do the same with regard to their disagreements about religion and the spiritual life?

The conciliatory conception of democracy offers an answer to both questions. Regarding the first, it states that reasonable citizens seek to *publicly* justify their intended exercise of political power in terms of reasons which other reasonable citizens could reasonably accept. This commitment to public justification precludes their invocation of religious beliefs as a dogmatic justification beyond the reach of the common reason of all reasonable citizens. Hence, reasonable citizens seek a different basis of justification, one that could be shared by all reasonable citizens. We do not have to deny that religious beliefs and ideals can *inform* such reasonable conceptions of justice and the intuitions motivating them. In fact, it would be quite implausible to assume that the public perspectives of citizens can be so fundamentally detached from their private perspectives that no commonalities remain. However, the crucial point is that the private perspective cannot be foundational to the public perspective in terms of its justificatory status.[6] If we thus sever the inferential links between both perspectives, there is no reason why we could not have both a conciliatory attitude toward disagreements about justice and a dogmatic attitude toward religious beliefs.

The answer to the second question, the effects of widespread disagreement of reasonable citizens about religion and the spiritual life, lies in the dynamic model of epistemic peerhood outlined in the preceding chapter. Recall that the model suggests that the dynamic of the permissible global up- and downgrading of epistemic agents is grounded in high-confidence dis/agreements.[7] Furthermore, this status of epistemic agents relative to each other is domain-specific. Hence, I can in principle be your peer in the domain of moral reasoning and not be your peer in the domain of astrophysics. Similarly, I can be your peer in the domain of political morality and not be your peer in the domain of spirituality. Moreover, assuming the absence of independent reasons, high-confidence dis/agreements determine the relative epistemic status in each domain. Hence, the shared framework of Democratic Public Reason (see Chap. 4) can speak in favor of the status of an epistemic peer in the domain of political morality, while the existence of high-confidence *dis*agreements in the domain of spirituality leads to an ascription of an asymmetrical epistemic status. The reasonable disagreement about comprehensive doctrines does not entail that "we should be hesitant and uncertain, much less skeptical, about our own beliefs."[8]

As the example of potentially irreconcilable disagreement about the permissibility of abortion shows, the conciliatory approach I advocate

---

[6] For this reason talk of a translation of arguments drawing on religious beliefs into a public justification makes the issue seem easier than it is. How do you translate the normative force of foundational religious premises?

[7] This assumes that there are no independent reasons for global up- or downgrading (see Chap. 4; Local and Global Downgrading and Independence and Chap. 6; Representative Democracy and the Fundamental Importance of Political Parties).

[8] Rawls (1996): p. 63; Rawls agrees with this conclusion.

might not be applicable to the whole range of contested issues at the center of political deliberation (though my suspicion is that there is a conciliatory perspective on many of them, including the abortion controversy). What I have shown is that at least in one important and paradigmatic case—disagreements about distributive justice—epistemic conciliation is possible and ought to be pursued by the reasonable citizens of deliberative democracies. I believe that the political struggle over the distribution of resources is of continued importance and enjoys a certain priority. This is because many other claims to justice have an important distributive dimension. Some dominant variants of feminism, that is, all those not *exclusively* concerned with the symbolic or discursive emancipation of women and/or liberation from gender norms and categories, for instance, are *also* about equal or preferential access to resources or positions enabling it (think equal pay, disadvantages incurred through maternity leave, or preferential hiring). Even the legality of abortion has a distributive component as one of the contested claims is the access to public health care and the uneven distribution of the costs and burdens of abortion policies.[9] The same holds, I believe, for many aspects of claims about the justice of race relations and minority rights. Of course, none of this is to say that demands of distributive justice are the only ones that really count, or even always dominant in these multifaceted struggles for justice. There is no need to claim a philosophically more charged version of the priority of distributive justice over other considerations of justice in order to underline the importance of the distributive dimension. However, it shows that the struggle for distributive justice is likely to remain a central aspect of democratic decision-making. It is no surprise, then, that distributive justice indeed enjoys a continued importance in the political life of existing democracy.[10]

Conciliatory Democracy and the Politics of Compromise One might also wonder whether the conciliatory conception of democracy is not just another version of a view advocating democracy as a method of reach-

---

[9] These are two of the ways in which the debate has and continues to be framed. Cf. Ferree et al. (2002): pp. 105ff.
[10] Cf. Fuchs and Klingemann (1989).

ing a compromise between conflicting preferences. So it will be useful to consider how the two views differ.

To start with, we can say that a compromise, just as epistemic conciliation, often demands splitting the difference. If two parties have conflicting preferences, the paradigm of a compromise says that we ought to accommodate both to an equal extent. So if we disagree about the justice of the tax rate, the right thing to do would be to compromise, that is, to seek middle ground. Two ideas could motivate us to do so. One is the idea that thus splitting the difference is fair. Such a compromise is indeed often seen as the paradigm case of fairness. If we both want the whole cake, it would be fair if we settled for one half in the end. Fairness is a moral concept and as such closely tied to the ideas of impartiality and reciprocity. We can thus say that we have moral reasons to seek a compromise between conflicting preferences. The other idea that could motivate us to seek this compromise is that it is prudent of us to do so. If we cannot get the whole cake and, unwilling to compromise, I might end up with no cake at all, it is prudent of me to settle for as much as I can get. If we assume equal bargaining power, this might be one half. Sometimes, we use the term "rational" to denote this prudent response to a choice situation. If we adopt this terminology, rationality and morality can conflict. If the distribution of bargaining power is in my favor, for instance, I might get a bigger piece. I might be able to force you to accept a compromise that splits the difference in a way that is not fair. Note, however, that there can be moral reasons to accept a pragmatic compromise. We might, for instance, be in disagreement about the question to what a fair division of the cake amounts. Maybe someone else made it and told you to share it fairly with me. However, it is your birthday cake and you insist that, therefore, you should get a bigger share. Yet I insist that to share it fairly is to share it evenly. Assume that we both believe that our respective positions are indeed the most reasonable. For pragmatic reasons, we might then accept a compromise between reasonable conceptions of fairness.[11] These points are familiar enough. What is important is that in both cases, it is

---

[11] Indeed, Cabuela May insists that these moral pragmatic reasons are the only reasons we have for accepting compromises between our own *moral* convictions and those of others. Cf. Cabuela May (2005).

practical reasons, fairness and prudence which motivate seeking middle ground between conflicting preferences. Politics, in this picture, is the arena in which citizens fight over conflicting preferences and a process which ushers in compromises between them.

A second characteristic of this idea of a compromise is that both parties, albeit willing to seek middle ground, would rather see their preferences prevail. A person motivated by considerations of fairness would still prefer that the other person did not have their conflicting preferences. And the prudent person would of course also rather see their preferences satisfied all the way. Neither person desires, *in the final analysis*, to split the difference. Even the person who believes that overall, the moral thing to do is to seek a compromise between positions reflecting different conceptions of justice, would prefer if all participants shared their own conception of justice. It is this conception of justice after all which this person regards as the most reasonable. If the outcome deviates, they are still willing to accept it, yet only as less than ideal, as just that, a compromise. For both the prudent and the moral person we might thus speak of *an unwilling willingness to compromise*.[12]

The idea of epistemic conciliation at the root of the conciliatory conception of democracy differs on both points. The reason it offers to seek middle ground between conflicting judgments is not practical but theoretical. It is rational for them to seek middle ground in the theoretical sense of rationality. Epistemic conciliation denotes a doxastic response to disagreement. If their beliefs are symmetrical in the required sense, parties to political disagreement seek to conciliate *their judgments*. Where the issue at stake has a scalar dimension, conciliation consists in moving along this scale until reaching the conciliatory position. In that respect, epistemic conciliation is similar to the idea of a compromise. However, the difference lies in the fact that opponents agree that moving to a middle ground is rational and not a normative demand or a strategic maneuver to ensure peaceful cooperation or the maximal satisfaction of their

---

[12] One philosopher explains: "Political compromise occurs when a political agent invokes the fact of disagreement as a reason to accept an alternative that she perceives to be worse on its own merits than her initial position" (Cabuela May (2005): p. 318). This also holds for what Henry Richardson calls "deep compromises," a term which he uses to denote a compromise that affects the ends of the compromising actors; cf. Richardson (2002): pp. 147ff.

preferences given their bargaining position. Instead, they believe that the conciliatory position is rational given their epistemic circumstances.

With respect to the second characteristic of a compromise, the parties' unwilling willingness to compromise, the idea of epistemic conciliation also differs. This difference is already indicated in the very term "conciliation," which does not leave room for a residue of bitterness or regret. In the paradigm cases of epistemic conciliation introduced in Chap. 4, both parties agree that it is rational to give up their original judgment because it is no longer justified given their epistemic circumstances. Because it is rational for reasonable citizens to conciliate their judgments with the conflicting judgments of those whom they regard as equal epistemic authorities, they ought to endorse a conciliatory judgment as the most rational judgment. This leads to a demand of deference which I shall address in more detail later (see Chap. 7; The Ambitiousness of Conciliatory Democracy and Weak Deference).

A third difference between the idea of a compromise and the idea of epistemic conciliation might lie in their applicability to different political conflicts. There might be more conflicts to which we can apply the idea of a compromise than conflicts to which the idea of epistemic conciliation can be applied. Most deliberative democrats believe that even though politics ought to aspire to the ideal of deliberation, bargaining is an irreducible part of politics even under ideal circumstances. In other words, sometimes politics is a brute clash of preferences and a bargain has to be struck between them. Notice that even in cases that make bargaining necessary, however, there are judgments involved which function as a backdoor through which the demand of epistemic conciliation might enter the picture. If we adopt the fairness model of compromise, citizens enter the bargaining arena with the belief that a certain distribution of preference satisfaction is fair and thus mutually acceptable. They do not simply try to satisfy their preferences to the greatest extent possible but to the extent that they believe they are entitled to given their beliefs about fairness. They then aim to strike a bargain which brings the outcome as close as possible to their idea of a fair compromise. Thus described, bargaining is not immune to the idea of epistemic conciliation. There exists a scale along which citizens can conciliate their judgments about what fairness demands of them.

More generally, the possibility of compromises, just as of epistemic conciliation, depends on the availability of a scalar dimension to the conflict at hand. A familiar distinction between two ideal types of political conflict is between "more or less" and "either/or" conflicts. While the former are conflicts, for example, about the distribution of resources, the latter can be conflicts which run along ethnic, linguistic, or religious lines. However, we might also want to include in the latter class such cases as the conflict over the permissibility of abortion. Either we allow abortion or we do not. The conflict is heavily polarized and the frontlines seem clear. I have explored the conflict over abortion and suggested that conciliation, and we can now add compromise, is possible if we dig deeper and do not let the appearance of an irreconcilable either/or-type conflict deceive us. *How permissive* should the state be with respect to abortion? *Up until what point* in the pregnancy should abortion be legal? *How much support* should the state give to those who consider an abortion? Or finally, *how neutral* does the state have to remain, assuming that it is not an all or nothing affair? All these questions allow for positions which are on different points on a scale and thus open the door for epistemic conciliation and/or political compromise. When conflicts arise, they often *start out* with an apparent exclusive choice between irreconcilable positions. It is only when we try very hard and bring our experiences of past conflicts to bear on new ones that compromise emerges as an additional option. This is why we sometimes talk of the art of compromise. And part of mastering this art is the ability to conceive scalar dimensions to conflicts which previously appeared to confront us as a simple either/or question. Epistemic conciliation requires very similar skills and it is part of the constructive function of public deliberation to conceive issues in a way that allows for them to be mapped on a scale along which compromise is possible (see also The Median Voter Lost in Space? below). Thus says Alfred O. Hirschman:

> I suspect [...] that the category of either-or or nondivisible conflicts is essentially a convenient label for a vast array of new and unfamiliar problems having quite different degrees of manageability. These conflicts can only be properly mapped out as we experience them. [...] What is

actually required to make progress with the novel problems that a society encounters on its road is political entrepreneurship, imagination, patience here, impatience there, and other varieties of virtù and fortuna.[13]

One important lesson to be learned from this discussion is that, in spite of the differences between the ideas of epistemic conciliation and of fair compromise, there exists considerable overlap. In certain paradigmatic cases, the outcomes they recommend might be indistinguishable. The difference thus lies in what motivates these ideas. As we have seen, it is moral considerations on the one hand and epistemological considerations on the other. That the two might often recommend the same outcomes is then a very happy result for a democratic theory. It suggests that what we are morally required to do (to split the difference fairly) might also be what is rational for us to do given our epistemic circumstances. Hence, it suggests that the normative and the epistemic dimensions of the significance of political disagreement are often congruent. This point will become even more evident in the epistemic argument for democracy, which I present in subsequent sections. The argument uses spatial models of voting and party competition, which are usually associated with bargaining and the ability of democratic systems to produce (fair) compromises.

Why Democracy?

The argument so far has been that reasonable citizens regarding each other as equal epistemic authorities ought to conciliate their conflicting judgments about justice. All along, I have indicated that this result—in tandem with the normative commitment to treat other reasonable citizens as equal normative authorities—leads us to endorse a view of democracy which I called the conciliatory conception of democracy.

Up until now, however, I have left open the question as to why my arguments lead us to endorse *any* view of democracy. After all, it is not obvious that epistemic conciliation and democracy go hand in hand. Are elections and rule by the *majority* not an essential part of democracy?

---

[13] Hirschman (1994): p. 216.

In fact, minimalist conceptions assert that democracy is nothing more than "a system in which parties lose elections."[14] In other words, isn't democracy all about the rule of a majority over a minority? We have already complemented this picture of democracy with an ideal of democracy as a deliberative enterprise of citizens who argue about policy and seek to justify their stances on important issues in terms of reasons reasonably acceptable to other reasonable citizens (see Chap. 2), and I shall return to the role and value of deliberation later (see Chap. 7; The Normative and the Epistemic Dimension of Conciliatory Democracy). However, even if the majority endorses one reasonable conception of justice at the expense of its reasonable alternatives, the democratic process does not track the ideal of epistemic conciliation. The question remains, then, how exactly epistemic conciliation and democratic decision-making relate. In what follows, I not only argue that democracy as an institutionalized decision-making procedure which enables majorities to rule over minorities does not run counter to the ideal of epistemic conciliation. I even maintain that *democracy is uniquely positioned to track the epistemic conciliation of the conflicting judgments of democratic citizens*. While democratic institutions do in no way guarantee perfect conciliation, they are the only political decision-making institutions which have a tendency to *most nearly get it right* and do so due to their inbuilt, systemic features. Notice that because the conciliatory outcome is the most rational to endorse for all reasonable citizens, the argument I have outlined amounts to a bestness-tracking claim. A complex array of democratic decision-making institutions produces outcomes which track the *most* reasonable of a set of reasonably acceptable options (see Chap. 2; Bestness and Majority Rule). As I shall demonstrate later, furthermore, democracy can achieve both issue-specific and comprehensive epistemic conciliation of the conflicting judgments of its citizens and their conceptions of a just society (see Chap. 6; Issue-Specific and Comprehensive Epistemic Conciliation). A further issue is whether this bestness-tracking claim is reasonably acceptable to all reasonable citizens, which I have introduced as a requirement for a publicly justifiable conception of democratic legitimacy (see Chap. 2).

---

[14] Przeworski (1991): p. 10.

My assertions might strike many philosophers as counterintuitive. Political philosophy has a long history of debating the merits of majority rule understood as the right of the majority to get its way in cases of conflicting interests or opinions.[15] Many with stronger leanings toward political science, especially the public choice theorists among them, on the other hand, might become only little excited about my assertion. The reason is that the conciliatory effects of democratic decision-making institutions are a staple of their discipline (although they probably would not call them by that name). Unsurprisingly, then, my argument for the conciliatory properties of democracy rests on the insights of public choice theory, which has played a significant part in broadening the understanding of political processes. More specifically, I draw on two aspects which are of fundamental importance when it comes to the understanding of democracy and democratic decision-making. The first is the Median Voter Theorem first formulated by Duncan Black; the second is the spatial model of party competition developed by Anthony Downs.[16] While Black focuses on the decision-making of committees on specific issues, Downs takes into view the democratic process more broadly and focuses on electoral competition between political parties. The results of both theories are strikingly similar, however. Majority rule and party competition lead to the promotion of median positions in decision-making. In other words, they lead to results that closely approximate epistemic conciliation of conflicting judgments.

However useful they might be for political scientists and for my argument, public choice theory in general and Downs's elitist conception of democracy as competition between party leaders in particular have a problematic relationship with contemporary political philosophy. When philosophers engage with public choice theory at all, it is because they perceive its results as a threat to their favorite conception of democracy.[17] Furthermore, elitist conceptions à la Downs and Schumpeter along with minimalist conceptions à la Przeworski have long been the target

---

[15] For recent examples, see Barry (1991), Waldron (1999, 2006), and Christiano (1996): Chap. 6 and (2008).
[16] Cf. Black (1948) and Downs (1957).
[17] Cf. Riker (1982) who formulates the threat he takes public choice theory to pose for mandate theories of democracy.

of attacks by more civic-minded philosophers who advanced deliberative conceptions of democracy. What I attempt in this chapter, then, is to reconcile public choice theory and Downs's spatial model of party competition with civic conceptions of democracy, such as that of deliberative democracy. As I shall demonstrate below, the conciliatory conception of democracy, which is of course itself a civic conception, makes productive use of both. As we shall also see, this requires making some important changes to Downs's original model.

My discussion of the Median Voter Theorem and the spatial model of party competition adds two important facets to the philosophical debate about the merits and nature of democracy. First, it shows that the rule of the majority does not ordinarily mean the rule of just any majority over a randomly constituted minority. Second, it reintroduces political parties as actors of major importance in modern democracies to the philosophical discourse. As I will show, both aspects have undeservingly received relatively little attention in political philosophy. This holds for political parties especially, which political philosophers, if they paid them any attention at all, have all too often displayed in an all too unfavorable light. Hence, the resources these philosophers provide for developing the argument for conciliatory democracy are limited. Fortunately then for my argument, this is very different for the field of public choice theory to which I shall turn presently.

Enter the Median Voter The cornerstone of my argument for democracy revolves around the concept of the median voter. The definition of the median voter is that of the voter who in reference to a one-dimensional issue space has as many voters to the left of his preference position as he does to the right. In the epistemic framework I have advocated, the median voter can thus be conceptualized as the voter who endorses a judgment that expresses, or is close to, the conciliatory position between disagreeing peers. If democratic institutions viewed in their real-world complexity can be shown to produce policies that correspond to the preferences of the median voter, then the epistemic argument for democracy can get off the ground. Hence, I demonstrate in this section that the theoretical analysis of the dynamic of democratic decision-making helps us to understand that democracy has precisely this tendency. Furthermore, these theoretical results are backed up by empirical findings of many important studies in this field.

The Rule of the Majority and the Spatial Model of Voting The idea of a median voter and the mechanics of this tendency toward conciliation require an exposition of what is known as the spatial theory of voting. Recall the example of the five legislators who have to determine the rate of income tax. Next, imagine that the tax rates are a point on a line starting from 0 (for a 0 % tax on income) on the left side to 10 (for a 100 % tax on income). Each of the legislators now has a preferred point on the line (their preferred income tax rate) and their preferences for alternative tax rates decline continuously when moving away on the scale in either direction.

According to this picture, Legislator 1 prefers a tax rate of approximately 35 %, Legislator 2 of approximately 45 %, Legislator 3 of 60 %, Legislator 4 of approximately 75 %, and Legislator 5 of approximately 85 %. Furthermore, the legislators' preferences are single-peaked, meaning the utility functions representing their preferences have a maximum at some point and decline from this point on either side. For any rate y that is not the maximum point, we can now define a preferred-to-y set for each legislator. As the name suggests, this set includes all the rates that a legislator prefers to y. For instance, Legislator 5's preferred-to-y set is $P_5(y)$.

In a next step, we can do this for all legislators. If we do, we will realize that the preferred-to-y sets of some legislators overlap, that is, each prefers an alternative to y. Some of these alternatives are preferred by a majority. This is, of course, what interests us. The set of alternatives preferred to y by a majority is called the *winset of y*. The winset for a point x is *empty* when there is no alternative that any majority prefers to x. All in all, there are 16 different majority coalitions. In our example, however, only one of them has an overlapping preferred-to-y set (Legislators 3, 4, and 5). It is now crucial to note a peculiar aspect of the above constellation. Namely, any point that is *not* the ideal point of the median voter is defeated by a majority. This is because for any point to the left of this point it holds true that a majority prefers the ideal point of the median voter (L3–5);

and for any point to the right of it, it holds true that a different majority (L1–3) prefers the ideal point of the median voter. Hence, the ideal point of the median voter has an empty winset and will be chosen by the majority.[18] We have arrived at Black's Median Voter Theorem (MVT), which states the following:

> If members of group G have single-peaked preferences, then the ideal point of the median voter has an empty winset.

Nothing of the above changes the fact that in a democracy a majority rules over a minority. However, this is only part of the truth. The spatial analysis of voting suggests that what is missing in this description is the fact that (in most cases) a *centrist* majority rules over *more extreme* minorities. Quite surprisingly, then, unconstrained majority rule might just be the best method of decision-making to foster epistemic conciliation of the judgments of legislators.[19]

Notice that if a decision is to reflect perfect conciliation of the judgments of those making it, the result should reflect the mean of their preferences, a tax rate of approximately 60 % in this case. Our example is engineered to achieve this result. The result could be off, however, if the median voter had a different position on the issue. The argument for democracy thus makes the more modest claim that democracy *most nearly* gets it right as the median preference has a particularly strong impact on the decision-making.

Cycling Majorities Black's MVT is an answer to a problem posed by another famous theorem which keeps public choice theorists busy to this day. This latter theorem is usually called Arrow's Impossibility Theorem.[20] The huge impact this theorem has had on the development of democratic theory in political science and philosophy is owed to the fact that it seemingly undermines a basic assumption most people have (or had) about

---

[18] For an illustration of this points, see, for example, Shepsle and Bonchek (1997): pp. 83ff.
[19] See also McGann (2004).
[20] However, the theorem was originally formulated by Condorcet and rediscovered by Charles Dodgson in 1884 only to be forgotten again. Eventually, it was Duncan Black (and not Kenneth Arrow!) who was the first to rediscover it and the writings of Condorcet, Borda, and Dodgson in the twentieth century; cf. Rowley (2004): p. 203f.

democracy: that its institutions reliably aggregate the preferences of citizens and produce something like the "will of the people." In brief, the theorem states that—given certain conditions which democratic institutions ought to satisfy—the decisions reached by majority rule are inherently unstable. More specifically, it states that no single alternative will be undefeated in pairwise voting. Imagine three voters *V1–3* who have different, transitive preference orderings over outcomes *A*, *B*, and *C*. *V1* prefers *A* over *B* and *B* over *C* (and, since the condition of transitivity holds, also *A* over *C*). *V2* prefers *B* over *A* and *A* over *C*. And *V3* prefers *C* over *B* and *B* over *A*.

V1	V2	V3
A	B	C
B	C	A
C	A	B

Notice that the preference ordering of each voter is transitive (*V1:* $A > B > C$; *V2:* $B > C > A$; *V3:* $C > A > B$). In a preference distribution such as this, the problem emerges when we employ majority rule in an effort to aggregate these individual preference orderings into a collective preference ordering that fulfills the condition of transitivity. Put simply, this cannot be done. For if we put the alternatives before us to a pairwise vote, we will get $A > B$ and $B > C$ but *not* $A > C$ (instead $C > A$). Hence, at the aggregate level, the preference order is not transitive and every alternative has a non-empty winset.[21] This is a troubling result because it shows that given certain conditions and preference orderings, majority rule engenders cycling majorities. Hence, it does not render stable outcomes because there is no one decision that most satisfies all preferences and, for the same reason, majority rule does not seem to reveal anything like "the will of the people."[22]

However, while the possibility cannot be denied under the conditions specified, not even the mathematical analysis shows preference cycles to

---

[21] Another way of phrasing this problem in the public choice lingo is to say that no alternative is the Condorcet winner. All these formulations express the simple idea that for each policy adopted there exists a majority that prefers a different policy.

[22] Hence, Riker's rejection of "populism," the idea that the people articulate their "will" through elections, in favor of a brand of liberalism which views elections simply as a device to get rid of political elites; cf. Riker (1982).

be very common.[23] Others have analyzed the real-world cases offered as examples for such cycles and concluded that only one of a total of 26 alleged cases was a credible case of a cycle of sincere preferences and all others failed attempts at strategic voting.[24] Furthermore, the large number of studies employing the spatial model of voting suggests that in most ordinary cases voter preferences can be mapped on a one-dimensional issue space while satisfying the single-peakedness condition.[25] In light of these findings, Robert Goodin succinctly remarks: "Proving that something is possible is one thing. Proving that it is probable quite another. In assessing the practical significance of formal theorems, it behoves us to bear that difference constantly in mind."[26] As we have seen, however, the MVT provides a different answer to the problem of cycling majorities. It shows that if preferences are single-peaked and the alternatives at stake can be presented in a one-dimensional space, the alternative most preferred by the median voter beats every other alternative in pairwise voting (has an empty winset and is the Condorcet winner) and the procedure results in a transitive preference ordering at the aggregate level.

The Median Voter Lost in Space? One of the major problems that besets attempts to make use of the MVT in the analysis of politics is the multidimensionality of the policy issue space. Oftentimes, dimensions cannot be separated as neatly as our model demands. Very often in politics, it is guns versus butter; choices in one dimension influence choices made in another, opening up the question as to whether stable equilibria exist under these circumstances. Similarly, one might conceive the ideological space in which political parties and voters situate themselves as multidimensional. The central conflict lines of modern societies are not only socioeconomically defined. Historically, they also appear in the traditional sets of center/periphery, church/state, agriculture/industry, workers/capitalists, and in more recent times also in constellations of materialist/post-materialist

---

[23] Cf. Niemi and Weisberg (1968).
[24] Cf. Mackie (2003).
[25] Cf. Poole and Romer (1985) and Poole and Rosenthal (1997).
[26] Goodin (2007): p. 194.

values.[27] Furthermore, how one positions oneself in one dimension affects one's stance on matters in another dimension.[28]

Consequently, the question arises as to whether the spatial model of voting can be extended to a multidimensional space, or whether the assumption of a single dimension can be made plausible. However, various studies suggest that it can be fruitful to pursue a multidimensional approach which employs a single left–right dimension along which preferences of parties and voters are then located. This is not to deny that the policy space is indeed multidimensional. What the approach proposes as an alternative is to model on a single dimension the vast majority of differences along a number of dimensions. The key to this maneuver is the high degree of correlation frequently observed among different dimensions. Analyzing the ratings various interest groups gave to members of the House of Representatives in a multidimensional policy space, Poole and Romer (1985) found that it only took three dimensions to acquire the predictive power inherent in the ratings.[29] Furthermore, a single liberal–conservative dimension sufficed to obtain 94% of the predictive power. Another study analyzing every roll call vote in the House and Senate between 1789 and 1985 had similarly encouraging results regarding the employment of a single dimension.[30] With these findings in mind, we can thus attempt to map these correlated dimensions on a single left–right dimension as shown in Figs. 5.1 and 5.2.

In addition to the conflation of various correlated dimensions into a single left–right dimension, we can also observe that a single dimension can "take over" and render other dimensions insignificant with regard to electoral competition.[31] Interestingly for my focus on epistemic conciliation about distributive justice, one of the, and in many cases *the*,

---

[27] Cf. Lipset and Rokkan (1967): p. 50 and Dalton (2006): p. 134.
[28] A troubling example is the effect of racism on redistributive policies; cf. Lee and Roemer (2006).
[29] Cf. Poole and Romer (1985).
[30] Cf. Poole and Rosenthal (1997).
[31] Cf. Roemer (2001). Roemer develops a sophisticated model of electoral competition which takes intra-party competition between various factions into account. It should be noted, however, that his model is committed to multidimensionality. See also Roemer (2006) for a broader perspective on multiparty electoral competition.

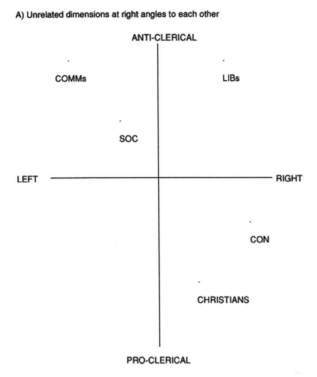

Fig. 5.1 Unrelated dimensions at right angles to each other
Source: McDonald and Budge (2005): p. 44

dominant conflict line in *all* 29 European party systems in the 1990s runs along the socioeconomic dimension.[32] This means that even if we do not attempt to conflate all or most salient dimensions into a single left–right dimension, the socioeconomic one is very likely to figure very prominently in electoral competition between parties and the conciliatory tendency of the process is thus likely to show itself here.

One important condition for the one-dimensional model to work (and for the looming danger of cycling majorities to be thwarted) is that all political actors share a perception of the political space as one-dimensional

---

[32] Cf. Siaroff (2000): p. 21f.

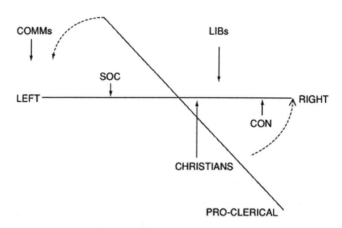

Fig. 5.2 Correlated dimensions, showing party positions projected on the principle left–right dimension
Source: McDonald and Budge (2005): p. 45

and share a perception of the dimension along which conflicting alternatives are to be placed. Thus, Riker remarked: "If, by reason of discussion, debate, civic education and political socialization, voters have a common view of the political dimension (as evidenced by single-peakedness), then a transitive outcome is guaranteed."[33] Interestingly, we see this condition fulfilled in various surveys probing the matter.[34] Citizens and party supporters are highly reliable in their self-placements and the placement of parties along a single dimension.[35] Furthermore, they show once again that issues surrounding the role of the government and the economy dominate the common perception of a left–right dimension. To a significant extent, democracies' work of comprehensive epistemic conciliation, then, is done along this single left–right dimension.

---

[33] Riker (1982): p. 128.
[34] Cf. Castles and Mair (1984), Huber and Inglehart (1995), and Benoit and Laver 2005).
[35] Cf. Gabel and Huber (2000) who check the self-placements of party supporters against the placements of parties by experts.

References

Barry, B. (1991). Is Democracy Special? In B. Barry (Ed.), *Democracy and Power: Essays in Political Theory 1*. Oxford: Oxford University Press.
Benoit, K., & Laver, M. (2005). *Party Policy in Modern Democracies*. London: Routledge.
Black, D. (1948). On the Rationale of Group Decision Making. *Journal of Political Economy*, 56(1), 23–34.
Cabuela May, S. (2005). Principled Compromise and the Abortion Controversy. *Philosophy & Public Affairs*, 33(4), 317–348.
Castles, F. G., & Mair, P. (1984). Left–Right Political Scales: Some 'Expert' Judgments. *European Journal of Political Research*, 12(1), 73–88.
Christiano, T. (1996). *The Rule of the Many: Fundamental Issues in Democratic Theory*. Boulder, CO: Westview Press.
Christiano, T. (Ed.). (2008). *The Constitution of Equality: Democratic Authority and its Limits*. Oxford: Oxford University Press.
Dalton, R. J. (2006). Social Modernization and the End of Ideology Debate: Patterns of Ideological Polarization. *Japanese Journal of Political Science*, 7, 1–22.
Downs, A. (1957). *An Economic Theory of Democracy*. New York: Harper and Row.
Feldman, R. (2006). Epistemological puzzles about disagreement. In S. Hetherington (Ed.), *Epistemology Futures* (pp. 216–236). Oxford: Oxford University Press.
Ferree, M. M., Gamson, W. A., Gerhards, J., & Rucht, D. (2002). *Shaping Abortion Discourse. Democracy and the Public Sphere in Germany and the United States*. Cambridge: Cambridge University Press.
Fuchs, D., & Klingemann, H.-D. (1989). The Left-Right Schema. In K. M. Jennigns, J. W. van Denth, et al. (Eds.), *Continuities in Political Action: A Longitudinal Study of Political Orientations in Three Western Democracies* (pp. 32–72). Berlin: de Gruyter.
Gabel, J., & Huber, J. (2000). Putting Parties in Their Places. *American Journal of Political Science*, 44, 94–103.
Goodin, R. E. (2007). Political Science. In R. E. Goodin, P. Pettit, & T. Pogge (Eds.), *A Companion to Contemporary Political Philosophy* (2nd ed., Vol. I, pp. 183–214). Oxford: Blackwell.
Gutman, A., & Thompson, D. (1996). *Democracy and Disagreement*. Cambridge, MA: Harvard University Press.
Hirschman, A. O. (1994). Social Conflicts as Pillars of Democratic Market Society. *Political Theory*, 22(2), 203–218.

Huber, J. D., & Inglehart, R. (1995). Expert Interpretations of Party Space and Party Locations in 42 Societies. *Party Politics, 1*, 73–111.
Lee, W., & Roemer, J. E. (2006). Racism and Redistribution in the United States: A Solution to the Problem of American Exceptionalism. *Journal of Public Economic, 90*, 1027–1052.
Lipset, S. M., & Rokkan, S. (1967). *Party systems and voter alignments: cross-national perspectives.* New York: Free Press.
Mackie, G. (2003). *Democracy Defended.* Cambridge: Cambridge University Press.
McDonald, M. D., & Budge, I. (2005). *Elections, Parties, Democracy: Conferring the Median Mandate.* Oxford: Oxford University Press.
McGann, A. J. (2004). The Tyranny of the Supermajority. *Journal of Theoretical Politics, 16*(1), 53–77.
Niemi, R. G., & Weisberg, H. F. (1968). A mathematical solution for the probability of the paradox of voting. *Behavioral Science, 13*(4), 317–323.
Poole, K. T., & Romer, T. (1985). Patterns of political action committee contributions to the 1980 campaigns for the United States House of Representatives. *Public Choice, 47*(1), 63–111.
Poole, K. T., & Rosenthal, H. (1997). *Congress: A Political-Economic History of Roll Call Voting.* Oxford: Oxford University Press.
Przeworski, A. (1991). *Democracy and the Market: Political and Economic Reforms in Eastern Europe and Latin America.* Cambridge: Cambridge University Press.
Rawls, J. (1996). *Political Liberalism* (2nd ed.). New York: Columbia University Press.
Richardson, H. S. (2002). *Democratic Autonomy: Public Reasoning about the Ends of policy.* Oxford: Oxford University Press.
Riker, W. H. (1982). *Liberalism Against Populism: A Confrontation Between the Theory of Democracy and the Theory of Social Science.* San Francisco: W. H. Freeman.
Roemer, J. E. (2001). *Political Competition.* Cambridge, MA: Harvard University Press.
Roemer, J. E. (2006). Modeling Party Competition in General Elections. In B. R. Weingast & D. A. Wittman (Eds.), *The Oxford Handbook of Political Economy* (pp. 1110–1131). Oxford: Oxford University Press.
Rowley, C. K. (2004). Public Choice from the Perspective of the History of Thought. In C. K. Rowley & F. Schneider (Eds.), *The Encyclopedia of Public Choice* (pp. 201–214). New York: Kluwer.
Shepsle, K. A., & Bonchek, M. S. (1997). *Analyzing Politics: Rationality, Behavior and Institutions.* New York: W.W. Norton.

Sher, G. (1981). Subsidized Abortion: Moral Rights and Moral Compromise. *Philosophy & Public Affairs, 10*(4), 361–372.

Siaroff, A. (2000). *Comparative European Party Systems: An Analysis of Parliamentary Elections Since 1945.* London: Routledge.

Waldron, J. (1999). *Law and Disagreement.* Oxford: Oxford University Press.

Waldron, J. (2006). The Core of the Case Against Judicial Review. *The Yale Law Journal, 115,* 1346–1406.

6

Representative Democracy and the Role of Political Parties

As has become clear, the Median Voter Theorem (MVT) is an important result of public choice theory supporting a conciliatory conception of democracy. However, it cannot be the end of the story. Modern democracies are not direct but representative democracies (although direct democratic elements are present to varying degrees, of course). Hence, before legislators get to vote, they have to be elected. Furthermore, voters in modern representative democracies do not vote for their representatives in a direct manner. Instead, they cast their vote for a political party.[1] And it is the victorious political parties that will make up the government and legislate and execute specific policies. This is a crucial—and often neglected—aspect of modern democracy. Indeed, it has been pointed out that

> [p]arties alone operate in elections as well as in governments. They are consequently in a unique position to transform broad popular preferences

---

This section is partly based on considerations first offered in Ebeling (2016).

[1] Cf. Gallagher et al. (2005): p. 72f.

© The Author(s) 2017
M. Ebeling, *Conciliatory Democracy*,
DOI 10.1057/978-1-137-57743-6_6

into specific actions, thus providing the main channel through which democratic States can be made responsive (and responsible) to their citizens. Studying the way parties do this is just as essential as the analysis of their electoral strategies for an understanding of democratic processes. It is also vital to the justification of parliamentary democracy against other types of political system.[2]

The Darlings of Political Science, the Orphans of Political Philosophy

The thoroughgoing appreciation of the importance of the political parties to the workings of modern democracy stands in stark contrast to the stepmotherly treatment they receive from the side of political philosophy.[3] However, even when philosophers have discussed parties more prominently, the latter were usually presented in an unfavorable light. Hence, to the extent that they are discussed at all, political parties have a notoriously bad reputation in political philosophy. As Nancy Rosenblum aptly puts it in her important contribution on the subject, "[i]f parties are the orphans of political philosophy, they are the darlings of political science."[4]

With few exceptions, throughout its history, the emphasis in political philosophy has been on parties as representatives of private interests, opposed to the common interest of the community. As parts pitted against the hole, they were discussed under the heading of "factions." Hence, Thomas Madison defines a faction as "a number of citizens, whether amounting to a majority or minority of the whole, who are united and actuated by some common impulse of passion, or of interest, adverse to the rights of other citizens, or to the permanent and aggregate interests of the community."[5] In his view, parties (or factions) are the necessary evil of politics that we can only hope to neutralize by means of institutional design but which we can never eradicate completely. Rousseau, in whose lineage I placed the conciliatory conception of democracy in the opening chapter, equally considered political associations united by

---

[2] Budge and Keman (1990): p. 1.
[3] This appreciation does not always lead to a favorable view of their role, of course. See, for example, von Beyme's critique of the modern democratic state as a "party state" in von Beyme (1993).
[4] Rosenblum (2008): p. 3.
[5] Hamilton et al. (2003): Federalist No. 10.

a common aim exclusively as potential threats to the exercise of political power according to the (truly) general will (see Chap. 1; Background Conditions). He claims that the shared interest on the basis of which the members of such associations unite gives rise to a general will, a *volonté générale* that is restricted to them. While its structure is analogous to the general will of society at large, it is not congruent with it. The shared interests of privately associated members are not the same fundamental interests universally shared across society. The general will of the former is thus a general will that is, albeit general, nevertheless particular in relation to the general will of society. We might also want to call it *a shared particular will*. Rousseau views such associations—we might also call them factions or parties—as latently dangerous for the prospect of a free society because the particular general will of its members has the potential to replace their *truly* general will which has its grounds in their fundamental interests they share with all other members of society. This, however, is obviously true for any particular will of individuals. What makes the case of private wills united in this way especially pernicious, then, is not this potential as such. Rather, it is the fact that the particular will is united with a large number of others. As I have shown in Chap. 1, Rousseau had a theory of how the particular wills of individuals are neutralized by political procedures *if* no large group with a shared particular will exists (see Chap. 1; The Epistemic Dimension of the Procedure Explained). If such a group does exist, however, the procedures no longer protect the society from laws that violate their fundamental, shared interests. With this in mind, Rousseau stated that "[w]hen particular interests begin to make themselves felt and sectional societies begin to exert an influence over the greater society, the common interest becomes corrupted" and "the meanest interest impudently flaunts the sacred name of the public good" (SC, IV.1.4). The chapter demonstrated that, for Rousseau, political disagreement is a problem which deeply affects the vision of a free society regulated by the general will of its members. He thought that it was a manageable one, however, because he adhered to a view of a well-ordered society as simple in its structure and of the general will as fully evident to all reasonable citizens (see Chap. 1; The Simplicity Assumption). According to this vision, the problematic effects of disagreement on the theoretical level are of little importance because it will not be a prevalent feature of a free society in its ideal state.

I have criticized this aspect of his theory as overly simplistic; and I have advanced arguments for why we ought to allow political disagreement to enter into a theory of democracy as a permanent and central feature of the political life of even the most ideal society (see the section The (Un)Reasonableness of Political Disagreement in Chap. 3). Other philosophers have shared this insight (albeit not the particular arguments supporting it) but have seen it as a regrettable fact about the human condition. Prominent examples are the writings of the Federalists who see the inevitability of disagreement as routed in human nature. Human reasoning, they say, is fallible and often biased, and the diversity of faculties inevitably leads to differences in property which are the most durable source of factions.[6] All that we can do in what they considered a dismal situation is to limit the impact factions would have on public life.[7]

This contrasts starkly with what must count as minority views in political philosophy. These views confer a positive connotation on disagreement and the role of political parties in the dynamic it unfolds in the political arena. Enlisting Mill's idea, which conceives parties as engaged in "a serious conflict of opposing reasons,"[8] each party "deriving its utility from the deficiencies of the other,"[9] Rosenblum develops what she calls a Proto-Millian defense of parties.[10] She also points to the "social function of antagonism," which Mill ascribed to the clash of conflicting opinions. Mill states that

> [t]ruth is so much a question of the reconciling and combining of opposites, that very few have minds sufficiently capacious and impartial to make the adjustment with an approach to correctness, and it has to be made by the rough process of a struggle between combatants fighting under hostile banners.[11]

---

[6] Cf. ibid.
[7] Cf. Hamilton et al. (2003): Federalist No. 51.
[8] Quoted in Rosenblum (2008): p. 9.
[9] Ibid.
[10] Cf. Rosenblum (2008): Chap. 3. She calls the defense "Proto-Millian" because Mill did not share the optimistic vision that parties can in fact deliver "the serious conflict of opposing reasons" which his positive view of social antagonism prescribed.
[11] Quoted in Rosenblum (2008): p. 145.

When it comes to the great practical concerns of life, progress does not "superadd" but substitutes one partial and incomplete truth or prevailing opinion for another fragment more adapted to the needs of the time than the one it displaces.

In Mill's vision of "reconciling and combining of opposites" there still resonates the idea that opposites can be reconciled through reasoned debate. I have argued above, however, that we ought to expect decentered deliberation about sufficiently complex issues to produce disagreement (see Chap. 3; The (Un)Reasonableness of Political Disagreement). Thus, if we take the likelihood of persistent rational and reasonable political disagreement seriously, this "reconciling and combining of opposites" has to take a different form. Opposites can only be conciliated when one adopts a self-reflective stance and steps back and distances oneself from the reasons one endorses. And an awareness of the fact of political disagreement, I have furthermore argued, can undermine the confidence one has in one's first-order reasons and make the pursuit of epistemic conciliation rational. For this reason, I shall later defend Hume's "moment of appreciation"[12] against Rosenblum's own Proto-Millian defense (see Chap. 7; A Room Full of Humeans).

I now proceed to argue for the claim that political parties play an essential role in the epistemic conciliation of the conflicting judgments of citizens. Hence, the conciliatory conception of democracy crucially depends on political parties and their role in the political process *properly carried out*. The last remark hints at the fact that this conception conceives them not as "united and actuated by some common impulse of passion, or of interest, adverse to the rights of other citizens, or to the permanent and aggregate interests of the community."[13] Instead, the conception conceives their role in a Burkean fashion describing them in a positive light. Burke famously defines a party as "a body of men united for promoting by their joint endeavours the national interest upon some particular principle in which they all agreed."[14] Citizens can disagree about their conception of the common good and the vision of a just society. It is the role of parties to organize and channel this conflict of opinion.

---

[12] Cf. Rosenblum (2008): pp. 136ff.
[13] Hamilton et al. (2003): Federalist No. 10.
[14] Burke (1770): p. 134.

The aim of this section, then, is and has been to replace the negative picture of political parties in the mainstream of political philosophy with a vision of democracy which sees them as legitimate institutions forming an integral part of democracy. This defense ties together a comprehensive philosophical vision of democracy and theoretical and empirical insights which I borrow from political science and public choice theory. The key idea of this enterprise is that political parties do not have to be the necessary evil of politics. Instead, they can be a force for the good in the political process of a democratic society. While some philosophers have articulated this insight in former times, it has been neglected in contemporary political and specifically democratic theory, which adopts too narrow a focus on deliberation and grassroots participation.[15] Undoubtedly, the reorientation of political theory away from minimalist and elitist conceptions is on the whole a laudable endeavor, and much good has come of it. However, the way reason enters politics is not *only* through the deliberative input and participation of the independent citizen or their representatives. To a large extent, citizens and their representatives both rely on political parties for their epistemic resources. Political parties are political-epistemic machines producing epistemic benefits for the electorate at large and their representatives. Party platforms, furthermore, express the basic values shared by their supporters. Instead of being the spokespersons of private interests opposed to the common good, they can thus be the spokespersons of citizens united by a conception of the common good. We can conceive these "parties of principle" in a much more positive light. This does not mean, of course, that private interests do not receive uptake in party programs. However, the idea is that the party platform expresses these interests in a way that is compatible with the criterion of reciprocity of advantage (see Chap. 2). They are expressions of a shared reasonable conception of justice which other reasonable citizens can perceive as treating them as equals in a substantive sense even though they might disagree with the way this commitment is spelled out. Crucially, however, this conception of justice shared by these partisans of justice is already a collective achievement. First, this is because it is the

---

[15] There is a growing literature sharing this aim: see, for example, Muirhead (2006, 2010), Biezen and Saward (2008), Rosenblum (2008), White and Ypi (2010), and Weinstock (2015).

product of a collective effort of reasoning and the pooling of resources that make possible a sufficiently coherent and sufficiently specific conception of justice in a complex social world in the first place. Second, it reflects epistemic conciliation of the judgments of members of a subsection of society.

The Fundamental Importance of Political Parties Unlike most philosophers, political scientists have long recognized the importance of political parties for modern representative democracies. In fact, they have done so from the days when political science first emerged as an academic discipline.[16] Subsequently, they have a long tradition of thoroughly analyzing their role in the democratic process. The fact that since the end of the Second World War approximately 11,500 academic publications have appeared on the subject in Western Europe alone bears witness to this.[17] The intimate relation political parties bear to democracy has even led some to remark that "political parties created democracy [...] modern democracy is unthinkable save in terms of parties."[18]

The analysis of both government and parliament, each one of them core democratic institutions of the democratic system of government, and their relationship is overshadowed by the fundamental importance of political parties as "both of these institutions, like nearly every other aspect of political life, are dominated by political parties."[19] Among the manifold results of this engagement with political parties is the insight that they perform many important functions, such as the mobilization of the electorate, the recruitment of political personnel, and the articulation and aggregation of interests.[20] In addition, they fulfill a crucial role in the process of representation as "the political party is the primary vehicle ensuring that citizen preferences are reflected in government policy."[21]

---

[16] Examples are the classic works of Ostrogorski (1991 [1902]), Michels (1968 [1911]), and Weber (1978 [1922]).
[17] Cf. Gunther et al. (2002): p. 2.
[18] Schattschneider (1942): p. 3.
[19] Gallagher et al. (2005): p. 58.
[20] Cf. Klingemann et al. (1994): p. 5; see also Clark et al. (2008): Chap. 13.
[21] Clark et al. (2008): p. 8.

Furthermore, they are important with respect to a basic element of democracy, namely the accountability of decision-makers to the electorate. The multitude of actors involved in decision-making in modern democracies makes it often virtually impossible to allocate responsibility for a political decision to an individual, be it a representative, a government figure, or a member of the bureaucracy. Parties, on the other hand, are collectives of people who together stand for a political decision reached through an otherwise complex process. It is "political parties [who] have to rule and take responsibility for their decision."[22] Some political scientist even maintain that "the only way collective responsibility has ever existed, and can exist given our institutions, is through the agency of the political party."[23]

Party Ideology and Programs In the conciliatory conception of democracy, another one of their functions becomes especially important. Party ideologies are based on certain fundamental values which their supporters endorse. They represent an attempt to structure these value judgments in a way that allows for a formulation of a consistent vision of a just society. In other words, they stand for different conceptions of justice endorsed by the citizenry. Party ideology is thus a vital attribute of political parties. As Klaus von Beyme noted, "[o]ver the longer term only parties based on an ideology have succeeded in establishing themselves."[24] The formulation of party ideologies and programs is the result of their members' collective effort of reasoned engagement with the social world.

Furthermore, parties translate the value judgments included in party ideology into policy programs (recall the argument from institutional expertise I offered in Chap. 3). This is another crucial step in reaching not only a *sufficiently coherent* but also a *sufficiently specific* vision of a just society. Political scientists have advanced this point earlier, remarking that

---

[22] Klingemann et al. (1994): p. 7.
[23] Fiorina (1980): p. 26.
[24] von Beyme (1985): p. 29.

[t]o offer the electorate a choice, they have to package seemingly disparate claims into more or less coherent bundles. In effect, they create predetermined bargains. When multiple parties present the voters with different bundles of issues and solutions, voters have a choice. They choose from within a more or less crystallized, active policy agenda.[25]

In all this, parties play the role of *collective epistemic agents*, that is, an entity capable of rational belief formation, to whom a range of beliefs is attributed, and which is made up of individual epistemic agents who individually do not hold all of the beliefs attributed to the collective agents but do so only collectively.[26] In modern democracies, such collective epistemic agents, not individuals, are the bearers of political expertise.

Importantly, voters do not necessarily have to be aware of the many details of the policy alternatives they face in their electoral choice. Often it is enough that they trust the political party they identify with on the more abstract level of party ideology to work out a set of policy proposals consistent with it. It serves to recall Rousseau's remark that "the evidence [of the common good] can be in the natural and political laws only when they are considered in abstraction. In any particular government, which is a composite of so many diverse elements, this evidence necessarily disappears" (LtoM, 1). It is the business of parties to incorporate expert knowledge and integrate various public policy proposals and proposals for institutional reform in a way that they can be regarded as expressions of a sufficiently coherent moral outlook on the shared social world of citizens.[27] As Alan Ware notes, "[i]deologies provide a kind of guide to the 'policy world' that enables voters to make more informed voting decisions than they would otherwise; parties have an incentive to develop

---

[25] Klingemann et al. (1994): p. 8.

[26] I do not claim, however, that the beliefs attributed to a party are in any significant sense independent from the beliefs of its members or that a party's rational belief formation is in any significant sense independent from the rational belief formation of its members, but only that rationally formed beliefs of a relevant subset of the party's members are attributed to the party as a collective entity without it being the case that all members hold the belief or form it in a rational manner. For a stronger thesis about collective epistemic agency, see Deborah Tollefsen, "Organizations as True Believers," Journal of Social Philosophy 33 (2002): 395–410.

[27] For a congenial idea on the vital role of platforms (of political parties) as guides to the just provision and distribution of intermediate goods as the relevant objects of public policy, see Weinstock (2015).

an ideology because the simplified understandings of the political world that ideologies provide will assist voters in making their decisions."[28] The locus classicus for this notion of ideology as information shortcut is Anthony Downs's economic theory of democracy, which I shall discuss in detail shortly.

Before further elaborating the argument, however, I should offer a more thorough defense of the claim that in the institutional landscape of modern democracy, parties are in a unique position to translate the abstract value judgments of citizens into a sufficiently coherent and sufficiently specific conception of justice. The claim has to be defended with respect to other institutional and non-institutional mechanisms through which citizens exercise their political agency.

First, those deliberative democrats who continue to neglect the role of political parties might simply invoke the epistemic benefits of public deliberation among the citizenry at large. It is certainly true that public deliberation increases the political competence of individuals with respect to the knowledge relevant to the issues at stake and with respect to their moral agency more generally.[29] Furthermore, deliberation in "mini-publics" can increase what Niemeyer calls the intersubjective consistency of participants, that is, it can help to establish "an overall correlation between subjectivity and preferences relationship across the whole range of discourse elements and preferences."[30] Yet, as is the case in the quoted article, this only holds for preferences concerning isolated issues. It might of course also be true more generally. However, it seems fair to regard the claim that it might do so for all (potential) preferences regarding all (potential) issues as a gross overestimation of the capacities of collective public deliberation and individual cognitive abilities. Other methods of democratic decision-making such as direct democracy and collective agency below the level of that of political parties face similar problems as do the deliberative innovations of creating various "mini-publics" and deliberative fora. The principal reason why they cannot replace political parties and take over their funda-

---

[28] Ware (1996): p. 320.
[29] See the practice-based argument in Chap. 3 and Benhabib (1996): pp. 71f.
[30] Niemeyer (2011): p. 109.

mental role as collective epistemic agents is that they do not address the political world in its comprehensiveness. They decide one issue at a time without the coherence of decision-making required for a specific conception of justice to shape the social world. Furthermore, they lack the interest and the cognitive resources of doing so.[31] As I have argued above, even if an individual or a small group were to take the reins for a sustained period of time, they could not overcome the obstacles posed by the complexity of the task of advancing the justice of society. In modern democracy as we know it and as theorists of democracy envision it, political parties are the only (collective) epistemic agents up to the task. They ease the cognitive burdens of individuals when charged with producing a sufficiently coherent and sufficiently specific conception of a just society. The public deliberation of individuals lacks the structure of debates in political parties whose members aim collectively at producing a shared vision of a just society and do so with the procedural apparatus of votes and specialized discussion groups who later bring their insights together in a multilayered process of integration. In this way, parties stabilize public debate and "help to provide structure to an otherwise unstable policy-making process."[32] In all of this, political parties are distinct from interest groups and social movements representing particular interests or opinions detached from an encompassing conception of a just society.

Recently, philosophers have brought up to date and advertised a systemic approach to deliberative democracy which lay dormant in the deliberative tradition.[33] Roughly put, the idea is that an institutional differentiation characterizes modern democracies, which makes it possible for other modes of decision-making and agency to be combined with public deliberation in various fora without the democratic system losing its overall "deliberative" character. Some of the reasons why these theorists endorse this systemic approach are decidedly epistemic: they allude to "the many factual contingencies and competing

---

[31] White and Ypi reject public deliberation as a substitute for political parties also on motivational grounds, cf. White and Ypi (2010): p. 820.
[32] Clark et al. (2008): p. 3.
[33] Cf. Mansbridge et al. (2012).

normative requirements" and the necessity of collective action in politics, which requires "the alignments of will" that make a division of epistemic labor between various agents necessary.[34] This epistemic argument also justifies partisanship and information heuristics entering the picture.[35]

Furthermore, proponents of this approach also explicitly name political parties as a node in the deliberative system.[36] Parties are also given a role in the democratization of expertise and as trusted proxies signaling to citizens that the authority granted to experts is justified.[37] The systemic approach to deliberative democracy, then, makes the underlying orientation toward deliberation and deliberative standards of legitimacy of a normative conception of democracy compatible with the role of political parties in the decision-making process. This systemic turn indicates another stage in the coming of age of deliberative democracy.[38] However, it names political parties in the same breath as many other institutions, which together form a deliberative system. At no point is the fundamental role of political parties which singles them out and makes them unique in the institutional landscape of modern democracy acknowledged. One might guess that this is a last residue of aversion to partisanship and institutions that are not part of the wave of deliberative innovations that came out of the deliberative turn in political philosophy.[39]

The Spatial Model of Party Competition One of the godfathers of Public Choice theory, Anthony Downs, was particularly occupied with the analysis of party competition within the framework of a spatial model of policy preferences. Drawing on models prevalent in the discipline of economics, he analogized the competition of political parties to Hotelling's spatial model of open-market competition of private

---

[34] Ibid., p. 5.
[35] Ibid., p. 6.
[36] Ibid., p. 10.
[37] Ibid., p.15.
[38] Cf. Bohman (1998).
[39] See also Ebeling, M., Wolkenstein, F. (manuscript). Deliberative Agency and Democratic Legitimacy.

businesses for consumer.[40] His idea was that the leaders of political parties use their parties as vehicles for their goal of obtaining power. Hence, his definition of a political party reads thus: "[A] political party is a team of men seeking to control the governing apparatus by gaining office in a duly constituted election."[41] Within the market/democracy analogy, they are the businessmen (and -women) who offer their product (the party program) to potential costumers (the voters) who then invest their resources (their votes) in the product of their choice.[42] With a few more assumptions, he then develops a very neat and slender theory of party competition which entails powerful predictions for the behavior of political parties.

Some of his key assumptions are similar to the ones which have already made an appearance in the analysis of majoritarian voting procedures in Chap. 5. This should come as no surprise as both models share the assumption that agents, whether legislators or voters, aim at utility maximization. More specifically, they will vote for the option closest to their single-peaked preference in a one-dimensional issue space. However, Downs now expands the spatial model of voting to a spatial model of party competition. The first additional assumption I have already mentioned: political parties are run by elites whose aim is to obtain posts in government. The way to achieve this is to win elections; and in order to win an election, one has to win votes. Hence, political parties are vote-winning parties, that is, their principle aim is to maximize their share of the votes. Furthermore, voters are assumed to be competent enough to identify the party which is closest to their preferences. This they do with the help of the particular ideologies political parties proclaim to stand for. Party ideologies provide information shortcuts for voters who consequently do not have to be familiar with the details of policy-making but can identify the party closest to their position in the issue space in a more coarse-grained manner. They thus minimize the costs of obtaining information for voters.

---

[40] Cf. Hotelling (1929).
[41] Downs (1957): p. 25.
[42] Notice that he conceives voting as an investment decision.

It is important to understand, however, that the Downsian model of party competition is not only an expansion of Black's MVT but builds on top of it a game-theoretic model. This model employs quite detailed assumptions about institutions such as electoral systems and the number of political parties as well as about the substantive motives of actors such as office-seeking party elites and their strategic interactions.[43]

Based on his modest (though by no means unimpeachable) assumptions, Downs made far-reaching predictions. Having in mind the example of the political system of the USA with its combination of single-member district (SMD) elections and a two-party system, he predicted the convergence of party programs on the position of the median voter. The rationale behind this becomes obvious in Fig. 6.1.

This figure describes a two-party competition for a maximum share of votes in a society where the majority of voters share a centrist ideology. Because there is no party to the left of Party A, its leaders can safely assume that everybody on that side will vote for their party. Reversely, the same holds for Party B. Hence, both parties have a motive to edge as closely as possible to the position of the other party. Because both parties share this motive, the predicted result is that they arrive at almost indistinguishable positions *just to the right* and *just to the left* of the median voter. In fact, they will be so close to each other that they effectively converge on the median voter's position. Politics, in the words of Anthony Downs, eventually loses its ideological impregnation and becomes Tweedledee-Tweedledum politics.[44]

According to Downs, party competition in a society will have a different form, however, where the ideological distribution of voters is multimodal or in an electoral system which aims at proportional representation (PR). Here, parties who abandon the fringes and focus exclusively on centrist voters will much sooner face competitors to their right and to

---

[43] Cf. Grofman (2004a, b): p. 44. Downs's model is sometimes mistakenly identified as the MVT even in such venerable publications as *The Oxford Handbook of Political Economy*. See Stephen Ansolabehere's entry on Voters, Candidates, and Parties, p. 35.
[44] Cf. Downs (1957): Chap. 8.

6 Representative Democracy and the Role of Political Parties

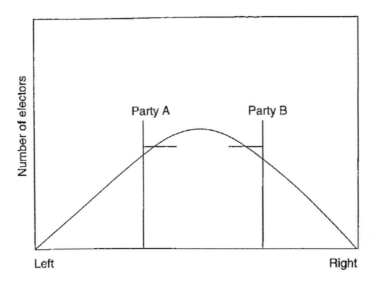

Fig. 6.1 Two-party competition with centrist majority
Source: Budge (2006): p. 424

their left (Fig. 6.2). Furthermore, he predicted that this constellation will foster the persistence of ideological positions among parties.

Because the spectrum of parties is likely to become more populated in PR systems,[45] Downs thought that the correct identification of those parties closest to one's preference would become more difficult, thus undermining the condition that voters are adequately informed in this sense. If we put this worry aside for a moment, we can see another problem with PR. As a system for electing the government, PR is often credited with a broader spectrum of options from which voters can choose relative to SMD systems with a unimodal ideological distribution. However, while an opportunity for meaningful choice is a desirable attribute of the electoral landscape, it harbors a problem for the approach I pursue. According to the theory outlined thus far, multiparty systems with more than two parties will not produce the same centripetal effects on the level of party competition as a two-party competition in single-member districts.

---

[45] This effect is known as Duverger's law, named after Maurice Duverger; cf. Duverger (1954).

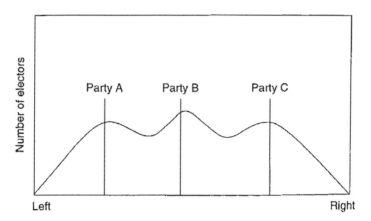

Fig. 6.2 Party competition with multimodel voter distribution
Source: Budge (2006): p. 425

Coalition Formation in Representative Democracies This problem, however, is not as grave as it seems. What we observe in the systems under discussion is simply that the convergence takes place at a later stage, the stage of coalition formation. The pressure toward epistemic conciliation kicks in when parties endorsing different visions of society have to agree on a common government program.[46]

Taking coalition formation into account is enlightening for another reason. Even single-party governments, which do not have to enter into complicated negotiations with other parties to convert their electoral success to access power and the opportunity to shape public policy, are not exempt from the pressure to form coalitions. Only in their case, the pressure comes from the opposing factions within their own ranks. For this reason, "even singly-party majority governments are more accurately seen as being supported by parliamentary coalitions formed on the basis of bargaining between senior politicians—except in this case the bargaining takes place *within* rather than *between* parties."[47] The idea can be generalized as it applies to all political parties, even those which are not

---

[46] Bargaining theory lends additional support to this observation; cf. Laver and Schofield (1990).
[47] Gallagher et al. (2005): p. 382.

in a position to form a government exclusively from their ranks. This reinforces the point I made above that every political party is a roof under which many individuals gather whose views and values are close enough for them to associate with each other yet so disparate that the emerging party ideology reflects lower-level epistemic conciliation of their judgments that conflict within a shared normative framework. Hence,

> [i]n a very real sense [...] the notion of any government as a coalition of diverse interests is fundamental to all political systems. In Britain (and in the United States), such coalition[s] of interests are found for the most part inside political parties as a result of the distorting effects of the plurality electoral system. In most continental European countries, election results are translated more or less proportionally into parliamentary seat distributions, and so bargaining to form a government takes place both within and between political parties.[48]

The Spatial Model of Party Competition Under Scrutiny After having laid out Downs's spatial model of party competition so far, it is time to ask whether it holds up to the empirical data. The answer is that it does not. Well, at least its most drastic predictions do not correspond to empirical reality. The *complete* convergence of the ideological positions of political parties in a two-party system with SMDs is not what we actually observe. Instead, we observe a gap between party ideologies that is relatively stable over time (Fig. 6.3). However, we do observe that the movement of party ideologies along a left–right scale is correlated with that of the opposing party.

In the case of multiparty competition in a proportional electoral system, on the other hand, Downs's prediction of a stable ideological distance between parties receives strong backing from empirical evidence (Figs. 6.4 and 6.5).

The lack of fit between theory and facts in the case of a two-party competition obviously calls for an explanation, and any explanation will have

---

[48] Ibid.

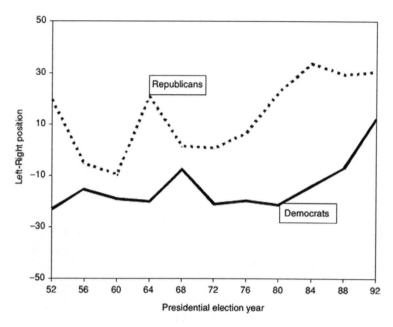

Fig. 6.3 American party movements on a left–right scale, 1952–1992
Source: McDonald and Budge (2005): p. 63

to either alter the theoretical edifice or take into account more institutional details. Both types of explanations have been offered in the literature. An example of the latter type takes into account the candidate selection process within parties. If we stick to the example of the American electoral system, party candidates face primaries in which they have to contest with other candidates coming from different points of the ideological spectrum of their own party. According to the theory, the candidate closest to the party median will receive the majority of votes. In order to win the election, however, the candidate will have to move closer to the median of the electorate as a whole.[49] The result will then be a position that lies somewhere between the party median and the general median.

---

[49] This dynamic is most easily observed in US politics with widely reported on primaries for the nomination of the presidential candidates of the two major parties. In the case of the 2012 presidential elections in the US., a common observation was that the median of the Republican Party forced Mitt Romney to a position too far right to then credibly move far enough to the overall median position to beat Barack Obama.

6 Representative Democracy and the Role of Political Parties

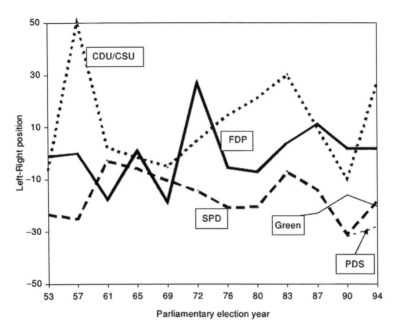

Fig. 6.4 German party movements on a left–right scale, 1953–1994
Source: McDonald and Budge (2005): p. 64

Another alteration is the introduction of the possibility of entry of a third party. Taking this possibility into account, the equilibrium outcome of a two-party competition is the ideological positioning of both parties in such a manner that a third party does not have an incentive to take part in the competition.[50] Also, if we make more complex assumptions about the motivation of voters, we can allow for the possibility of vote abstention because voters are alienated (the candidates are two far away from their ideal points) or indifferent (the candidates' positions are too close to each other), thus drastically reducing the benefit of voting and cost of abstention. Yet another explanation introduces the significance of factors that are not directly related to expectations of what policies the candidate might pursue. Instead, for example, the perceived competence of the

---

[50] Cf. Palfrey (1984).

222 Conciliatory Democracy

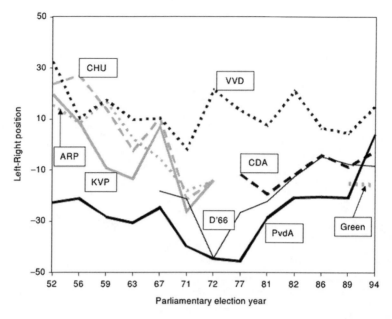

Fig. 6.5 Dutch party movements on a left–right scale, 1952–1994
Source: McDonald and Budge (2005): p. 65

candidates is allowed to play a role. In such a model, the candidate who scores lower in this category will actually increase their chance of winning by moving away from the median.[51] Furthermore, the risk aversion of political parties might lead them to adopt ideologically distinguishable positions.[52] Finally, another crucial alteration aims at the fundamentals of Downs's model. It is the replacement of the assumption that politicians are exclusively concerned with obtaining a public office with the assumption that they are primarily concerned with implementing their preferred policies. This concern for policies closer to their ideal point introduces another reason for non-convergence.[53] I will return to this point below.

---

[51] Cf. Ansolabehere et al. (2000) and Wittman (2005).
[52] Cf. Grofman (2004b): p. 38.
[53] Cf. Wittman (1983). If we adopt a citizen–candidate model according to which citizens only bother to run for public office if this results in a greater chance to influence the course of policy-making in their favor, convergence of two parties is not an equilibrium outcome because at least one party would lose interest in competing altogether; cf. Besley and Coate (1997).

The Paradox of Voting Apart from the countervailing data, another well-noted difficulty is the question of why self-interested voters would actually take the trouble to drag their feet to the polling booth to cast their vote. Given the minimal return on their investment, that is, the chance to actually influence the outcome of the election and thus receive a pay-off from their action, and the cost of even making the effort, it seems that rational, utility-maximizing actors would abstain from rather than participate in the democratic process.[54]

Again, different replies have been offered in the vast literature on the subject. Some propose an analysis of the rationality of individuals embedded in groups with the same interests.[55] Others offer a more complex view of the decision rules involved in rational decision-making. At least one of these, minimax regret decision-making, results in rational participation.[56] One of the earliest and most important contributions introduced a constant term to Downs's mathematical formulation of the basis of rational participation that results in a direct utility gain from voting. This direct utility gain is meant to capture the citizen's sense of duty. However, what looks like a subtle alteration of the Downsian analysis in fact fundamentally shifts the overall character of his theory. First off, the theory no longer views voting in terms of an investment decision but in terms of a consumption decision. Second, as voting is now no longer explained exclusively in terms of the pursuit of selfish preferences, it abandons the original impetus of elitist theories to provide a more "realistic" account of democracy. We shall revisit this point below.

The Problem of Rational Ignorance Yet another difficulty with Downs's model is the problem of rational ignorance. It is similar to the paradox of non-voting, which is not very surprising given that it has its roots in the

---

[54] This problematic entailment of his theory was already noted by Downs. He introduced the long-term participation value of maintaining a democratic system which increases not only the benefit of voting for the correct party but the benefit of voting per se even if one makes an uninformed or misinformed choice. Cf. Downs (1957): Chap. 14.

[55] Coate and Conlin (2004) develop a group rule utilitarianism resting on John Harsanyi's work on rule utilitarianism.

[56] Ferejohn and Fiorina (1974) model and contrast expected utility maximizers, minimax regret decision makers, and maximin decision makers.

same considerations regarding utility maximization and the cost–benefit analysis of political participation. Only now, the resulting question is: why should citizens make an effort to obtain information about candidates and parties at all? Given that such an effort is costly, that is, it will cost time, and the benefits are bound to be minimal, rationally behaving citizens would not undertake it. This result would fundamentally undermine a function democracy is meant to fulfill in Downs's model, namely the responsiveness of the elite's decision-making to the preferences of the electorate. The problem is threefold. First, the votes of citizens would not reflect their preferences because they would not know which party is more likely to fulfill them. They would vote more or less randomly for any candidate. This entails, second, that the effort of politicians to compete for votes by offering a political program that satisfies a maximum number of voters would be stunned. Because they lack information about the relative proximity of the candidates' positions to their own optimum, the electorate would not be able to reward such efforts. And, third, voters could be easily fooled by candidates who misrepresent their true intentions.

The problem with our model is not only that it renders predictions that are refuted by the empirical evidence.[57] It touches on a point which lies at a deeper level. When writing *An Economic Theory of Democracy*, Downs explicitly referred to Joseph Schumpeter's elitist theory of democracy with which he shared many basic assumptions.[58] However, Downs thought that the virtue of democracy is not just, as is the case in Schumpeter's conception, that voters can reject or accept the elites who govern them. Instead, the theory sees the main benefit of the democratic struggle for power between political parties in the *responsiveness* to the preferences of the electorate this process guarantees. However, if voters are rationally ignorant, the mechanism that was to ensure this responsiveness—the vote maximization of parties closest to the preference of the median—is dysfunctional.[59]

---

[57] See, for example, the early refutation in Key (1966).
[58] Cf. Downs (1957): p. 29, *fn* 11.
[59] Not only did Schumpeter think that voters are misinformed, but he also thought that their preferences are the result of manipulation by political elites. Hence, responsiveness could not even appear as an important benefit in his theory. I return to this below.

Since the problem of rational ignorance follows as straightforwardly from Downs's basic assumptions as does the paradox of voting, it has also received a good deal of scholarly attention. Most answers focus on the fact that voters actually need only very little information to make a decision with a very high likelihood of being correct. Of the various information shortcuts voters can and do use in their decision-making are the endorsements parties receive from interest and other groups and, most importantly, the party label. Which party a politician belongs to is an especially strong variable in explaining their voting behavior.[60] Other reliable clues they receive are polling results and endorsements.[61]

Even though these are important insights (see also the argument from institutional expertise in Chap. 3), the problem remains that the cost of even obtaining very little information would usually outweigh the benefits accrued in a model of voting resting on self-interested utility-maximizers as conceived by Downs. Hence, something has to be included in the model over and above the fact that information need not at all be comprehensive in order to make an informed choice. After we have already learned that various theorists have expanded the model with auxiliary assumptions about the citizens' motivation to participate based on a sense of duty, it is only natural to invoke them again at this point to make the theory consistent with its aim to explain the responsiveness to median voter preferences in democratic systems. I have already mentioned, however, that this extension of the motivational set affects the theory in fundamental ways. What we get after making these changes is a theory of democracy that is much more in tune with the ideas driving the civic conception of conciliatory democracy.

Political Parties and Government Policy Another worry that besets the model and my use of it is that political parties are not the actors we ought to focus on when discussing the output and performance of democratic systems of government. Critics of the analysis in these terms and of modern systems of government generally come from different corners. There is the (neo-)Marxist camp, which views the democratic process as

---

[60] Cf. Brady and Sniderman (1985), Page and Shapiro (1992), and Ansolabehere et al. (2001).
[61] Cf. McKelvey and Ordeshook (1985, 1986).

a cover-up for the power of capital, the equally long-standing Webberian critique of "the logic of bureaucracy," and neo-corporatist theories which attribute a decisive influence on policy-making to interest groups. Some of the empirical evidence seems to underline the view that parties and electoral competition between them do not exert much influence on, for instance, the dynamics of social welfare expenditures.[62] The implications of these findings are not as straightforward as they may seem, however. Significant differences can be found when one analyzes *how and with what effect* these expenditures are made.[63] Some political scientists evaluating the fields of social welfare, income distribution, and economics show that party control of government is a significant factor.[64] This holds especially when control of the relevant ministries is taken into account. They conclude that their theory views "parties as significant, if not *the* significant actors within parliamentary democracies."[65] Others second this positive evaluation in another important respect. They show that parties largely implement policies that correspond to preelection party programs. Hence, public statements do indeed correspond to intentions of which policies to implement.[66] These scholars state that "[t]he strong congruence that we found between election programs and later policy mean[s] that the policy process is more democratic and probably more orderly than many critics have claimed—and this is so because of the contributions of political parties."[67] The central conclusion these authors reach is that "party programs generally function according to the requirements of democratic theory."[68] These empirical findings encourage the idea that democratic systems are equipped to perform the task of epistemic conciliation of citizens' conflicting judgments about justice.

---

[62] The increase in public expenditure on public welfare seems to be determined primarily by economic variables and population growth; cf. Jackman (1972) and Wilensky (1975).

[63] Here, one can observe different levels of poverty, inequality, and social instability, which can be described as a result of liberal, corporatist, and social-democratic welfare regimes. Cf. Esping-Andersen (1990): Chap. 5 and Goodin et al. (1999).

[64] Cf. Budge and Keman (1990).

[65] Ibid., p. 189.

[66] Klingemann et al. (1994): p. 254.

[67] Klingemann et al. (1994): p. 2.

[68] Klingemann et al. (1994): p. 254.

The Adaptation of the Spatial Model

As we have seen, the theory of democracy and party competition as Downs originally presented it struggled to explain vital elements of democracy, elements which are in fact presuppositions of both the supposed benefit of democracy—responsiveness to citizens' preferences—and of stable democratic systems. These were (1) the participation of (2) sufficiently informed citizens.

As I said in the introductory paragraph of this chapter, one core motivation of the deliberative democracy movement was to reinstate civic conceptions in lieu of minimalist conceptions and elitist conceptions of democracy. I have also stated my belief that this theoretical and genuinely political motivation has gotten in the way of an appreciation of the potential of rational choice models within civic conceptions of democracy. This is an unfortunate consequence of a step in the right direction. Instead of a wholesale rejection of the general approach of the opposed position, the debate should center on the conception of the motives and interests of citizens and the aims of democratic decision-making. While the conciliatory conception of democracy is itself a civic conception with strong participatory and deliberative elements, it does appreciate the results of public choice theory and attempts to conceive them in neutral terms. As I have outlined above (see Chap. 4; The Idea of a Well-Ordered Society and an Expanded Conception of Reasonableness), citizens are reasonable when (1) their votes are determined by their sincere judgments about the justice of the public choices confronting them; (2) they give motivational primacy to the common good; (3) they actively seek to justify their judgments in terms of reasons other reasonable citizens could accept; (4) they share a commitment to treat others as equal normative authorities and regard them as equal epistemic authorities; (5) they are *meta-rational* with respect to the low-confidence disagreements they have with other reasonable citizens; and (6) they stay within the bounds of Democratic Public Reason. Hence, the fundamental assumptions of early public choice theories have to be reformed in crucial ways.

Narrow and Wide Conceptions of Self-Interest and Conceptions of Rationality Public choice approaches are often associated with a narrow conception of self-interest according to which actors try to maximize their egocentric preferences and, if they conflict conflict and given the opportunity do so, at the expense of altruistic motives. Anthony Downs adheres to this view of human nature. In a first step, however, he defines "rational" merely in terms of choosing the right, that is, economically sensible, means to chosen ends. In his conception, then, rationality is a formal relation that holds between political means and ends. Thus, whether we define these ends in terms of narrow or wide conceptions of self-interest is not determined by this conception of rationality alone. Accordingly, Downs at one point defines rational action as "action which is efficiently design[ed] to achieve the consciously selected political and economic ends of the actor."[69]

It is only in a second step that Downs specifies his conception of rationality not only in terms of this formal relation but in terms of certain substantive ends: "Throughout our model, we assume that every agent acts in accordance with this view of human nature. Thus, whenever we speak of rational behavior, we always mean rational behavior directed primarily toward selfish ends."[70] This postulate he calls *the self-interest axiom*.

Hence, at the root of giving narrowly conceived self-interest center stage in his theory of democracy is a conception of human nature which he deems more realistic and of superior explanatory power than civic conceptions. He shares this "insight" with Schumpeter and approvingly quotes him as saying:

> In observing human societies we do not as a rule find it difficult to specify, at least in a rough commonsense manner, the various ends that the societies under study struggle to attain. These ends may be said to provide the rationale or meaning of corresponding individual activities. But it does not follow that the social meaning of a type of activity will necessarily provide

---

[69] Downs (1957): p. 20. It is noteworthy that he introduces the example of a monk whose consciously chosen end is to reach a state of mystic contemplation of God to explain the economic conception of rationality at the root of the political one. Cf. Downs (1957): p. 5.
[70] Downs (1957): p. 27.

the motive power, hence the explanation of the latter. If it does not, a theory that contents itself with an analysis of the social end or need to be served cannot be accepted as an adequate account of the activities that serve it. For instance, the reason why there is such a thing as economic activity is of course that people want to eat, to clothe themselves and so on. To provide the means to satisfy those wants is the social end or meaning of production. Nevertheless we all agree that this proposition would make a most unrealistic starting point for a theory of economic activity in commercial society and that we shall do much better if we start from propositions about profits. Similarly, the social meaning or function of parliamentary activity is no doubt to turn out legislation and, in part, administrative measures. But in order to understand how democratic politics serve this social end, we must start from the competitive struggle for power and office and realize that the social function is fulfilled, as it were, incidentally—in the same sense as production is incidental to the making of profits.[71]

"This brilliant insight," says Downs, "summarizes our [Downs's] whole approach to the functioning of government."[72] Indeed, Schumpeter's influence on Downs in this regard can hardly be overstated. Downs goes so far as stating that Schumpeter's application of this reasoning to politics "forms the inspiration and foundation of our [Downs's] whole thesis."[73]

The basic idea is that the selfish behavior of a collectivity of agents can produce social benefits which were not part of their individual motivational sets.[74] In their adulation of free markets, Schumpeter and Downs were both led to conceive democracy as functioning analogously. The more "realistic" premise of utility-maximizing behavior where utility is defined in terms of narrowly conceived self-interest replaces "the classical view" of democracy which conceives citizens as *individually and collectively* pursuing the common good of society. Downs subsequently extended this logic to an analysis of the motivational grounds of the behavior of politicians, famously stating that they act "solely in order to

---

[71] Schumpeter ([1943] 2003): p. 282; quoted in Downs (1957): p. 29.
[72] Downs (1957): p. 29.
[73] Downs (1957): p. 29, *fn* 11.
[74] This idea, of course, goes back to Adam Smith's invisible hand and it is little wonder that Downs explicitly traces it back to his *The Wealth of Nations*; cf. Downs (1957): p. 28.

attain the *income, prestige,* and *power* which comes from being in office"[75] and for "love of conflict, i.e., the thrill of the game."[76] From this follows "the fundamental hypothesis of our [Downs's] model: parties formulate policies in order to win elections, rather than win elections to formulate policies."[77]

It was only over 30 years after the publication of *An Economic Theory of Democracy* that Downs eventually admitted that it neglected the necessary role of social values for stable democratic practices and introduced the following axiom:

> *Normal adult citizens can both recognize and pursue their own interests and the interests of society as a whole with reasonable accuracy and effectiveness, if they have access to sufficient, reliable, and relevant information.*[78]

However, he continued to maintain that

> *individuals in all societies tend—when they can—to give higher priority to serving their own interests, and the interests of those dearest to them, than the interests of others not so linked to themselves—even at the cost of sacrificing or exploiting others to benefit themselves.*[79]

This emphasis of narrow self-interest as the motivational basis of citizens is the primary reason why philosophers drawn to more civic conceptions have rejected the analytical tools provided by rational choice approaches. Representative of a broader trend, some assert that "methodological individualism nurtures the normative belief that politics should attend and respond to the needs, wants, and preferences of individuals."[80] The methodological individualism of rational choice approaches, it is claimed, stands in opposition to the idea that democracy and political life in general can have a transformative effect on citizens and ought to aim at the

---

[75] Downs (1957): p. 28.
[76] Downs (1957): p. 30.
[77] Downs (1957): p. 28.
[78] Downs (1991): p. 148.
[79] Downs (1991): p. 149.
[80] Petracca (1991): p. 178.

6 Representative Democracy and the Role of Political Parties

pursuit of wisdom, knowledge, virtue, and justice.[81] This claim, however, is evidence of a drastic misunderstanding of rational choice approaches. While it is quite true that their early proponents, among them Schumpeter and Downs, rejected such ideas, their opposition was not an inherent feature of their approaches as such. Instead, it grew out of a conviction that some of the motivational premises, or conceptions of human nature are untenable.[82] Agreeing with Hume in that "in contriving every system of government [...], every man ought to be supposed a knave, and to have no other end, in all his actions, than private interest,"[83] they subsequently place their approaches in a different tradition of political thought, one where "realism" beats "idealism."

As we have seen, however, there are two layers to Downs's conception of rationality. First, he focuses on the formal relation between means and ends, and only secondly does he add a substantive conception of rational ends. Importantly, these two layers are logically independent. In their standard work on public choice, Shepsle and Bonchek note that far from being wed to a narrow conception of self-interest, the approach allows for a wide conception of self-interest and a broader, laxer conception of human nature. They state accordingly that

> [m]odern man and woman are economic and social animals. While one cannot deny the strong influence of material, economic wants on individual preferences, additional important sources of preference include religious values, moral precepts, ideological dispositions, altruistic impulses, and a sense of common destiny with a family, clan, tribe, ethnic group, or other community.
>
> The individuals who populate our model world are assumed to have preferences derived from any and all of these various sources. [...]
>
> We shall occasionally say that people who act in accord with their preferences are *self-interested*. As already noted, this does not require us to assume that people are selfish in the ordinary sense of that word. [...] We assume

---

[81] Ibid.
[82] Consider also this quote from Mancur Olson: "Indeed, unless the number of individuals in a group is quite small, or unless there is coercion or some other special device to make individuals act in their common interest, *rational self-interested individuals will not act to achieve their common or group interests*" (Olsen [1965] 2002: p. 2; emphasis in the original).
[83] Hume (1994): p. 24.

that people pursue the things they regard as important, which may include empathy for family, friends, whales, trees, or random strangers.[84]

This definition of self-interest is so wide that it is almost empty. Hence, one could claim that something is lost that made the original approach so attractive, namely the idea that with very few, rather austere assumptions about the motivational basis of individual behavior we can construe an encompassing theory of politics. On the other hand, something is gained by dropping these limiting assumptions and with them the aim to incorporate into a theory of politics an explanation of *why* people vote and other political actors act the way they do.[85] To put it bluntly, we do not even want to know. What we do want to know is how democratic politics works in *even more* abstract terms. And on this question, the model continues to deliver.

The Motivation of Voters Without leaving the framework of Public Choice theory, we can thus replace the narrow conception of self-interest employed in the original model with a wide conception that includes other-regarding motives. The conciliatory conception, just like many other civic conceptions, regards the role of citizen and voter as analogous to holding a public office, a role which places constraints on the behavior of those executing it. It conceives voters as public good–oriented and as promoting their conception of justice in the public realm. Furthermore, the argument for democracy I develop ultimately grounds the right to participate as an equal in collective decision-making on the commitment of reasonable citizens to regard and treat other reasonable citizens as equal epistemic and equal normative authorities (see Chaps. 2 and 3). The equal standing as citizen and the equal weight of the vote are thus inherently bound up with public good–oriented reasoning.[86] However, it is not only from this epistemic-normative perspective that this conception of voting

---

[84] Shepsle and Bonchek (1997): p. 16f.
[85] The original model did not provide an explanation for why people vote their narrow self-interest either. Instead, it was assumed to be self-evidently true.
[86] Recall the definition of equal epistemic authorities as prima facie equally reliable judges of the rightness of political decisions according to a procedure-independent criterion of rightness (reliable in an epistemic sense).

is more adequate. It also receives empirical support.[87] Hence, whatever the merit of a "realistic" conception of democracy may be, the assumption of narrowly self-interested behavior does not seem to be any more self-evident and realistic than the proposed alternative.

Vote-Winning versus Policy-Seeking Parties In order to turn the spatial model of party competition into a fertile ground for a conception of conciliatory democracy, we not only need to adopt a wide conception of the self-interest of voters but an adequate conception of the motivation of party elites and their relationship with the party base and the electorate at large. As stated, Downs assumed that parties are steered by party elites who have no other aim than to win a seat in government. In other words, they are office-seeking. This he takes to follow from his self-interest axiom. In order to obtain their goal and make the median voter's preference congruent with the party platform, they manipulate the party platform (and in the Schumpeterian conception voter preferences as well). From the perspective of conciliatory democracy and other civic conceptions, two things are wrong with this picture. The first is that the motivation of party elites ought to be an interest to advance their preferred conception of justice rather than the aim of winning office. The second is that the model assumes party competition to be driven by elites engaging in a top-down manipulation of party platforms. I will return to this second point in the next section and focus on the first one for now.

The "neutralization" of self-interest in an analysis of public choice allows us to move beyond the interest elites might have in power, prestige, and income. Just as we can conceive voters as motivated by an interest in advancing their conception of the common good, we can conceive politicians as motivated in the same way. Indeed, political scientists have adopted a broader conception of the motives of party elites not only because of these idealizing tendencies in certain democratic theories but also because of the empirical finding that party elites are in fact often

---

[87] See, for example, Kramer (1983) and Rohrschneider (1988).

motivated by more idealist aims than material rewards for themselves.[88] They now conceive political parties and party elites as *also* driven by an aim to implement certain policies.[89] These attempts to disambiguate the motivations of political parties resulted in ideal types of policy-seeking, vote-seeking, and office-seeking parties, which were defined thus:

> A policy-seeking party is one which gives primary emphasis to pursuit of policy goals, a vote-seeking party is one whose principal aim is to maximize votes and win elections, while an office-seeking party is primarily interested in securing the benefits of office—getting its leaders into government, enjoying access to patronage, etc.—even if this means sharing power with others or pursuing strategies which fail to maximize its share of the vote.[90]

As we can see from Table 6.1, policy-seeking parties are associated with high levels of participation and inclusion of party members in the formulation of policy goals and an ongoing debate between them that is intense, protracted, and issue-focused. And the author does not fail to note that "[t]he policy-seeking party corresponds to a civics book image of what many people think that parties should be like in a liberal democracy. Policy-seeking parties are issue-oriented and, quite simply, give priority to their policies."[91]

Interestingly and crucially for our purposes, in many important respects the conception of parties as policy-seeking does not fundamentally alter the results of the predictions of the original model of party competition.[92] Policy-seeking parties will have an incentive to win votes just as well; for only when they win an election will they have the opportunity to implement their preferred policy. And in order to win votes, they have to expose themselves to the same centripetal dynamics of party competition

---

[88] Among the first to do so were Wittman (1973, 1983) and Calvert (1985).
[89] Some cite the consistent records of parties in government as evidence for the prevalence of policy-seeking parties. See, for example, Budge and Keman (1990): p. 144.
[90] Wolinetz (2002): p. 149f.
[91] Wolinetz (2002): p. 150.
[92] Variations in the motivation of candidates and voters do affect the Downsian model and resulting equilibria. The emphasis here is on "fundamentally." The general conciliatory implication of the model is left intact by the various ways of modeling these motivations. For an overview, see Duggan (2006).

6 Representative Democracy and the Role of Political Parties

Table 6.1 Policy-, vote-, and office-seeking parties

Possible indicators	Parties		
	Policy-seeking	Vote-seeking	Office-seeking
Internal policy debate % of time spent at party meetings	High	Low	Low
Character of debate	Intense, protracted, issue-focused	Pro forma, diffuse, unfocused	Pro forma, diffuse, unfocused
Extent and level of involvement	Extensive; most levels of party involved	Confined to leadership or policy committee; compartmentalized	Confined to leadership or policy committee; compartmentalized
Consistency of policy positions assumed	High	Medium to low, prone to change depending on leader's directions, electoral opportunity structure	Medium to low
Election campaigns			
Prominence of policy	High	Varies	Low
Determination of strategy	Follows from policies	Policies developed to fit strategy, maximize votes	Varies, preference for low-risk strategies
Use of new electoral techniques	Low to medium	High	Low to medium
Infrastructure to support policies (e.g., research bureaus, think-tanks, affiliated organizations)	Present	Either minimal or at disposal of leaders, office-holders	Either minimal or at disposal of leaders, office-holders

Source: Wolinetz (2002): p. 155

already analyzed. A move closer to the preference of the median might, of course, incurs the cost of not being able to implement the policies which the party prefers the most. However, an electoral victory based on a more centrist position enables them to implement policies which are closer to their ideal point than those who would be adopted by a party that is closer to but on the opposite side of the median. Hence, the policy-seeking assumption does not in any fundamental way alter the predictions of the spatial model of party competition.[93] We can thus conclude that the model does allow for an idealized conception of the motivations of political parties. Parties can indeed be seen, as one classic definition has it, as "alliances in conflicts over policies and value commitments within the larger body politic."[94]

Elite Manipulation and Exogenous versus Endogenous Preferences The second point regarding the party elites' top-down manipulation of party platforms has already been addressed in passing with the substitution of office-seeking with policy-seeking parties in the model. The image of office-seeking parties is firmly associated with elitist conceptions of democracy. Party leaders will be the only ones to come into office in case of an electoral victory. The classic examples are of course the elitist theories of Schumpeter and Downs. However, this point also touches on a related issue on which both took opposite stands. While Downs took the preferences of voters as given, that is, as exogenous to the political process, Schumpeter and later critics of Downs (who nevertheless adhere to the elitist picture) argued that party elites manipulate not only their party's platform but also voter preferences. They do so to such a degree that talk of voters' preferences as important variables in democratic decision-making is rendered almost empty. Schumpeter "emphasizes the periodic submission of elites to an otherwise unspecified voter

---

[93] In some models, such as Whitman's, it does alter the predictions slightly as policy-seeking parties might be less inclined to give up their ideological commitments in order to maximize votes. See also Kollman et al. (1992), whose simulations allow candidates to give weight to their own ideologies when choosing positions, and to have imperfect information on voters' preferences and nevertheless predict convergence on centralist positions.
[94] Lipset (1967): p. 117.

judgment."[95] Downs, on the other hand, "stresses the capacity of elites to respond readily and sympathetically to demands. Thus, government 'approved by' the people (Schumpeter) is not the same thing as government 'responsive to' the people (Downs)."[96]

A civic conception of democracy, however, has to reject both the arbitrary changes in party platforms and the manipulation of voter preferences. In a "citizens' democracy," this is the wrong picture of the role of political parties. Political parties are instruments of citizens to further their political aims, which are primarily defined in terms of the motivation to inject their conception of justice into the political process. Such policy-seeking parties do not endorse party programs because a detached party elite defines them with the sole aim of winning a majority of the vote. Party programs emerge out of a participatory, deliberative, and inclusive process. Hence, a civic conception of democracy replaces the elitist top-down picture with a bottom-up conception of political parties and party programs.

Voters' preferences are then conceived as endogenous in the sense that they are shaped and molded by the participatory practices of intra-party deliberation.[97] Importantly, however, this effect of the political process on their preferences is benign. It does not undermine the idea that party competition serves to make their *authentic* preferences efficacious in the political arena. The endogenous genesis of preferences only becomes malign when it is the result of elite manipulation, which has a distorting effect on voters' preferences so that the notion of their *authentic* preferences loses its meaning. Hence, the important question is not whether preferences are exogenous or endogenous to the political process but whether the political process has a *manipulative* effect on the formation of preferences. These points, however, are logically independent. The alteration of preferences does not necessarily obliterate the idea that party platforms are a medium for the authentic preferences of citizens. If

---

[95] Bartolini (2002): p. 88.
[96] Ibid.
[97] Along with the general negligence of the role of political parties in deliberative conceptions of democracy, intra-party deliberation has received almost no scholarly attention. For an exception to the rule, see Wolkenstein (2016).

we replace the idea of top-down manipulation inherent in Schumpeter's elitist conception of democracy with the idea of a bottom-up creation of party platforms or a deliberative cycle between party elites and the party base in a conception of civic democracy, we bypass the issue of exogenous versus endogenous preferences.

The Nature of Rationality Another objection sometimes voiced against theories of rational choice concerns the conception of practical rationality at work in such approaches. Public choice theory is a variant of rational choice theory and as such it does, of course, employ a conception of practical rationality. As we have seen, public choice theorists usually think of practical rationality as instrumental rationality. This is confirmed once again by Shepsle and Bonchek (1997) who point out that "[r]ationality is associated with both this capacity to order [preferences] *and* an aptitude to choose from the top of the order."[98] They go on to state that

> [t]he very existence of a "top" to a preference ordering, and individuals with sufficient sense to choose it if given half the chance, is the reason that most of us working in this tradition think of rationality as consisting of *maximizing* behavior. Individuals in social situations are thought to be seeking some goal, pursuing some objective, aiming to do the best they can according to their own lights.[99]

In the description of public choice theorists, then, rationality appears as a property of individuals who maximize their utility. While it would be ludicrous to deny that the idea of instrumental rationality associated with such maximizing behavior is part and parcel of the concept of practical rationality, the adoption of the model of rational choice need not entail the claim that the instrumental conception of practical rationality is exhaustive of the concept.[100] Thus, the adoption of the rational choice

---

[98] Shepsle and Bonchek (1997): p. 30; emphasis in the original.
[99] Shepsle and Bonchek (1997): p. 31f.
[100] Habermas's theory of communicative action, for instance, does not reject the idea of instrumental rationality. It supplements the idea with a conception of communicative rationality (or "reason") and aims to defend its practical significance precisely against an understanding of practical rationality as exhausted by the instrumental conception. It is this understanding which he perceives as misguided and indeed as morally and politically pernicious. His theory is an example, then, that

model does not per se entail a claim about the nature of the interests of rational agents, about the values they ought to pursue, or about the substantive aims of collective decision-making procedures.

Issue-Specific and Comprehensive Epistemic Conciliation The epistemic argument for democracy makes the case that democratic institutions have an inbuilt tendency to produce conciliatory government policies. I have presented the MVT, which concerns committee decision-making and a spatial model of party competition built on top of it. In the case of committee decision-making on a single, insular issue, the MVT suggests that the median position will win the day. The spatial theory of party competition I have discussed at some length now, on the other hand, proposes that the democratic process more broadly conceived will render the epistemic conciliation it reaches more comprehensive. This comprehensive conciliation implicates many issues and policies which are at stake in the ideological stand-off between parties. In fully functioning modern democracies, then, epistemic conciliation happens on a grand scale.[101]

This concludes my epistemic argument for democracy. I have argued that democratic institutions have a strong tendency to produce outcomes that reflect median voter positions and are thus likely to reflect conciliatory judgments of reasonable citizens. Furthermore, the adaptation of public choice approaches to the conciliatory conception reconciles the former with civic conceptions of democracy and democratic decision-making with the deliberative component of democracy. The conciliatory conception gives citizens reasons to accept democratic outcomes that are not exclusively based on normative considerations. Instead, they derive directly from their rational insight that political disagreement among

---

the instrumental conception has its place in a theory of practical rationality as long as it does not make the strong claim that other conceptions of rational action are obliterate. Cf. Habermas (1984).

[101] Recall the example I used in the previous chapter. See also the composition of the left–right dimension in Klingemann et al. (1994): p. 40. The authors include stands on economic policies, foreign policy and defense, and endorsements of "traditional morality."

equal epistemic authorities calls for epistemic conciliation and a reflective attitude of intellectual humility.

Which Democracy? The Epistemic Perspective To complete the argument for a democratic system of decision-making based on the tendency of democratic systems to produce conciliatory outcomes, I will make an attempt to disambiguate which set of democratic institutions are most likely to advance the goal of conciliating the judgments of reasonable citizens. I thus turn to the question of which set of democratic institutions the conciliatory conceptions recommends. So far, I have mainly discussed elections, political parties, and majoritarian decision-making in the legislative body, which I have noted often requires coalition-building between parties.

The interaction between the various elements of the democratic process, that is, elections, choices offered by disparate party programs, and coalition formation is important for a simple reason. At each stage we are confronted with a potentially inaccurate transcription of voters' preferences, including of course the median preference, to the next stage. This is first because no electoral system, including all of the various electoral rules aiming at PR, is capable of producing an absolutely accurate representation of the spectrum of preferences present in society. And second, it is because the next element—the choices party programs offer to voters—does not converge on the median voter preference but pulls away from it (toward the party median). Hence, the median party in parliament is bound to be unrepresentative of the median preference of the general population. Finally, it is important because the necessity to form a winning coalition with at least one other party can drive the median party in parliament even further away from the median of the electorate. However, at the same time these potentially reinforcing malign effects of the mechanics of political representation offer the hope that things go the opposite way. Instead of being reinforcing, the biases and distorting effects of each stage can cancel each other out (Fig. 6.6).

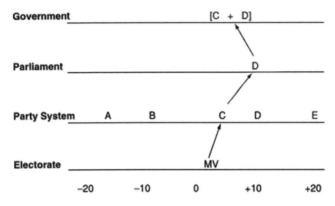

Fig. 6.6 Hypothetical conditions at four stages on the representational process used to illustrate how distortions and biases are evaluated. Conditions: (1) the median voter, MV, is located at +3; (2) Party C is located at +5 and is the party closest to the median voter; (3) Party D, at +10, becomes the parliamentary median through mistranslation from the electoral system; (4) Party C and Party D form the government, and their weighted mean position is +8
Source: McDonald and Budge (2005): p. 123

The evidence seems to support this optimistic reading.[102] However, the question remains whether a specific set of institutions can help us to keep the distortions at a minimum. The stage I want to focus on is the electoral stage. This focus has two reasons. First, it determines how accurately the relative weight of votes is represented in the legislature. Second, it is strongly linked to the number of political parties which enter into the electoral competition and thus to the choices voters can effectively make.

For instance, ought we to opt for SMD electoral systems which can effectively engender rule by a plurality of citizens and are most likely to foster two-party competition? Or ought we to push for PR systems much more likely to result in multiparty competition with a subsequent need for coalition-building? When we compare SMD systems with PR systems in each electoral cycle, the evidence suggests that the latter are superior in accommodating median voter preferences.[103] If we broaden the time horizon, however, we see that SMD systems—without the need for

---

[102] Cf. McDonald and Budge (2005).
[103] Cf. Powell (2006).

coalition-building between parties—are also bound to produce conciliatory effects. The difference is that these effects only become recognizable over time. This is largely owed to the changes in government between two parties both of which are on average farther away from the median than coalition governments in PR systems but which pull government policy in opposite directions.[104] In sum, however, McDonald and Budge note that "PR systems are likely to get it more nearly right in the first place, and to the extent they do not, there is more compensation for missteps in the process."[105] Hence, PR systems better approximate the ideal of epistemic conciliation.

The presentation of the epistemic argument for democracy might lead some to conclude that the conciliatory conception is in essence a conservative, status quo–oriented conception of democracy. This assessment might derive from the focus I have laid on the "traditional" institutions of democracy, elections, and multiparty competition. This focus, of course, has not been coincidental. I do indeed believe that deliberative conceptions—with all the praise they deserve—should move closer to an appreciation of these traditional institutions. However, this is not to deny the legitimacy of their criticism of elitist and minimalist conceptions of democracy with their *exclusive* focus on electoral competition between elites. The aim should rather be to reconcile the foci of democratic theory on the traditional and progressive elements of democracies. In the preceding chapters, I endorsed the emphasis on public deliberation. It should also be remembered that it is only from the conclusions I drew from my discussion of the equal epistemic authority of citizens thus engaged that the epistemic argument in support of the (traditional) democratic institutions of elections and multiparty competition got off the ground (see Chap. 3; The Practice-Based Argument). Far from leaving either side behind on opposite riverbanks of democratic theory, the conciliatory conception of democracy is the bridge that unites them.

---

[104] Cf. McDonald et al. (1999).
[105] McDonald and Budge (2005): p. 135.

References

Ansolabehere, S., de Figuereido, J., & Snyder, J. M., Jr. (2000). Valence Politics. *Public Choice, 103*, 327–336.

Ansolabehere, S., Snyder, J. M., & Stewart, C., III. (2001). Candidate Positions in US House Elections. *American Journal of Political Science, 45*, 136–159.

Bartolini, S. (2002). Electoral and Party Competition: Analytical Dimensions and Empirical Problems. In R. Gunther, J. Ramón-Montero, & J. J. Linz (Eds.), *Political Parties Old Concepts and New Challenges* (pp. 84–113). Oxford: Oxford University Press.

Benhabib, S. (1996). Toward a Deliberative Model of Legitimacy. In S. Benhabib (Ed.), *Democracy and Difference. Contesting the Boundaries of the Political*. Princeton, NJ: Princeton University Press.

Besley, T., & Coate, S. (1997). An Economic Model of Representative Democracy. *Quarterly Journal of Economics, 112*, 85–114.

Biezen, I., & Saward, M. (2008). Democratic Theorists and Party Scholars: Why They Don't Talk to Each Other, and Why They Should. *Perspectives on Politics, 6*, 21–35.

Bohman, J. (1998). Survey Article: The Coming of Age of Deliberative Democracy. *The Journal of Philosophy, 6*(3), 400–425.

Brady, H., & Sniderman, P. (1985). Attitude Attribution: a Group Basis for Political Reasoning. *American Political Science Review, 79*, 1061–1978.

Budge, I. (2006). Identifying dimensions and locating parties: Methodological and conceptual problems. In R. S. Katz & W. Crotty (Eds.), *Handbook of Party Politics* (pp. 422–435). London: Sage.

Budge, I., & Keman, H. E. (1990). *Parties and Democracy: Coalition Formation and Government Functioning in 22 Democracies*. Oxford: Oxford University Press.

Burke, E. (1770). Thoughts on the Causes of the Present Discontents. In L. I. Bredvorld & R. G. Ross (Eds.), *The Philosophy of Edmund Burke*. Ann Arbour, MI: University of Michigan Press.

Calvert, R. L. (1985). Robustness of the Multidimensional Voting Model: Candidate Motivations, Uncertainty, and Convergence. *American Journal of Political Science, 29*, 69–95.

Clark, W. R., Gloder, M., & Golder, S. (2008). *Principles of Comparative Politics*. Thousand Oaks, CA: CQ Press.

Coate, S., & Conlin, M. (2004). A Group Rule: Utilitarian Approach to Voter Turnout: Theory and Evidence. *The American Economic Review, 94*(5), 1476–1504.

Downs, A. (1957). *An Economic Theory of Democracy.* New York: Harper and Row.

Downs, A. (1991). Social Values and Democracy. In K. R. Monroe (Ed.), *The Economic Approach to Politics. A Critical Reassessment of the Theory of Rational Action.* New York: HarperCollins.

Duggan, J. (2006). Candidate Objectives and Electoral Equilibrium. In R. E. Goodin (Ed.), *The Oxford Handbook of Political Science* (pp. 64–84). Oxford: Oxford University Press.

Duverger, M. (1954). *Political Parties: Their Organization and Activities in a Modern State* (B. North & R. North, Trans.). New York: John Wiley.

Ebeling, M. (2016). Epistemic Political Egalitarianism, Political Parties, and Conciliatory Democracy. *Political Theory, 44*(5), 629–656.

Esping-Andersen, G. (1990). *The Three Worlds of Welfare Capitalism.* Princeton, NJ: Princeton University Press.

Ferejohn, J. A., & Fiorina, M. P. (1974). The Paradox of Not Voting: A Decision Theoretic Analysis. *The American Political Science Review, 68,* 525–536.

Fiorina, M. (1980). The Decline of Collective Responsibility in American Politics. *Daedalus, 109*(Summer), 25–45.

Gallagher, M., Laver, M., & Mair, P. (2005). *Representative Government in Modern Europe.* New York: Open University Press.

Goodin, R. E., Headey, B., Muffels, R., & Dirven, H.-J. (1999). *The Real Worlds of Welfare Capitalism.* Cambridge: Cambridge University Press.

Grofman, B. (2004a). Black's Single-Peakedness Condition. In C. K. Rowley & F. Schneider (Eds.), *The Encyclopedia of Public Choice* (Vol. 2, pp. 43–45). New York: Kluwer.

Grofman, B. (2004b). Reflections on Public Choice. *Public Choice, 118*(1/2), 31–51.

Gunther, R., Ramón-Montero, J., & Linz, J. J. (2002). Introduction. In R. Gunther, J. Ramón-Montero, & J. J. Linz (Eds.), *Political Parties: Old Concepts and New Challenges* (pp. 1–35). Oxford: Oxford University Press.

Habermas, J. (1984). *A Theory of Communicative Action* (Vol. I–II, T. McCarthy, Trans.). Boston, MA: Beacon Press. This work originally appeared in German under the title *Theorie des Kommunikativen Handelns, Bd. I-II,* Suhrkamp Verlag, Frankfurt a.M., Germany, 1981.

Hamilton, A., Madison, J., & Jay, J. (2003). The Federalist. In T. Ball (Ed.), *Hamilton, Madison and Jay: The Federalist with Letters of "Brutus"* (pp. 1–433). Cambridge: Cambridge University Press.

Hotelling, H. (1929). Stability in Competition. *Economic Journal, 39*, 41–57.
Hume, D. (1994). Political Essays. In K. Haaknossen (Ed.), *Hume: Political Essays*. Cambridge: Cambridge University Press.
Jackman, R. (1972). *Politics and Social Equality*. New York: Wiley.
Key, V. O. (1966). *The Responsible Electorate: Rationality in Presidential Voting, 1936–1960*. Cambridge, MA: Belknap Press.
Klingemann, H.-D., Hofferbert, R. I., & Budge, I. (1994). *Parties, Policies, and Democracy*. Boulder, CO: Westview Press.
Kollman, K., Miller, J. H., & Page, S. E. (1992). Adaptive Parties and Spatial Elections. *American Political Science Review, 86*(4), 929–937.
Kramer, G. H. (1983). The Ecological Fallacy Revisited: Aggregate- versus Individual-level Findings on Economics and Elections, and Sociotropic Voting. *American Political Science Review, 77*, 92–111.
Laver, M., & Schofield, N. (1990). *Multiparty Government: The Politics of Coalition in Europe*. Oxford: Oxford University Press.
Lipset, S. M. (1967). *Consensus and Conflict: Essays in Political Sociology*. Brunswick, NJ: Transaction.
Mansbridge, J., Bohman, J., Chambers, S., Christiano, T., Fung, A., Parkinson, J., Thompson, D. F., & Warren, M. E. (2012). A Systemic Approach to Deliberative Democracy. In J. Mansbridge & J. Parkinson (Eds.), *Deliberative Systems* (pp. 1–26). Cambridge: Cambridge University Press.
McDonald, M.D., Budge, I., Hofferbert, R.I. (1999). Party mandate theory and time series analysis: A theoretical and methodological response. *Electoral Studies, 18*, 587–596.
McDonald, M. D., & Budge, I. (2005). *Elections, Parties, Democracy: Conferring the Median Mandate*. Oxford: Oxford University Press.
McKelvey, R., & Ordeshook, P. (1985). Sequential Elections with Limited Information. *American Journal of Political Science, 29*, 480–512.
McKelvey, R., & Ordeshook, P. (1986). Information, Electoral Equilibria, and the Democratic Ideal. *Journal of Politics, 48*, 909–937.
Michels, R. (1968). *Political Parties: A Sociological Study of the Oligarchical Tendencies of Modern Democracy*. New York: Free Press.
Muirhead, R. (2006). A Defence of Party Spirit. *Perspectives on Politics, 4*, 713–727.
Muirhead, R. (2010). Can Deliberative Democracy Be Partisan? *Critical Review, 22*, 129–157.
Niemeyer, S. (2011). The Emancipatory Effect of Deliberation: Empirical Lessons from Mini-Publics. *Politics & Society, 39*, 103–140.

Olsen, M. ([1965] 2002). *The Logic of Collective Action. Public Goods and the Theory of Groups*. Cambridge, MA: Harvard University Press.

Ostrogorski, M. (1991). In S. M. Lipset (Ed.), *Democracy and the Organization of Political Parties*. New Brunswick, NJ: Transaction.

Page, B., & Shapiro, R. (1992). *The Rational Public*. Chicago: University of Chicago Press.

Palfrey, T. R. (1984). Spatial equilibrium with Entry. *Review of Economic Studies, 51*, 139–156.

Petracca, M. P. (1991). The Rational Actor Approach to Politics: Science, Self-Interest, and Normative Democratic Theory. In K. R. Monroe (Ed.), *The Economic Approach to Politics. A Critical Reassessment of the Theory of Rational Action* (pp. 171–204). New York: HarperCollins.

Powell, G. B. (2006). Election Laws and Representative Government. *British Journal of Political Science, 36*, 291–315.

Rohrschneider, R. (1988). Citizens' Attitudes toward Environmental Issues: Selfish or Selfless? *Comparative Political Studies, 21*(3), 347–367.

Rosenblum, N. L. (2008). *On the Side of Angels: An Appreciation of Parties and Partisanship*. Princeton, NJ: Princeton University Press.

Schattschneider, E. E. (1942). *Party Government*. New York: Holt, Rinehart & Winston.

Schumpeter, J. A. ([1943] 2003). *Capitalism, Socialism, and Democracy*. London: Routledge.

Shepsle, K. A., & Bonchek, M. S. (1997). *Analyzing Politics: Rationality, Behavior and Institutions*. New York: W.W. Norton.

von Beyme, K. (1985). *Political Parties in Western Democracies*. New York: St. Martin's Press.

von Beyme, K. (1993). *Die politische Klasse im Parteienstaat*. Frankfurt a.M.: Suhrkamp Verlag.

Ware, A. (1996). *Political Parties and Party Systems*. Oxford: Oxford University Press.

Weber, M. (1978). In G. Roth & K. Wittich (Ed.), *Economy and Society*. Berkeley, CA: University of California Press.

Weinstock, D. (2015). Integrating Intermediate Goods to Theories of Distributive Justice: The Importance of Platforms. *Res Publica, 21*, 171–183.

White, J., & Ypi, L. (2010). Rethinking the Modern Prince: Partisanship and the Democratic Ethos. *Political Studies, 58*, 809–828.

Wilensky, H. L. (1975). *The Welfare State and Equality*. Berkeley, CA: University of California Press.

Wittman, D. (1973). Parties as Utility Maximizers. *American Political Science Review, 67,* 490–498.
Wittman, D. (1983). Candidate Motivation: a Synthesis of Alternative Theories. *American Political Science Review, 77,* 142–157.
Wittman, D. (2005). Valence Characteristics, Costly Policy And The Median-crossing Property: a Diagrammatic Exposition. *Public Choice, 124,* 365–382.
Wolinetz, S. B. (2002). Beyond the Catch-All Party: Approaches to the Study of Parties and Party Organization in Contemporary Democracies. In R. Gunther, J. Ramón-Montero, & J. J. Linz (Eds.), *Political Parties. Old Concepts and New Challenges* (pp. 136–166). Oxford: Oxford University Press.
Wolkenstein, F. (2016). A Deliberative Model of Intra-Party Democracy. *Journal of Political Philosophy, 24*(3), 297–320.

7

Connecting the Dots

In the course of this book, we have covered a lot of ground. I started with an appraisal of Rousseau's insight that the political judgments of reasonable citizens have epistemic significance as equally reliable indicators of the general will. I also concurred with him in that democratic decision procedures have both a normative and an epistemic dimension. Furthermore, I reconstructed his doctrine of the general will as a conception of public reason grounded in the fundamental, shared interests of citizens, thus providing a shared basis of justification. His aim, I maintained, was to publicly justify the exercise of political power in accordance with the general will. The exercise of political power is legitimate, according to Rousseau, if and only if citizens as equal epistemic authorities and equal normative authorities exercise their sovereignty and express in the form of law their conception of the common good. These were the Rousseauian starting points of my exploration of the normative and epistemic significance of political disagreement.

A central aspect of his ideas which I rejected, however, is the claim that political judgments cease to possess epistemic significance when disagreement is widespread. According to Rousseau, the existence of widespread disagreement is evidence that the state is in decline and that the citizens' commitment to the common good is weakened. At least in societies as we know them, this assumption has no reasonable foundation.

I then introduced the ideal of deliberative democracy, which I presented as continuous with the Rousseauian idea that the exercise of political power is legitimate only when it aims at justice and when this aiming-at-justice is intelligible to the shared reason of citizens. The ideal of deliberative democracy extends this thought and states that this conception of legitimacy requires the actual deliberation of citizens. Legitimacy, in other words, presupposes not only public justifiability but actual public justification. If and only if citizens publicly invoke reasons to justify their intended exercise of political power which other reasonable citizens could reasonably accept can it enjoy legitimacy. I explored this normative dimension of deliberative democracy, and argued that what I called the deliberative standard of legitimacy (DSL) cannot be deliberative all the way down. When the moment of decision arrives, citizens, just as philosophers, have to turn to deliberation-independent criteria of legitimacy in order to justify the decision procedure they employ to overcome their deliberative disagreements. In other words, they have to play the role of the Rousseauian lawgiver. The question of which decision procedure the fundamental normative criterion of reasonable acceptability prescribes led me to invoke epistemic considerations. A reasonably acceptable decision procedure has to be fair and sensitive to the post-deliberative judgments of citizens. Having come this far, we saw that a variety of decision procedures satisfies this demand. This, I maintained, is a disappointment for anyone who expects a conception of democracy to tell the whole story of democracy, the part about deliberation and the part about decision procedures. A promising way to overcome this impasse, I then ventured, is to make a bestness-tracking claim in support of specific decision procedures: some procedures might be better than others at tracking the most reasonable among the set of reasonable options which emerge from deliberative processes. In the course of the discussion, however, we have seen that deliberative democrats have struggled to offer a reasonably acceptable argument in support of a bestness-tracking claim.

In an additional step, I defended the commitment to regard other reasonable citizens as equal epistemic authorities, that is, as prima facie equally reliable judges of the rightness of political decisions according to a procedure-independent criterion of rightness. I offered four arguments against moral elitism, the thesis that there are discernible differences in the reliability of the judgments of the reasonable citizens of a well-ordered society which figure in political decision-making. Synthesizing these arguments in a fifth argument, the debate room argument, has led to a further insight: even in ideal circumstances, we should expect the outcome of decentered deliberation about sufficiently complex issues to be widespread disagreement. Importantly, this disagreement need not be irrational, that is, the product of cognitive error, or unreasonable, that is, the product of insincere reasoning.

The question of how to react to such rational and reasonable disagreement about justice between equal epistemic authorities has thus become the center of attention. I explored various positions in the epistemological debate about "peer disagreement." In my discussion, the spotlight was on the *Equal Weight View* and a principle termed *Independence*. The Equal Weight View argues that peers ought to give equal weight to their judgments and ought to conciliate them in cases of disagreement. Independence states that the downgrading of the epistemic status of an opponent in a disagreement is only permissible when the reasons for doing so are independent from the reasoning that figures in the disagreement. I defended the Equal Weight View and Independence against a number of challenges when applied to insular disagreements in a given domain. However, problems emerged when I explored their entailments in cases of numerous disagreements. A strong reading of Independence has the untenable consequence of locking in the epistemic status of other epistemic agents. Working my way out of this predicament, I introduced the distinction between *local* and *global* downgrading. I then argued that the drivers of a permissible global up- and downgrading dynamic are high-confidence dis/agreements. This conclusion led me to propose a dynamic model of epistemic peerhood. Based on this model, I eventually presented an epistemic conception of public reason, which I called *Democratic Public Reason* as the shared epistemic framework of reasonable citizens.

The Epistemic Authority of Democracy Within this epistemic framework, I then argued, epistemic conciliation of conflicting judgments is the rational reaction to political disagreement. The epistemic component of an argument for democracy builds on the claim that modern democracies have a unique tendency to produce outcomes which correspond to conciliatory judgments. Importantly, the claim is not that this correspondence is always perfect. It is the more modest claim that of all available reasonably acceptable methods of decision-making in large societies, they are the most likely to get it right. Furthermore, because in large societies citizens cannot know what the conciliatory judgment would be without consulting the procedure, their best bet to act on conciliatory judgments is to accept the outcomes of democratic decision-making. In other words, it is *rational* to accept the outcomes of democratic procedures. Thus, in addition to its moral authority, democracy has *epistemic authority* over citizens.

This epistemic authority arises from the epistemic significance of political disagreement. The fact that political disagreement exists between reasonable citizens (who regard each other as equal epistemic authorities) is evidence which undermines the justificatory relation between their first-order evidence and their original belief about the merits of the proposal at stake in democratic decision-making. The awareness of this second-order evidence and its epistemic significance gives citizens an *independent reason*, that is, a reason that is independent from the belief-forming process which led to their disagreement, to accept conciliatory outcomes as epistemically authoritative. Because this relation holds, the epistemic authority of democracy is reasonably acceptable to all reasonable citizens.

The Ambitiousness of Conciliatory Democracy and Weak Deference This result immediately leads to the question of how strong this authority is. Should citizens generally and always defer to the outcomes of the bestness-tracking procedures we have specified? The answer is "yes and no." We do not want a theory to make the implausibly strong claim that citizens ought to regard outcomes as true or correct or the most reasonable without any qualifications to the claim. A theory which would make such a claim would deny that it can be rational for citizens to revise their decisions. It would thus fly in the face of reality—not simply because of the fact that democracies often revise decisions, but because it is an epistemic virtue that they do. Quite simply, citizens often have reasons to revise a decision which trump whatever (epistemic) reasons the procedure might have given them for accepting it earlier. Hence, the deference claim needs to be modified in two respects. The claim can only be that the procedure gives citizens a reason to accept outcomes as *the most rational course of action*, not as true or the most reasonable of all things considered, and to do so only *temporarily*. This is exactly what the conciliatory conception does. It claims that the reasonable citizens of a well-ordered society can have independent reasons to accept the outcomes of democratic decision-making as *the most rational course of action given the state of deliberation when the decision is taken*. Recall that in decentered deliberation about sufficiently complex issues, one does not know the reasons other reasonable citizens have for disagreeing with one's own judgment (see Chap. 3; The Debate Room Argument). Given the fact that they regard each other as equal epistemic authorities with respect to their epistemic role in decision-making and thus assign equal weight to their judgments, it is rational for them to seek to conciliate their judgments and subsequently endorse the result as the most rational course of action. This, however, does not preclude citizens from continuously injecting their first-order judgments and the first-order evidence supporting them into an ongoing process of deliberation. If they change the judgment of a sufficient number of other citizens, the decision might be overturned and a different outcome will then appear to be the most rational to accept given the state of deliberation at *that* moment. Hence, the demand of weak deference thus conceived does *not* demand of citizens that they stop evaluating outcomes according to their own reasons or completely suppress their perspective of *how things seem to them*. What it does demand, however, is that they become self-reflectively aware of their own biases, of their lack of complete information, their lack of knowledge about the global validity status of arguments in decentered deliberation and that they consequently adopt an attitude of intellectual humility vis-à-vis their own judgments and those of other reasonable citizens.

A Room Full of Humeans Given these constraints on and distortions of their belief-forming process, the conciliatory conception of democracy furthermore demands of citizens that they step back from their emotional engagement in political debate and do not allow the emotional intensity of political debate and of political disagreement to swamp their awareness of the precarious epistemic status of many of their judgments about the justice of the social and political arrangements of their societies. Their awareness of the fact of disagreement, moreover, gives them reason to conciliate their judgments with those of citizens whom they regard as equal epistemic authorities on the issues at stake. They understand that "extremes of all kinds are to be avoided, and though no one will ever please either faction by moderate opinions, it is there we are most likely to meet with truth and certainty."[1] This is the insight that Hume brings to the philosophical analysis of political conflict. Unlike Mill, who believes that "reconciling and combing" opposing positions is the work of reasoned debate, I believe with Hume that it is more often a result of democratic procedures which conciliates judgments without, at the moment of decision-making, looking at the dependent reasons of citizens. Reasoned debate surely has the potential to help us overcome disagreement and produce consensus on some questions. However, it is most likely to do so when the question is not overly complex and the ensuing debate not "entropic" (see Chap. 3; Global Consensus and The Entropy of Reason). Once citizens of diverse backgrounds face complex issues in a decentered deliberative setting, the expectation that reasoned debate will have these reconciling effects is no longer justified (see Chap. 3; The Debate Room Argument). We thus have reason to reject Rosenblum's Proto-Millian defense of political parties and adopt a Humean picture of how multiparty competition produces outcomes with a strong tendency to track conciliatory judgments (see Chap. 6; The Darlings of Political Science, the Orphans of Political Philosophy). In this picture, furthermore, citizens can adopt an outsider's perspective and at least temporarily detach themselves from the beliefs they advocate in the political process and understand the rationality of conciliating their judgments with the conflicting judgments of other reasonable citizens. For Hume, "[p]olitical moderation depends on the capacity to adopt the standpoint of the impartial observer, if only episodically."[2] Nancy Rosenblum reconstructs Hume's view on the matter more fully, stating that, according to him,

---

[1] Hume (1994): p. 247.
[2] Rosenblum (2008): p. 140.

[i]t is possible to "persuade each that its antagonist may possibly be sometimes in the right [,] ... that neither side are ... so fully supported by reason as they endeavor to flatter themselves," and that "there are on both sides wise men who meant well to their country." This expectation is demanding. It demands a sense of fallibility and accompanying humility, for one thing (not "so fully supported by reason as they endeavor to flatter themselves"). It demands a generous estimate of the opposition's intentions, for another ("there are on both sides wise men who meant well to their country"). Hume escalates his demand even further: partisans must also "persuade each that its antagonist may possibly be sometimes in the right."[3]

Rosenblum, however, finds that "[t]he striking thing here is that Hume would impress the impartial observer's view on partisans themselves."[4] She has a hard time accepting that "Hume reflected that with all their defects, partisans might nonetheless be injected with 'a small tincture of Pyrrhonism' and hesitation;"[5] and her principal reason for rejection this proposition is that "Hume's pose is phenomenologically alien."[6]

But is it really? Given the current political climate in the USA and many other democracies around the globe, it is hard to deny the unwillingness of many to adopt an impartial stance, even if only temporarily. Yet, if this is the final word, it is a conclusion that should trouble us deeply. If citizens (1) did not find the persistence of disagreement with other citizens an epistemically unsettling fact and could *not* "persuade each that their antagonist may possibly be sometimes in the right" and (2) could not even believe that those they disagree with "meant well," democracy would be in a dire state. It would be a state of disintegration of the political community. For what else should we think of a society of citizens who can no longer have even a modicum of trust that their adversaries in political debate argue sincerely, and of a society of citizens who lack any self-reflective awareness of their own fallibility? This, I venture, should strike us as "phenomenologically alien." I thus maintain with Rousseau that reasonable citizens "should be wary of [their] own reason" (PE, 6)

---

[3] Ibid.; She quotes from: Hume (1994): p. 206f.
[4] Rosenblum (2008): p. 139.
[5] Rosenblum (2008): p. 140; She takes the quote from Whelan (1985): p. 330.
[6] Rosenblum (2008): p. 142.

and with Hume that the fact of disagreement can make citizens aware that "neither side are [...] so fully supported by reason as they endeavor to flatter themselves."[7] Thus, reasonable citizens could and should endorse the conciliatory conception of democracy.

Having reached this conclusion, I shall now use the remainder of this chapter to elucidate the status of the conciliatory conception as an ideal theory of democracy and to subsequently clarify the relation which holds between its normative and its epistemic dimension. This point also concerns the role of public deliberation in the normative and epistemic framework of conciliatory democracy.

Ideal versus Non-Ideal Theory The conciliatory conception of democracy is an ideal theory in two respects. First, it is an ideal theory because it assumes that citizens exhibit certain moral virtues. The most important among them is that they are motivated to promote what they regard as the most reasonable conception of justice in the public realm and in political decision-making. Second, it is an ideal theory because it assumes that citizens exhibit certain epistemic virtues. The most important among them is that they are meta-rational, that is, that they understand and accept the implications of the epistemology of peer disagreement and take them into account in their reaction to political disagreements with those whom they regard as equal epistemic authorities.

Hence, the ideal character of the conciliatory conception of democracy defended here ought not to be in doubt. What might throw the reader off track, however, is the considerable space and significance I grant to rational choice and game theoretical approaches in my argument. At least in the field of political philosophy, there is an engrained view that weds such approaches to a narrow conception of self-interest and subsequently places them in the "realistic" camp of political theory.[8] Hence, some readers otherwise sympathetic to my argument might rebel at a perceived inconsistency between an ideal conception and its realistic building block. I have attempted

---

[7] Hume (1994): 206f.
[8] As we have seen, the disciplines of political science and economics have long moved passed the idea that rational choice approaches should be thus limited.

to allay such fears of a thus polluted conception at some length. As I have shown, we can give up the narrow conception of self-interest and inject all the idealizations which the conciliatory conception assumes without losing any of the insights of rational choice approaches. They are analytical tools which help us to understand and predict political outcomes given certain premises about the motivational basis of political agents. The conciliatory conception fills in the motivation of reasonable citizens to promote what they regard as the most reasonable conception of justice in political decision-making. The fact that we can use different assumptions about the motivations of the functionaries of political parties in the models discussed without undermining the tendency of democratic decision-making within the context of these institutions to produce outcomes reflecting the epistemic conciliation of citizens' judgments makes the model all the more "realistic."

The Normative and the Epistemic Dimension of Conciliatory Democracy
It is now the time for an exposition of the relation of the normative and the epistemic dimensions of the conciliatory conception of democracy. I started from a postulation of a normative commitment which states that in order to be legitimate, the exercise of political power has to be justifiable to citizens: "[I]ntelligible justifications in social and political life must be available in principle for everyone."[9] The ultimate aim of any justifiable political order, I then maintained, is *justice*. Therefore, the exercise of political power has to aim at justice. Furthermore, this aspect of the exercise of political power has to be intelligible to citizens: it is not enough that justice is done; it has to be seen to be done. This introduces the requirement of the *publicity of justice*: the aiming-at-justice of the exercise of political power has to be *intelligible* to reasonable citizens. Only when it is does this exercise enjoy *legitimacy*.

However, citizens of contemporary societies are in disagreement about what justice demands. Therefore, it will not do to claim, as Rousseau did, that to the reasonable citizens of a well-ordered society the common good is fully evident or that they can reach nearly unanimous judgments about its demands. Instead, citizens have to make an active effort to justify their exercise of political power to each other. Only if they thus make it *intelligible*

---

[9] Waldron (1987): p. 128.

to each other that their actions aim at justice, or what they take it to be, can their exercise of political power be legitimate. In a next step, I declared my allegiance to the idea that the reasonable pluralism of conceptions of justice entails the further requirement of *reciprocity of justification*: citizens ought to justify their exercise of political power, or how they intend to exercise it, with reference to reasons all reasonable citizens could accept. In that sense, the justification they offer has to be *public*; it has to be *accessible* to all reasonable citizens. This requirement entails that citizens do not draw on sources of authority, for example, sectarian doctrines, which lie beyond the reach of the common reason of citizens. What survives this filter imposed on justifying reasons is an idea which is at the heart of every reasonable conception of justice fit for publicly justifying the exercise of political power. This is the idea of *reciprocity of advantage*: reasonable conceptions of justice promote the interest of each as equals.[10]

We can now conceive the role of public deliberation against this background. Public deliberation is a practice of normative justification. It is a social practice that makes intelligible to other reasonable citizens that one's intended exercise of political power can be justified in terms of reasons other reasonable citizens could reasonably accept. However, this is only one way in which deliberation enters into the normative dimension of conciliatory democracy. Another way in which it enters into the normative justification of democracy is through its epistemic properties. Living in a complex and pluralistic society imposes epistemic burdens on citizens who want to exercise political power justly. In order to be just toward others, one has to make an active effort to get to know their perspectives, access their localized knowledge, and so on. The epistemic burdens require that they engage in public deliberation. Only if they expose their beliefs about justice and about the consequences of their actions to public scrutiny can they gain any confidence at all that their intended exercise of political power tracks justice. Hence, because public deliberation plays this important epistemic role in increasing the reliability of the belief-forming process, citizens have to engage in public deliberation in order to be just. Because this is the case,

---

[10] One way of specifying this idea is to say that it is instantiated when "all who are engaged in cooperation and who do their part as the rules and procedure require, are to benefit in an appropriate way as assessed by a suitable benchmark of comparison [i.e., of equality]" (Rawls 1996: p. 16).

the epistemic dimension overlaps with the normative: in order to make the aiming-at-justice of one's intended exercise of political power intelligible, one has to justify it in public deliberation. And *part of the evidence* that one's actions aim at justice is to engage in public deliberation (in order to harvest its epistemic benefits).[11]

Even under ideal conditions, however, we cannot expect decentered deliberation about sufficiently complex issues to usher in consensus (see Chap. 3; The (Un)Reasonableness of Political Disagreement). Deliberation as a decision-making procedure is incomplete. I have argued that in the face of the persistence of moral disagreement, deliberative democrats are mistaken if they conceive the legitimacy of democratic decision-making as tied to deliberation all the way down (see Chap. 2). In place of such a thoroughly *deliberative* standard of legitimacy, I have suggested that it is the task of political philosophy to face up to persistent political disagreement and develop a conception of legitimacy which can stand its ground. As I have just explained, however, this does not mean that deliberation adds nothing to the normative dimension of conciliatory democracy. The opposite is the case. Yet when it comes to the moment of decision, when the talk is talked, political philosophers, just as citizens, need a normative fix point which continues to give them guidance. This normative fix point is the criterion of reasonable acceptability, and the justification of political decision procedures has to live up to it. Starting from this firm footing, we have been led to an ideal of political equality, one aspect of which is to give others equal influence over outcomes in political decision-making. This, furthermore, is congruent with the Rousseauian starting point of the commitment to treat reasonable citizens as equal normative authorities. At that point, a component of substantive legitimacy (re)enters the argument. Decision procedures ought to select among reasonably acceptable options which have survived ongoing deliberative processes. They do so when they display sensitivity to the "post-deliberative" judgments of reasonable citizens. Here, we thus have another point of contact with the epistemic dimension of deliberation. Even equality of influence and judgment-

---

[11] The conclusion refutes the claim that the role of deliberation is limited to the exchange of information with the aim of improving the quality of outcomes; cf. Michelman (1997) and Christiano (1997).

sensitivity combined, however, do not specify which out of a number of decision procedures fulfilling these criteria we ought to opt for.

At this point, I tentatively injected an additional epistemic component into the argument. If we can publicly justify that decision procedures track bestness, that is, select the most reasonable among the range of reasonable options which emerge from public deliberation, this bestness-tracking claim can help us to specify which among a number of reasonably acceptable decision procedures we ought to endorse. Notice that this claim is itself also subject to the normative criterion of reasonable acceptability. Once again, we find the normative and the epistemic dimension of the conciliatory conception intertwined. For a bestness-tracking claim to pass the hurdle of reasonable acceptability, it would have to enjoy the support of independent reasons. For in order to justify the claim to those citizens who find themselves in the minority after decisions have been taken, it is not enough to simply *tell them* that the majority judgment was more reasonable than their own. The fact that this is the case needs to be made intelligible to them without appealing to reasons which they could reasonably reject as *better* reasons than the ones they have for rejecting the outcome. Hence, the normative dimension of conciliatory democracy points to a justification of a bestness-tracking claim which draws on reasons that are independent of the reasoning of reasonable citizens about the rightness of an outcome.

It is this point which we might consider the most important point of contact of both dimensions. The epistemic dimension of conciliatory democracy rests inter alia on the (reasonable) commitment of reasonable citizens to regard each other as equal epistemic authorities. Because they subsequently do not arbitrarily favor their own judgments but assign equal weight to each other's judgments, they regard their political disagreement as second-order evidence, which undermines the evidential connection between their first-order evidence and their original judgment. The correct assessment of the epistemic significance of this evidence, the very fact of disagreement, gives them a second-order reason to conciliate their judgments. Because modern democratic systems feature a robust tendency to produce outcomes which correspond to conciliatory judgments, all reasonable citizens have second-order reasons to endorse them as the rational course of action (given the state of an ongoing deliberative process at that point in time).

Normative or Epistemic? One might still ask: is the conciliatory conception of democracy a normative *or* an epistemic conception of democracy? Is the fundamental value political equality *or* getting it right?

The answer to these questions is that the conciliatory conception is squarely both. It is a conception of democracy which interlaces the normative and the epistemic dimension of democracy and treats both as irreducible components. This should come as no surprise because it attempts to accommodate the normative *and* the epistemic significance of disagreement. The presumed dichotomy between political equality and getting it right is misleading. Instead, the conciliatory conception gives citizens who aim to treat each other both formally and substantively as political equals reasons to regard the conciliatory outcomes of democratic decision procedures as the rational course of action.

Some people might not be satisfied with this answer because they still think that one dimension has to be fundamental to the enterprise. And, in one respect, this is correct. The normative dimension is fundamental to the enterprise because the normative criterion of reasonable acceptability sets the bar for the epistemic dimension to become a component of *a justification of a certain conception of democracy*. In that sense, the epistemic dimension is embedded in the normative outlook I have adopted throughout this book.

But the epistemic dimension is also in an important aspect independent from the normative dimension. *As a theory of how the reasonable citizens of a well-ordered society ought to react rationally to their political disagreements with other reasonable citizens whom they regard as equal epistemic authorities*, it does not rely on any normative import whatsoever.

In my view, it is a point in favor of the conception that it interlaces the epistemic and normative dimensions when it presents itself as a publicly justifiable conception of democracy, and that it keeps the dimensions separate when it addresses the normative and epistemic significance of political disagreement from the point of view of reasonable citizens.

Thus, retracing the evolution of the argument for the conciliatory conception of democracy, we can see that the normative and the epistemic dimensions are intertwined in numerous ways. Furthermore, we can see that the reactions of reasonable citizens to political disagreement between equal normative authorities and equal epistemic authorities are congruent. Both commitments lead them to endorse democratic decision procedures. This is without a doubt a very happy result for an epistemologically informed conception of democracy. Is it also a result that speaks to the citizens of contemporary democratic societies given their experiences with the democratic experiment? Probably not. Yet it shows what democracy can be at its best, something for which it is worthwhile to strive, namely a society of citizens who respect each other as equal normative and epistemic authorities about justice, who work together to uphold the institutions that enable them to make competent decisions, and who accept the outcomes of democratic decision-making at least in part because they possess the virtue of intellectual humility.

References

Christiano, T. (1997). The Significance of Public Deliberation. In J. Bohman & W. Rehg (Eds.), *Deliberative Democracy Essays on Reason and Politics* (pp. 243–279). Cambridge, MA: MIT Press.
Hume, D. (1994). Political Essays. In K. Haaknossen (Ed.), *Hume: Political Essays*. Cambridge: Cambridge University Press.
Michelman, F. I. (1997). How Can the People Ever Make the Laws? A Critique of Deliberative Democracy. In J. Bohman & W. Rehg (Eds.), *Deliberative Democracy Essays on Reason and Politics* (pp. 145–173). Cambridge, MA: MIT Press.
Rawls, J. (1996). *Political Liberalism* (2nd ed.). New York: Columbia University Press.
Rosenblum, N. L. (2008). *On the Side of Angels: An Appreciation of Parties and Partisanship*. Princeton, NJ: Princeton University Press.
Waldron, J. (1987). Theoretical Foundations of Liberalism. *The Philosophical Quarterly, 37*(147), 127–150.
Whelan, F. (1985). *Order and Artifice in Hume's Political Philosophy*. Princeton, NJ: Princeton University Press.

Bibliography

Anderson, E. (2008). An Epistemic Defense of Democracy: David Estlund's Democratic Authority. *Episteme. A Journal of Social Epistemology, 5*(1), 129–139.

Ansolabehere, S. (2006). Voters, Candidates, and Parties. In B. R. Weingast & D. A. Wittman (Eds.), *The Oxford Handbook of Political Economy* (pp. 29–50). Oxford: Oxford University Press.

Arrow, K. J. (1963). *Social Choice and Individual Values* (2nd ed.). New Haven, CT: Yale University Press.

Arrow, K. J. (1969). Values and Collective Decision Making. In P. Laslett & W. G. Runciman (Eds.), *Philosophy, Politics and Society* (pp. 215–232). Oxford: Blackwell.

Cohen, J. (1993). Moral Pluralism and Political Consensus. In D. Copp, J. Hampton, & J. Roemer (Eds.), *The Idea of Democracy* (pp. 270–291). Cambridge: Cambridge University Press.

Darwall, S., Gibbard, A., & Railton, P. (1992). Toward Fin de siècle Ethics: Some Trends. *The Philosophical Review, 101*(1), 115–189.

de Condorcet, N. ([1785] 1976). Essay on the Application of Mathematics to the Theory of Decision-Making. In K. M. Baker (Ed.), *Condorcet Selected Writings*. Indianapolis, IN: Bobs-Merrill.

Enoch, D. (2009). How is Moral Disagreement a Problem for Realism? *Ethics, 13*(1), 15–50.

Hobbes, T. (1991). Man and Citizen. In B. Gert (Ed.), *De Homine* (C. T. Wood, T. S. K. Scott-Craig, & B. Gert, Trans.); and *De Cive* (T. Hobbes & B. Gert, Trans.). Indianapolis, IN: Hackett.

Korsgaard, C. (1994). *The Sources of Normativity*. Cambridge: Cambridge University Press.

Landemore, H. (2014). Democracy as Heuristic: the Ecological Rationality of Political Equality. *The Good Society, 23*(2), 160–178.

McDonald, M. D., Mendes, S., & Budge, I. (2004). What Are Elections For? Conferring the Median Mandate. *British Journal of Political Science, 34*, 1–26.

Nagel, T. (2002). *Concealment and Exposure and Other Essays*. Oxford: Oxford University Press.

Pettit, P. (1999). *Republicanism: A Theory of Freedom and Government*. Oxford: Oxford University Press.

Rawls, J. (1971). *A Theory of Justice*. Cambridge, MA: Harvard University Press.

Rousseau, J.-J. (1913). *A Discourse on Political Economy. The Social Contract and Discourses* (G. D. H. Cole, Trans.). London: J. M. Dent and Sons, Ltd.

Simmons, A. J. (1979). *Moral Principles and Political Obligations*. Princeton, NJ: Princeton University Press.

Simmons, A. J. (1995). *On the Edge of Anarchy. Locke, Consent, and the Limits of Society*. Princeton, NJ: Princeton University Press.

Simmons, A. J. (2001). *Justification and Legitimacy*. Cambridge: Cambridge University Press.

Simpson, M. (2006). *Rousseau's Theory of Freedom*. London: Continuum.

Index

D

decision procedures
 the argument from the presumption of rationality, 74–8
 bestness and majority rule, 73–4
 deliberative democracy and decision procedures, 58–9
 epistemic reasons for, 240–2
 majority rule and alternative decision procedures, 71–3
 motivation of voters, 232–3
 the paradox of voting, 223
 the problem of rational ignorance, 223–5
 Rousseau and the epistemic dimension of, 10–30
 Rousseau and the normative dimension of, 30–4
defeaters
 undercutting and rebutting, 81, 128
deliberation
 from deliberation to conciliation, 90–1
 as the final court of appeal, 60
 its two purposes, 40
democracy
 conciliatory, xxi–xiv, 169–71
 and abortion, 176–81
 the argument for, 188–98
 and cycling majorities, 193–5
 and epistemic conciliation about justice, 171–88
 and ideal *vs.* non-ideal theory, 256–7
 and intellectual humility as a political virtue, 253–6
 its ambitiousness, 252–3
 its epistemic authority, 251–2

democracy (*cont.*)
- its normative and epistemic dimension, 257–62
- and the median voter, 191–2
- and multidimensionality, 195–8
- and the politics of compromise, 183–8
- and religious dogmatism, 181–3
- and the rule of the majority
- and the spatial model of voting, 192–3
- deliberative democracy, xiv–xvii
- deliberation and sensitivity to preferences, 71
- from deliberation to conciliation, 90–1
- the epistemic dimension of, 66–82
- from justifiability to deliberation, 47–8
- majority rule and alternative decision procedures, 71–3
- the normative dimension of, 42–66
- procedural fairness and deliberation, 69–71
- and procedural legitimacy, 55–8
- Rousseau and, 39–42
- dependent *vs.* independent reasons, 78–82
- downgrading. *See* independence and downgrading

E

epistemic authority of citizens, xvii–xix
- the argument from institutional expertise, 110–12
- the argument from multidimensional complexity, 95–8
- the challenge of moral elitism, 92–112
- and deliberative democracy, 89–90
- J.S. Mill's epistemic political elitism, 102–9
- the local knowledge argument, 98–100
- Mill and the equal epistemic authority of citizens, 106–8
- the practice-based argument, 101–2
- Rousseau and the equal epistemic authority of citizens, 22, 32, 87–9
- their equal epistemic authority, 92–112

epistemic conciliation
- about justice as reaching a compromise along a scalar dimension, 169–88
- along a single left-right dimension, 198
- issue-specific *vs.* comprehensive epistemic conciliation, 239–40
- as splitting the difference in credence, 129

epistemic peerhood
- definition of, 127
- downgrading (*see* independence and downgrading)
- dynamic model of, 151–6
- equal weight view, 131–3
- and Rousseau, 24–6
- Rousseau's version of, 148–51

evidence
    first-order and second-order evidence, 24–5, 128–30
    (political) disagreement as second-order evidence, 24–6, 128
    procedure-dependent evidence as second-order evidence, 21–4
    second-order evidence as undercutting defeater, 128
    testimony as second-order evidence, 128

G
general will
    background conditions, 12–15
    as a conception of public reason, 3–5
    the content of, 6–7
    and decision procedures, 10–36
    the form of, 5–6
    law as the expression of, 8–9
    legitimacy without procedures?, 28–30
    procedure-independent *vs.* procedure-dependent access to, 21–4
    the scope of the, 7–8
    the simplicity assumption, 27–8

I
independence and downgrading, 137–51
    the argument from personal information, 144–5
    the argument from the opacity of evidence, 146
    the case against independence, 140–1, 148
    Independence (the principle), 138–40
    independence and the strength of first-order evidence, 141
    local and global downgrading, 138–40
    the many disagreements objection, 147–8
    the permissibility of downgrading anti-democrats, 162–6
    spinelessness, 147
    the substance of the disagreement, 143–4
    the independent reasoning condition, 135
intellectual humility
    hume and, 253–6
    as a political virtue (*see* democracy, conciliatory)
    Rousseau and, 17–19

J
justice
    as reciprocity and the general will, 9–10
justification
    citizens as agents and subjects of, 104–6
    justifiability and public justification, 47–8, 53
    and legitimacy (*see* legitimacy)
    publicity of j. as accessibility, 53

L

legitimacy
- consensus conception of DSL, 48–51
- and deliberation, 257–60
- and deliberation as the final court of appeal, 61–2
- deliberative standard of (DSL), 48–66
- DSL and the sense of emptiness, 60–1
- the epistemic circularity of the consensus conception of DSL, 51–2
- the ideal of deliberation and the moment of decision, 58–9
- Principle of Provisionality, 62–6
- procedural legitimacy and the limits of DSL, 55–8
- reasonable acceptability conception DSL, 52–5

M

Median Voter, 191
- the Median Voter Theorem, 192–3
- and the problem of cycling majorities, 193–8

moral deference
- and conciliatory democracy (*see* democracy, conciliatory)
- (near) unanimity, and levels of confidence, 19–21

N

neutrality of justification, 42. *See also* reasonable acceptability

normative authority of citizens
- their equal normative authority, 32, 88

P

political disagreement
- and agnosticism, 172–3
- among representatives, 108–9
- consensus as the motivational requirement and telos of deliberation, 117–19
- the debate room argument, 113–15
- the epistemic significance of, 24–6
- the epistemology of, xix–xxi, 123–66
- global consensus and the entropy of reason, 115–17
- peer disagreement and, 157–66
- rational and reasonable disagreement and symmetrical evidence, 119–21
- the (un)reasonableness of, 112–21

political parties
- coalition formation in representative democracies, 218–19
- as collective epistemic agents, 211, 213
- elite manipulation and exogenous *vs.* endogenous preferences, 236–8
- fundamental importance of, 209–10
- and government policy, 225–6
- multi-party electoral competition, vii, xvii, xxiii, xxiv
- party ideology and programs, 210–14
- in political science and in political philosophy, 204–9
- the spatial model of party competition, 27–42, 214–23
- vote-winning *vs.* policy-seeking parties, 233–6

public reason
  democratic public reason, 157
  democratic public reason as the epistemic framework of disagreement, 159–62
  the general will as a conception of, 2–10, 249

R
reasonable acceptability, xv, xii, 39–40
  of decision procedures, 71–8
  and dependent and independent reasons, 78–82
  and neutrality, 54
  of outcomes and decision procedures, 67–9
  as publicity as accessibility, 53–4
  and public justification, xii, xv, 39–40
  and reasonable disagreement, 44–5

reasonable disagreement, 42. *See also* reasonable acceptability
reasonableness
  the idea of a well-ordered society and an expanded conception of, 158–9
reconstruction, method of, 44
  and the normative significance of political disagreement, 46
right reasons view, 130–1

S
sovereignty
  as the epistemic and normative authority of the people, 30–3

T
total evidence view, 133–5
  and Rousseau, 24–6